IGOR STRAVINSKY

Twentieth Century Composers

BY

DAVID EWEN

AUTHOR OF

"The Man with the Baton"

ILLUSTRATED

THOMAS Y. CROWELL COMPANY
PUBLISHERS : : NEW YORK

Printed in the United States of America

FOR

ISAAC GOLDBERG

to commemorate ten years
of friendship

PREFACE

MODERN music might very aptly be likened to a kaleidoscope. A kaleidoscope consists of many varicolored and symmetrical patterns, each supposedly independent of the other. Flip the kaleidoscope—and these many patterns and hues resolve themselves into one unified design.

So, too, modern music. At first glance it appears to be a baffling composition of many conflicting styles, each completely independent of the other: the atonality of Schönberg, the neo-classicism of Stravinsky and Hindemith, the post-impressionism of Loeffler and Delius, the romanticism of Elgar, the nationalism of de Falla, Béla Bartók and Vaughan-Williams, the jazz of George Gershwin. And yet, these diverse expressions are merely segments of a kaleidoscopic whole: the attempt on the part of present-day composers to give musical expression to the many facets of the pre-war and post-war world of the twentieth century.

At best, the various trends and movements of modern music, if viewed with the microscopic eye of the theoretician, is an abstruse subject, the dissection and analysis of which belong to the text-book. How modern composers have taken harmonic and contrapuntal laws and revised them is a fascinating subject—but only for students who are thoroughly intimate with musical theory. To the musical layman, not the technical analysis of the style of modern composers is of interest but its æsthetic implications; not the exact structure of Schönberg's twelve-tone system or the names of the unrelated keys employed by Bartók interests

vii

the average music-lover but rather the artistic aim of these methods and the success with which this aim is achieved.

Modern music is, after all, a palpitantly living subject. It is the artistic interpretation of the human experiences that have affected human existence during the past forty years. It is this living subject—not the technical one—that intrigues the musical layman. And it is with this subject that this book is concerned.

The present book has been designed particularly for the intelligent layman whose curiosity in modern music has been aroused by the numerous performances of modern works over the radio and in the concert-hall. It is, therefore, not the purpose of the author in the pages that follow to trace analytically the transformation of musical structure and technique in modern times. There exist any number of excellent treatises which have accomplished this with far greater clarity, erudition and grace than this author can ever hope to achieve. However, there exist few works which attempt to guide the musical layman—and light his way—through the treacherous alleys and dark corners of modern music.

The author hopes to give the layman a more intimate understanding of modern music from the point of view most easily assimilated and understood: that of the personalities themselves who have given shape and direction to this music. Thus the emphasis in this book is on biographical and personal material: the biographical material enabling the reader to understand the background and circumstances which have inspired the music, and the personal material giving the reader an intimate introduction to those personalities that gave voice to this music. The personal information was drawn from direct contact and conversations with many of these composers. Critical appraisal, however, is not sacrificed. The book discusses seventeen composers— not the seventeen greatest of our time, but seventeen whose work represents most accurately a cross-section of modern music. In any case, it is a noble representation of composers, and one of which any generation may justifiably be proud. In non-technical verbiage the author has attempted to explain to the reader the nature of each composer's style, to interpret the principal works of each composer and to evaluate his musical significance.

Some of the material included in this book appeared originally in prominent magazines. This material has, to be sure, been radically revised and amplified for the purposes of this book. However, for permission to reproduce it here the author is grateful to the editors of *American Music Lover, Chesterian* (London), *Coronet, Esquire, Menorah Journal, Monthly Musical Record* (London), *Musical Record* and *Musical Quarterly.*

CONTENTS

IGOR STRAVINSKY

I

IGOR STRAVINSKY

1.

ON MAY 29, 1913, a volcanic eruption rocked musical Paris.

The eruption was caused by the first performance of the *Sacre du Printemps (The Rite of Spring)* at the Théâtre des Champs Élysées, an offering of the Diaghilev Ballet Russe, headed by Nijinsky. However, it was not Diaghilev's original choreographic conception that caused the tremors among the audience, or even the exotic theme of the ballet itself, heightened by the bizarre settings and costume designs of Nicholas Roerich. Rather, it was the musical score, drenched with strange colors and defiantly new sounds, a score sublimely indifferent to tradition and heritage, fearlessly pronouncing a fresh vocabulary and what then appeared to be a strangely distorted one. The music was the work of the young Igor Stravinsky, who had already made his mark with two other ballets also presented by the Diaghilev troupe.

The music had not progressed beyond several minutes, under Pierre Monteux's baton, when a growling began to be heard in the audience. The music seemed to lack altogether that logic and coherence which is ordinarily expected of a creative work. There was no recognizable melody, only distorted lines of sound which zigzagged aimlessly, so it seemed, through a score complicated by a labyrinth of rhythm and sporadic outbursts of cacophony. As the sounds became more confused, restless movement was heard in the seats, some snickers from the audience, some smothered guffaws. Before long, the air of the theatre became charged with electric excitation, and the sparks of dissension ignited

3

the passion of the listeners. "A certain part of the audience," writes Carl van Vechten, who was a member of that historic assemblage, "was thrilled by what it considered to be a blasphemous attempt to destroy music as an art and, swept away with wrath, began, very soon after the rise of the curtain, to make cat-calls and to offer audible suggestions as to how the performance should proceed. The orchestra played unheard except occasionally, when a slight lull occurred. The young man seated behind me in a box stood up during the course of the ballet to enable him to see more clearly. The intense excitement under which he was laboring betrayed itself when he began to beat rhythmically on the top of my head with fists. My emotion was so great that I did not feel the blows for some time." [1]

While the music was in progress, a lady stretched into the box neighboring hers and slapped the face of a man who was hissing; her escort arose, cards were exchanged, and a duel took place the following morning.[2] Saint-Saëns viciously denounced the composer; André Capu, the critic, bellowed that it was all a colossal bluff, while at the same time Maurice Ravel was crying "genius" at his inattentive neighbors. The Austrian Ambassador laughed loudly in derision; Florent Schmitt, the composer, attacked him for his laughter. The Princesse de Pourtalès left her box exclaiming: "I am sixty years old, but this is the first time that anyone has dared to make a fool of me!" Another proud society lady rose majestically in her seat, contracted her capacious bosom and spat in the face of one of the demonstrators. In the wings, Stravinsky was clinging to Nijinsky's collar in an attempt to prevent the dancer from rushing upon the stage and expressing openly his contempt of the audience. And throughout it all, Claude Debussy, pale and trembling, was pleading to the audience to remain quiet and listen patiently to the music.

[1] *Music After the Great War,* by Carl van Vechten.
[2] As reported by Romola Nijinsky in her biography, *Nijinsky.*

2.

At the time of the *Sacre* "scandal," Igor Stravinsky was thirty-one years old, a brusque, ungainly young man, slight of build, whose somewhat awkward and self-conscious mannerisms had not as yet been polished by Parisian refinement. His upper lip was still clean-shaven, his face, in consequence, seeming longer and leaner than it has in more recent years. A *pince-nez*, perched at a sharp angle on the bridge of his nose, gave him a professorial appearance.

His reputation had been imposing even before the riot of the *Sacre* brought him world-wide notoriety. His name had already been linked with the rising futurist movement: in Rome, the redoubtable Marinetti had carried a banner in the streets proclaiming: "Down with Wagner; long live Stravinsky!" To a meagre handful of younger art-lovers, chafing under the bondage of formalism and tradition, the name of Stravinsky had already become a *shibboleth*. The *Sacre*, therefore, had established more firmly what *Petrushka* had first created two years before this—namely, Stravinsky's reputation as the *enfant terrible* in the music of his time.

The *Sacre du Printemps,* with its attendant riot, brought to a climax an artistic career that had been meteoric.

Igor Stravinsky was born in Oranienbaum, a suburb of St. Petersburg, on St. Igor's Day, June 5, 1882. At the time of Stravinsky's birth, Glinka, the father of Russian music, had been dead twenty-five years; his influence, however, had already produced the school of national music known as the "Russian Five." By 1882, the "Russian Five" were at the height of their creative growth (except Moussorgsky, who had died the year before). They had already formed, moulded, and developed a musical speech that Stravinsky was soon to inherit. Borodin was forty-eight; behind him was the composition of the *Symphony in B minor,* the *String Quartet in A* and the remarkable tone-poem, *In the Steppes of Central Asia.* Balakireff, aged forty-six, had already produced his *Tamara* and *Russ.* Moussorgsky's *Boris Godounoff* produced successfully eight years before, was still some two decades from acceptance as a Russian epic. Nikolai Rimsky-Korsakoff was the only one of the "Five" whose future still stretched before him; and Rimsky-Korsakoff, then in his thirty-ninth year, had already created the *Antar Symphony* and *Sniegouroutchka.* Stravinsky, therefore, was born at a time when musical activity was richly productive in Russia.

Igor Stravinsky's father, Feodor, was a well-known singer of the Maryinsky Theatre, who—as though to establish a more direct link between Igor and the traditions of the "Russian Five"—had been cast as the drunken monk in the first performance of *Boris Godounoff.*[3] Feodor Stravinsky, despite his artistic calling, was a practical, level-headed man. Long before Igor's birth he had decided that any child of his would be strongly discouraged from adopting art as a profession; for Igor, therefore, he had selected law. Feodor Stravinsky, moreover, possessed a strong streak of stubbornness together with his level head. In his early academic studies, Igor was very nearly hopeless (the schoolmaster at one time despatched a note to Feodor Stravinsky prophesying that Igor would never amount to anything!) while in his piano study he revealed an alert intelligence; but not even these facts could persuade the father to change the plans he had conceived. Clinging to them tenaciously, he saw Igor through preparatory school and finally into the University of St. Petersburg.

From his earliest years, Stravinsky showed unusual responsiveness to music. He received his first vivid musical impressions as a mere child, from performances of Glinka's *A Life for the Tsar* and *Russlan and Ludmilla,* and of Tchaikovsky's *Symphonie Pathètique;* these impressions were so vivid that Stravinsky never forgot them. He was

---

[3] Rimsky-Korsakoff refers to him frequently in *My Musical Life.*

a frequent visitor at the home of his uncle where performances of German works took place regularly. He likewise attended public concerts—particularly those of the Imperial Music Society, directed by Nápravnik, and of the Russian Symphony Orchestra (which, in 1885, had been founded by Belaiev).[4]

His music study, however, was spasmodic. As a child of nine he began to have piano lessons. Then, hearing one day a piano recital of Josef Hofmann, he was inspired to study the instrument with greater assiduity and industry. In a few years, he succeeded in attaining a supple technique.

During his University days, he received the permission of his father to begin the study of harmony under a private tutor. Dull exercises and implacable rules were of small attraction to him; in a short while, he discontinued the study. In his eighteenth year, he began to thumb a text on counterpoint, finding therein so much fascination that he assumed the study of the subject by himself. He achieved a remarkable knowledge of its technique, particularly in view of the fact that he studied it without the help of a teacher.

When Stravinsky was twenty years old, he left with his family for Bad Wildungen, Germany, for a prolonged holiday. While there, he heard that Rimsky-Korsakoff was in Heidelberg. A great admirer of the composer and teacher, Stravinsky left immediately for Heidelberg to consult Rimsky-Korsakoff about his own career. He performed for the master a few abortive piano pieces which he had recently composed. To Rimsky-Korsakoff, these pieces represented the self-conscious stammerings of an immature musical mind; however, behind them Rimsky-Korsakoff perceived an original message and the rudiments of an individual speech. He therefore urged Stravinsky to continue his musical activity, dissuaded him from entering the

---

[4] The same Belaiev who was soon to become the influential publisher of modern Russian music.

St. Petersburg Conservatory, whose rigid curriculum, he feared, might be unbearable to so headstrong a personality, and advised the young composer to submit to him whatever he produced.

Rimsky-Korsakoff's praise—couched though it was in a cautious and none too enthusiastic vocabulary—convinced Stravinsky, at last, that he could become a serious musician. He did not, as yet, abandon law. Instead, in his spare hours, he hurled himself with youthful zest into the artistic life of St. Petersburg. He read avidly the art-journal, *The World of Art,* edited by an apostle of modernism, Diaghilev. Frequently, he visited the exhibition of paintings which this very same Diaghilev arranged in St. Petersburg. And he became an enthusiastic member of a progressive musical society which regularly performed the chamber-works of such modern French composers as Debussy, César Franck, Paul Dukas, Chabrier and Gabriel Fauré.

Towards the close of 1903, Stravinsky had completed his first unified composition, a piano sonata. For a fortnight, he lived with Rimsky-Korsakoff, while the master carefully and patiently dissected the work and mercilessly disclosed its technical weaknesses. Rimsky-Korsakoff found that the composition, though the work of an undeveloped musician, possessed a strength of fibre and an intensity of speech not frequently discovered in a first-born work. He therefore no longer had any hesitancy in advising Stravinsky to take the final step—exchange the profession of law for that of music.

In 1906, Stravinsky was married to his cousin, a girl of unusual intelligence who was strongly instrumental in swaying him from a legal career to that of music. Early in 1905, upon completing his course at the University, he had definitely changed the direction of his life. Brushing aside the legal profession permanently, he began a two-year period of intensive study of instrumentation under Rimsky-

Korsakoff. And under the guidance of the master, he was converted from a raw student into a self-confident musician.

The first fruits of his studies with Rimsky-Korsakoff were the *Symphony in E-flat,* dedicated to his teacher, and a suite for voice and orchestra after three poems of Pushkin, entitled *Faune et Bergère,* both composed between 1906 and 1907. In these works, the future rebel had not yet begun to flaunt his defiance in the face of tradition. This was music strongly influenced by the idiom established by the "Russian Five," couched in orthodox forms. One critic found the *Symphony* a "straightforward work which is chiefly notable for its docile acquiescence in conventionality to a degree that almost contradicts the report of his chafing under academic restraint." The *Symphony* and the *Faune et Bergère* were first performed privately by the court orchestra in 1907. Shortly after this, the Belaiev concerts of the Russian Symphony Orchestra had the distinction of giving the first public performance of a work by Stravinsky when it introduced *Faune et Bergère.*

Stravinsky next set to work upon a *Scherzo fantastique,* for orchestra—inspired by Maurice Maeterlinck's *Life of the Bee*—and upon the first act of an opera, *Le Rossignol,* based on the famous fairy-tale of Andersen. Rimsky-Korsakoff saw the sketches of both compositions, approved of them highly, and for the first time enthusiastically prophesied a brilliant career for the young composer. In 1908, Stravinsky abandoned the composition of his opera to write the *Feu d'artifice (Fireworks),* music prepared in honor of the forthcoming marriage of Rimsky-Korsakoff's daughter, Sonia. He despatched the manuscript to the master as a surprise offering for the wedding. The master, however, never saw the work. The package was returned to Stravinsky unopened, "on account of the death of the addressee."

The death of Rimsky-Korsakoff was a hard blow to Stravinsky, who had lost a great teacher and a great friend. In expression of his profound sentiments, and as a gesture of farewell, Stravinsky composed a *Chant funèbre*.[5]

The winter of 1908 was a turning point in the career of Igor Stravinsky. At that time the Siloti concerts in St. Petersburg presented the *Scherzo fantastique* and the *Feu d'artifice*. In the audience was Diaghilev, increasingly famous sponsor of modern art and organizer of a new Russian ballet which was to be introduced to Paris the following year. Diaghilev, who possessed an uncanny sensitiveness to the presence of hitherto undetected genius, recognized that greatness lurked in the hidden corners of these works. Immature they were, to be sure; but Diaghilev had too penetrating a vision not to perceive behind their immaturity the growing stature of a striking individuality, particularly in the brilliantly orchestrated *Feu d'artifice*, of which Fokine, the ballet-master, once said that it always made him see vividly flames searing the skies. Diaghilev, therefore, approached Stravinsky after the concert, asked him if he would be interested in enlisting his talent in the Diaghilev ballet, and—as a first assignment—commissioned Stravinsky to orchestrate two Chopin pieces to be used in the ballet, *Chopiniana*.[6] Thus began a relationship which, continuing for two decades, was to have an enormous effect not only upon Stravinsky's artistic evolution but upon the development of modern music as well.

At the time of this first meeting with Stravinsky, Diaghilev was thirty-six years old, his reputation—after many tribulations—solidly established at last both in Russia and in Paris. In his youth he had revealed an alert and supple intelligence keenly sensitive to beauty in whatever form or medium it was expressed. He turned first to music, aspiring to become a composer, but—after a heart-breaking

[5] The *Chant funèbre*, together with many other Stravinsky papers, disappeared during the Revolution in Russia.

[6] Later renamed *Les Sylphides*.

interview with Rimsky-Korsakoff—was convinced that
musical creation was not his *forte*. From music he turned
to art and journalism. He founded and edited a progressive magazine, *The World of Art*, which publicized
European art-movements among the Russian intelligentzia;
and he inaugurated annual art exhibitions in which he introduced Russian art lovers for the first time to some of
the most characteristic products of the various schools of
modern European art.

Finally, after an extended period in which his principal
goal was the education of Russia in European art trends
(a period whose importance to Russia's artistic development should not be underestimated), Diaghilev suddenly
was imbued with a far more intoxicating mission. He had
recently rediscovered Russian art, and found therein artistic values and concepts which he felt were unique and
incomparable. He, therefore, appointed himself as the
prophet to introduce and interpret this art to the rest of
Europe.

In 1906, Diaghilev held an imposing exhibition of modern Russian painting in Paris. The tremendous success of
this venture gave Diaghilev the strength to expand his
program and redouble his activity. In 1907, he arranged
a series of historical concerts of Russian music in Paris,
consisting of the foremost examples of Russian symphonic
and operatic art. Glazunov, Rachmaninoff and Rimsky-
Korsakoff personally conducted programs of their own
works. Josef Hofmann played the piano concertos of
Scriabin and Liapounov, while Rachmaninoff performed his
own *Second Concerto*. Scenes from Borodin's *Prince Igor*
and Moussorgsky's *Boris Godounoff* were featured, with
Feodor Chaliapin making his first appearances in Paris.

But Diaghilev had only begun. In 1908, he brought to
Paris the complete Moussorgsky opera, *Boris Godounoff*,
with Feodor Chaliapin in the principal rôle—the scenery,
costumes and choreography personally supervised by

Diaghilev. This was the first indication Diaghilev had given of his instinctive knowledge of the theatre and of his genius for organization. *Boris Godounoff* was a decided success.

From opera to ballet was but a short step for Diaghilev. A casual conversation at a café, in which Diaghilev boasted of the unique distinction of Russian dancing, inspired him to bring its finest examples to Paris. In 1909, therefore, the Diaghilev Ballet Russe came into being in Paris. Fokine was ballet-master; the principal dancers included Karsavina, Anna Pavlova and Nijinsky. And from the very first the guiding genius was Diaghilev.

Diaghilev was no mere dabbler in the arts. In his own way he was as much a creator as those eminent collaborators whom he gathered under his wing for the Ballet Russe. A dilettante in the finest meaning of the word, he was, as his biographer wrote of him, "a master painter who never painted, a master musician who never wrote or played, a master dancer who never danced or devised the steps of a ballet." [7] An artistic instinct that seemed infallible, an impeccable taste, an insight of penetrating sharpness—these things combined to make him that organizing genius that could blend the innumerable parts of a ballet into a completely unified artistic whole. And like all true geniuses, Diaghilev had the power to electrify and inspire all those with whom he came into contact: members of his ballet frequently confessed that when Diaghilev was not witnessing a performance the quality of the dancing deteriorated noticeably.

It was this dynamic and revitalizing personality, this cultured and eclectic mind, broad enough to encompass all of the arts, who crossed Stravinsky's path in 1908.

How important an influence Diaghilev was in Stravinsky's evolution has been the subject for many copious

[7] *Diaghileff: His Artistic and Private Life,* by Arnold L. Haskell (in collaboration with Walter Nouvel).

paragraphs. Certainly it is ridiculous to assume that had there been no Diaghilev there would have been no Stravinsky—an assertion which many of Diaghilev's devotees have strongly and frequently reiterated. There are sufficient foreshadowings of the later Stravinsky in the *Scherzo fantastique* and *Feu d'artifice*—particularly in the nervous energy of the rhythms, the electrically charged instrumentation, and above all in the first signs of impatience and dissatisfaction with existing musical conventions—to convince us that Stravinsky would have made his mark without Diaghilev. However, it would be just as naïve to disregard Diaghilev's influence entirely. An immature genius does not almost over-night evolve into an integrated artist with a fully developed, highly personal vocabulary, without the influence of a powerful external stimulus. The only convincing explanation of why Stravinsky reached full maturity so rapidly, why two such works as *Feu d'artifice* and *L'Oiseau de feu (The Fire-Bird)* were separated by only two years, is—Diaghilev.

3.

Chopiniana—with the two Stravinsky orchestrations commissioned by Diaghilev—was featured in the inaugural season of the Ballet Russe at the Paris Opéra. The orchestration pleased Diaghilev considerably,—so much so that, several months later, in planning another season for his Ballet Russe he decided to yield to one of his characteristic extravagant gestures by placing his most important musical commission in the hands of this young and inexperienced composer—even though the foremost of Russian composers were eager to serve him.

Diaghilev had been revolving in his mind a plan to translate the famous legend of the Fire-Bird into a ballet. It is for this ballet that Stravinsky was commissioned to compose an original score.

During late winter of 1909 and early spring of 1910, Stravinsky worked industriously upon his first major assignment—the ballet-master Fokine, who fashioned the scenario of the *Fire-Bird,* almost indefatigably at his side. "They worked very closely together, phrase by phrase. Stravinsky brought him a beautiful cantilena on the entrance of the Tsarevitch into the garden of the girls with the golden apples. But Fokine disapproved. 'No, no!' he said. 'You bring him in like a tenor. Break the phrase where he merely shows his head on his first intrusion. Then make the curious swish of the garden's magic horse's return, and then, when he shows his hand again, bring in the full swing of the melody.' " [8]

Stravinsky's score was finally completed in May of 1910. One month later, on June 25th, it was given its première at the Paris Opéra by the Ballet Russe. The principal dancers included Fokine, Mme. Fokina, and Karsavina; the settings were designed by Bakst and Golovine; and the conductor was Gabriel Pierné.

The scenario of Fokine follows closely the traditional Russian legend, and serves admirably as the program for the concert suite, *L'Oiseau de feu,* which is usually performed in the symphony hall. Ivan Tsarevitch, roaming aimlessly one night, stumbles across the Fire-Bird and captures it as it is in the act of plucking golden fruit from a silver tree. As a reward for its release, the Fire-Bird presents Ivan with one of its glowing feathers, which he accepts. Suddenly, the thick darkness of the night dissipates. A castle comes clearly into view, from whose portals emerge thirteen maidens of surpassing beauty. Little realizing that they are being observed, they play with the silver tree and its golden fruit. Emerging from hiding, Ivan receives from one of the maidens a golden fruit as gift, and they dance out of sight. The night passes into dawn. Suddenly, Ivan realizes that the castle is the home

[8] Lincoln Kirstein in his biography, *Fokine.*

of the dreaded Kastcheï who captures wayfaring travelers
and subjects them to his spell. Determined to conquer this
monster, Ivan enters the castle, which is guarded by terrifying monsters. Kastcheï attempts to bewitch Ivan; but
his power is impotent before the magic feather that Ivan
holds in his hand. Then the Fire-Bird comes to view, reveals to Ivan a casket and informs him that Kastcheï's fate
is concealed therein. Ivan opens the casket, and withdraws
an egg which he smashes to the ground. Death emerges
from the smashed egg-shell and obsesses the body of
Kastcheï. As Kastcheï perishes, the castle suddenly disappears, and the maidens are freed from their bondage.
As a reward, Ivan receives in marriage the hand of the
most beautiful of the captive maidens.

L'Oiseau de feu was an instantaneous success, the most
substantial triumph of the 1910 season of the Ballet Russe.
Diaghilev was thrilled by Stravinsky's score, and knew
instantly that he had made no mistake in recruiting the
young composer as his principal music collaborator.
Some of the critics were puzzled by several of the more
unorthodox pages of Stravinsky's music, but for the most
part they found it full of power and beauty. A handful of
French musicians knew that with the *L'Oiseau* a formidable
musical creator had emerged. One of these was Claude
Debussy who, immediately after the first performance,
rushed backstage, embraced Stravinsky, and poured out
his effusive congratulations before the embarrassed young
composer.

L'Oiseau de feu was Stravinsky's first significant thrust
towards individuality and greatness. His first creative
period—the period of apprenticeship which produced the
Symphony, the *Scherzo fantastique* and *Feu d'artifice*—
was now definitely over. He was at last well started in
formulating his own idiom; he had begun to show those
personal mannerisms which were to become the revealing
fingerprints on all the works of his second period.

In these works of the middle phase of Stravinsky's artistic development—ranging from *L'Oiseau* to *Les Noces (The Wedding)*—Stravinsky is essentially the Russian, his musical speech heavy with a Russian accent. His second period stemmed from the soil of the "Russian Five," from Moussorgsky and Rimsky-Korsakoff particularly; *L'Oiseau de feu*, as a matter of fact, is a recognizable godson of Rimsky-Korsakoff's influence. Russian folk-music obsesses Stravinsky in the works of this time. While he borrows directly from folk-music only rarely, his melodic and harmonic material have an unmistakable Russian character. They are full of the spirit and color of Russian folk-song.

In comparison with *Le Sacre du Printemps* and *Les Noces*, *L'Oiseau de feu* may appear conservative, indeed. But, in 1910, it stung and pinched musical ears, unaccustomed to such brazen audacities. True, Stravinsky permitted himself the luxury of tender, delicate, often poignantly beautiful melody—as in the *Dance of the Princesses* and the *Berceuse*—which belongs more to the equipment of the "Russian Five" than to that of a rebel composer. Yet, at other moments, an already striking impatience with old norms asserts itself. In the *Dance of the King Kastcheï* there is already a rhythmic barbarism which, in its nervous energy and agitation, sweeps convention to the winds. The brusque leaps and starts of Stravinsky's later melodic line frequently pierce through the prevailingly smoother texture of *L'Oiseau*. And it has that characteristic Stravinsky orchestration, as luminous as flame.

The success of *L'Oiseau de feu* definitely established the Ballet Russe as an annual feature of the Paris theatrical season. In planning the 1911 season, therefore, Diaghilev inevitably looked upon Stravinsky to furnish him with a new score. There had already been some conversation between Stravinsky and Diaghilev about a ballet theme which was later to reach realization in *Le Sacre du Printemps*. Stravinsky, however, was mentally and physically too exhausted by the strain of composing *L'Oiseau* to undertake another arduous assignment. Instead, he sought relaxation by composing a work in a lighter vein, a sort of *Konzertstück* for piano and orchestra.

The one great obstacle facing Stravinsky, in the sketching of this work, was the selection of an appropriate programmatic title. *"Konzertstück"* was, after all, too effete a name for a work of such malicious irony as Stravinsky was etching; and Stravinsky felt that, unless he succeeded in finding a suitably descriptive designation for his work, its progress would be greatly retarded. For hours at a stretch he walked along the edge of the Lake of Geneva, whistling to himself snatches of his new music as he exhausted his imagination and experience for a title. When it finally came to him, it literally burst upon his consciousness when he least expected it. But it was precisely the theme for which, instinctively, he had been groping. He would call his new work *Petrushka* after the pathetic sawdust puppet, well known to the Russian fair.

The progress of *Petrushka* was temporarily interrupted in the spring of 1911 when Stravinsky suffered a severe illness, the result of nicotine poisoning. For a period, it was seriously thought that he was on the border of death. But in the end recovery brought him an altogether new zest for composition, and returning to the manuscript of *Petrushka* he felt the pen fly under his fingertips.

In the summer of 1911, Diaghilev visited Stravinsky at his home in Clarens, Switzerland, for the purpose of hearing portions of *Le Sacre,* which he believed Stravinsky to be composing at the time. At first very much surprised to hear that not *Le Sacre* but a substitute was awaiting him, Diaghilev nevertheless listened patiently to Stravinsky's exposition of the Petrushka subject, and to those portions which Stravinsky had already committed to paper. *Petrushka* instantly exhilarated and excited Diaghilev. He recognized in the subject a ballet cut to the pattern of the

Ballet Russe requirements; as he listened to sections of the music he envisioned in his mind's eye Nijinsky as Petrushka, capering to the pungent rhythmic patterns and the wittily satirical phrases of Stravinsky's music.

Stravinsky completed *Petrushka: Scènes burlesques en 4 tableaux* in Rome in May, 1911. On June 13, the Ballet Russe introduced it at the Châtelet, in Paris. Karsavina and Nijinsky were the principal dancers; the scenery was painted by Benois; Fokine was the ballet-master, and Pierre Monteux the conductor.

The scenario of Petrushka had been prepared by Alexandre Benois. "This ballet depicts the life of the lower classes in Russia with all its dissoluteness, barbarity, tragedy and misery. Petrushka is a sort of Polichinello, a poor hero always suffering from the cruelty of the police and every kind of wrong and unjust persecution. This represents symbolically the whole tragedy in the existence of the Russian people, a suffering from despotism and injustice. The scene is laid in the midst of the Russian carnival, and the streets are lined with booths, in one of which Petrushka plays a kind of humorous rôle. He is killed, but he appears again as a ghost on the roof of the booth to frighten his enemy, his old employer, an allusion to the despotic rule in Russia." [9]

Petrushka definitely established Stravinsky's fame. Once again, his unusual effects—now grown more startlingly original and bizarre—caused the raising of eyebrows. But many music critics could not deny Stravinsky's seductively fresh approach, the rich Slavic flavor of his musical material and, most important of all, his ability to give music an expressiveness which few, if any, of his contemporaries could equal. To the public at large, Stravinsky represented much more an intriguing but ephemeral novelty than a permanent influence; his music appeared

[9] This excerpt is quoted by Philip Hale in his admirable program notes on *Petrushka*. The source of this quotation, however is not given.

more original than important. But a handful of musicians
and art-lovers already accepted him as a prophet of the
future.

Following *Petrushka,* Stravinsky began work upon *Le
Sacre du Printemps.* Plans for *Le Sacre* had been conceived two years earlier, as Stravinsky himself informs us.
"One day, when I was finishing the last pages of *L'Oiseau
de feu* in St. Petersburg, I had a fleeting vision which came
to me as a complete surprise, my mind at the moment being
full of other things. I saw in imagination a solemn pagan
rite: sage elders, seated in a circle, watched a young girl
dance herself to death. They were sacrificing her to propiti-
ate the god of spring. Such was the theme of the *Sacre du
Printemps.* I must confess that this vision made a deep
impression upon me and I at once described it to my friend,
Nicholas Roerich, he being a painter who had specialized
in pagan subjects. He welcomed my inspiration with enthusiasm, and became my collaborator in this creation. In
Paris, I told Diaghilev about it, and he was at once carried
away by the idea, though its realization was delayed. . . ." [10]

The completion of *Le Sacre* was momentarily interrupted in the summer of 1912 when Stravinsky left with
Diaghilev for Bayreuth to witness a performance of Wagner's *Parsifal. Parsifal* sickened Stravinsky both as a
theatrical spectacle and as a musical score. His utter dis-
taste for Wagner's music has remained something of an
obsession with him throughout his career.

Le Sacre du Printemps, performed at the Théâtre des
Champs Élysées on May 29, 1913, definitely established
Stravinsky as a world figure in music—a man who from
that day became one of the most publicized and contro-
versial personalities of our generation. However, though
Le Sacre had been subject for derision and laughter, Stravinsky was convinced that he had produced an important
work; he insisted that he was right and his critics wrong.

[10] *Stravinsky: An Autobiography.*

And, slowly and inevitably, Stravinsky's faith in himself and in his work was to receive eloquent justification. On July 11, 1913, Pierre Monteux introduced the ballet to London; while there was some hissing, there was infinitely more applause. On April 5, 1914, Pierre Monteux conducted the music of the ballet at a symphonic concert at the Casino de Paris; the enthusiasm was stirring. Since that time, *Le Sacre du Printemps* has been accepted by the world of music as the crowning work of Stravinsky's career, and one of the indisputable monuments of twentieth century music.[11]

Two more important works, with roots deeply embedded in Russian tradition, succeeded *Le Sacre*. In 1914, Stravinsky completed his opera *Le Chant du rossignol (The Song of the Nightingale)*, the first act of which he had planned and sketched in Russia in 1909. S. Mitoussov fashioned the libretto after the Andersen fairy-tale. The opera was performed for the first time at the Paris Opéra in May of 1914, with only moderate success. During the War, Stravinsky converted the opera into a ballet, omitting much material from the first act. This ballet—with scenery by Matisse and choreography by Massine—was presented by the Ballet Russe in Paris on February 2, 1920. The orchestral suite drawn from the ballet has become familiar on orchestra programs.

Stravinsky's orchestral suite follows the narrative of the fairy-tale closely. The Emperor of China, hearing tales of the beautiful singing of a brown nightingale, invites it to his court. The bird sings so beautifully that the hearts of all the courtiers are softened and the eyes of the Emperor are filled with tears. But suddenly an envoy arrives bearing a mechanical nightingale which delights the entire court with its ingenious albeit stilted song. Heart-broken, the brown bird flies out of the palace and disappears. Enraged,

[11] As Cecil Gray wrote in 1929, *Le Sacre* is "one of the most conspicuous landmarks in the artistic life of our period."

the Emperor permanently banishes the nightingale from his empire. Shortly after this, the Emperor is at the threshold of death, and the physicians have given up all hope. One morning, the brown nightingale flies through the window and sings at the Emperor's bed so beautifully that she softens the heart of Death, who leaves the royal bedside. The courtiers return, expecting to find their Emperor dead, only to see him glowing with health and contentment.

The last of Stravinsky's important Russian works, bringing the second period to termination, was *Les Noces,* "scènes choréographiques Russes." *Les Noces* was composed during one of the most trying periods of Stravinsky's life. He began the first sketches in London in 1914, when the War suddenly forced him to flee with his family to Switzerland. There followed several years of great financial distress, heightened when the Russian revolutionists confiscated his last possessions. Troubles never coming single-handed, Stravinsky was also suffering excruciating pain as a result of intercostal neuralgia which made breathing difficult and which even brought on partial paralysis of the legs. At the same time, his spirits were depressed by the death of a younger brother and a nurse whom he had accepted as a foster-mother. In the midst of such confusion and bitterness—further heightened not a little by the inconvenience of being forced to compose a great part of his work in a cold Swiss attic, cluttered with empty Suchard chocolate boxes—Stravinsky created his tonal picture of a peasant wedding in Russia.

Les Noces, which was completed in 1917, did not receive its final instrumentation until 1923. On June 13, 1923, the Ballet Russe introduced it at the Paris Opéra to thunderous acclaim. It was esteemed as one of the greatest artistic triumphs of the Ballet Russe and one of Stravinsky's most vitally dynamic scores.

Stravinsky's middle creative period had spanned seven

years, in which five major works were produced. It is the opinion of more than one authority that it is in this period that Stravinsky fashioned his greatest music, music in which the abortive revolutions of the "Russian Five" were brought to their ultimate and inevitable destination. In these five works, harmonic language had been immeasurably enriched, contrapuntal writing had been stretched to its utmost flexibility, forms had become elastically supple, orchestration had been illuminated with electric brilliance, rhythm had been treated with a new and dynamic freshness. In these works, Stravinsky created an impression of irresistible energy. This music gives the listener the impression that it was created at white heat. The music sweeps relentlessly along like a typhoon. Stravinsky's works from *L'Oiseau de feu* through *Les Noces* are the irrepressible outbursts of creative genius.

4.

In 1919, Stravinsky took up his residence in Garches, in the environs of Paris, and from this time on his permanent home was France. At the same time, Stravinsky applied for French citizenship.

But in his music, he had already changed his nationality. Beginning with *Renard*—a "burlesque from Russian folk-tales" for four male voices and chamber orchestra, composed in 1917—a mystifying metamorphosis came over Stravinsky's style and idiom. Stravinsky had suddenly discarded the style of his magnificent second period as though it were a removable cloak, and assumed an altogether new and foreign one. Russian tradition and culture no longer dominated his thinking; from the composition of music that clearly showed its Slavic origins he turned to the creation of works whose polished surfaces reflected the elegance of French art. Most important of all, he had ceased being the defiant rebel, the fearless pioneer. Renouncing his former vitriolic style, he began to compose music with a simplified and lucid texture, in forms polished and refined. A cool counterpoint replaced his former tangled rhythms; his orchestration had now been peeled of several layers of color; the former nervous excitation now yielded to an aloof placidity. Stravinsky was composing "in the style of Handel and Scarlatti."

Renard launched Stravinsky upon his third period as a creator, a period even more radically different from the one that preceded it than the second had been from the first. With two burlesques—*L'Histoire du soldat,* for chamber orchestra, "a story to be read, played and danced" (introduced at Lausanne on September 28, 1918) and *Pulcinella,* a ballet based upon melodic material of Pergolesi (first performed by the Ballet Russe at the Paris Opéra on May 15, 1920)—and with the *Concerto for Piano and Orchestra,* composed in 1923-1924 and introduced in the latter year in Paris by Serge Koussevitzky with the composer at the piano, the new style reached crystallization. Stravinsky's music was now completely objective, unemotional, restrained; it was, in short, "pure" music. "I loathe orchestral effects as means of embellishment," Stravinsky said, a few years later, in an interview. "I have long since renounced the futilities of *brio*. I dislike cajoling the public; it inconveniences me. . . . The crowd expects the artist to tear out his entrails and exhibit them. That is what is held to be the noblest expression of art, and called personality, individuality, temperament, and so on." Certainly, Stravinsky had no further intention of indulging in emotional exhibitionism; the music of his new period was as impersonal as a slab of marble.

In 1925, Stravinsky crossed the ocean for the first time. The leading orchestras of America—including the New York Philharmonic Orchestra—were placed in his hands; in a series of guest concerts, Stravinsky conducted programs devoted to his own music. The regal reception which

America gave him showed clearly that, although Stravinsky had changed his æsthetic philosophy and reversed his
style completely, he was still, in the eyes of the music public of America, the most picturesque and glamorous figure
among the composers of our time.

In 1927, Stravinsky composed his first major work in
the new idiom, an opera-oratorio based upon Sophocles'
Œdipus Rex. In planning the work, Stravinsky felt
strongly that the text, to suit best the quality of his music,
must be in a classical tongue. Ancient Greek he discarded
as a language that was too dead. He therefore selected
Latin. Thus the text, which was written by Jean Cocteau,
was translated into Latin by Jean Daniélou. In this form it
was first performed by the Ballet Russe in Paris at the
Théâtre Sarah Bernhardt on May 30, 1927.

One year later, upon a commission from Mrs. Elizabeth
Sprague Coolidge, the eminent American patron of music,
Stravinsky composed another classical work—this time for
chamber orchestra, *Apollon Musagète*. *Apollon* was the
first work of Stravinsky to be given its world première in
America (it was performed at the concerts of the Library
of Congress in Washington, D. C., in May of 1928). It
was also the last work of Stravinsky featured by the Ballet
Russe. In 1929, Diaghilev died in Venice. And with
Diaghilev gone, Stravinsky's last link with the Ballet
Russe was permanently severed.

After *Apollon* came two more outstanding works. In
1930, Stravinsky composed the *Symphonie des Psaumes
(The Symphony of Psalms)*, for chorus and orchestra, inscribed to "the great glory of God" and dedicated to the
Boston Symphony Orchestra, which had commissioned the
work to celebrate the organization's fiftieth anniversary.
The *Symphonie*, however, was not given its first performance by the Boston Symphony Orchestra. Through a mis-
handling of the dates, it was first performed by the
Brussels Philharmonic Society on December 13, 1930, six

days before Koussevitzky introduced it in Boston. The
text of the *Symphonie* is from the Vulgate. In 1933-1934,
Stravinsky produced a "melodrama," *Perséphone,* for
chorus, orchestra, tenor and speaking voice, composed to a
text of André Gide. Commissioned by Ida Rubinstein, it
was introduced by her in Paris in April, 1934.

More recently, Stravinsky has composed a choreographic
drama—*Jeu de cartes en trois donnes (The Card Party)*
—dealing with the game of poker. Composed expressly
for the American Ballet, this work was first introduced
by that organization at the Metropolitan Opera House,
on April 27, 1937. The action of the ballet portrays a
game of cards by several choreographic and pantomimic
devices. The stage is set like a great club-room, but the
action, representing the card game, takes place on an
elevated, smaller stage. The face cards and the joker
are represented by solo dancers, costumed to the subject. This was the first time when a Stravinsky ballet
had had its world première in America. It was conducted
by himself. Two earlier ballets shared the program—
Apollon Musagète and *La Baiser de la Fée.*

There has been as much acrimonious disagreement about
the importance of Stravinsky's neo-classical idiom as there
was, in 1913, about the artistic importance of *Le Sacre.*
Today, as well as in 1913, Stravinsky is a subject for debate. On the one hand, there are many musicians who fer-
vently believe that Stravinsky's third period is the ultimate,
inevitable fulfillment of a lifelong artistic evolution. These
musicians feel strongly that Stravinsky has produced music
of transcendent quality; music finally denuded of overstuffed
costumes and meretricious jewelry, purged of hysterics and
emotional exhibitionism; music whose highest æsthetic value
lies in its purity, objective beauty and restraint.

But just so strongly does the opposing camp believe that
in this third period the genius of Stravinsky has entered
upon senescence. These critics feel that the great weakness

of Stravinsky's latest works rests in the consummate success with which the composer has achieved the ideal he has
set for himself: to reduce the body of music to a mere ugly
skeleton. Even in the most pretentious of his later works,
they feel, there are stretches of tonal aridity, as well as a
style that is effete and without character, devoid of any
vital message.

However, though Stravinsky's music may be subject for
violent difference of opinion, there can be no question that,
for more than three decades, he has held a magisterial
position over the composers of our time, exerting a cataclysmic influence upon the development of music. Just as in
1913, his cacophonies and his fresh rhythmic conceptions
led the way to revolt and opened an altogether new avenue
for musical expression (an avenue through which composers
everywhere have followed his lead), so five years later his
purity of writing pointed the way to a neo-classicism which
many younger and older composers were to adopt just as
readily. His outlook, his artistic aim, his style may undergo
complete reversal, but such is the force and strength of his
personality that he sways with him half of the music-world.
Whether one accepts the music of his later period or rejects
it, one cannot deny that as an influence in modern music
Stravinsky remains unique.

5.

Igor Stravinsky is small and thin; his chest appears
hollow. His face, long and lean, has an expression of inde-
finable sadness. His eyes have a particularly piercing
intensity which not even heavy lenses can obscure. An
aquiline nose descends sharply from a majestic brow, and
overlooks lips of uncompromising firmness. Upon his upper
lip the hair grows thin and sparse as though he had only
just begun to raise a moustache. He gives the impression
of excessive fragileness. However, he is not half so sus-

ceptible to illness as his puny body suggests or as he himself frankly believes. An inveterate hypochondriac, his frequent pains and indispositions are often more imaginary than actual.

When this author last visited Stravinsky, the composer was living in a spacious apartment in the Faubourg St. Honoré district of Paris, a few moments from the Champs Élysées. The family consists of four children: the two boys are Feodor, a capable painter, and Sviatoslav, a competent pianist (who, together with his father, gave the world première of the *Concerto* for two pianos in Paris in October of 1935); the two girls are Milena, who paints icons for churches, and Milka, who is still very young.

Stravinsky impresses friends and those with whom he comes into direct contact as a man of herculean energy. He is no longer a young man, and he has had a vigorous life. Yet his schedule would tax the endurance of one many years younger. His conductorial assignments force him to span virtually half a globe during a season. Yet he returns from each rigorous concert schedule and fatiguing succession of boats and trains as fresh as when he started—fresh enough, certainly, to hurl himself with his customary zest into producing a new composition, studying of new scores, increasing his musical equipment, perhaps even writing critical essays, or a book of memoirs.

Seated at his side, one instantly feels the enormous vitality of the man. He pours as much energy and zest into a casual conversation as he does into any of his endeavors— vigorously criticizing composers and their music, acridly condemning fads and fashions, electrically alive at every moment. As he talks, he diverts some of this endless energy into smoking cigarettes, stroking his moustache, and making staccato gestures of the wrists to punctuate his remarks. Occasionally, he shifts nervously in his chair, or paces the room. He seems incapable of being still a moment. He literally exhausts his listeners.

Stravinsky is enormously fond of conversation, and will discuss any musical subject with animation. Unless he is very familiar with his visitor, Stravinsky maintains a discreet but frigid silence where his own music is concerned. Not that Stravinsky is modest! As a matter of fact, he is quite convinced of the ultimate importance of his work, and has no hesitation in telling you about it; at one time he went so far as to say (refusing, however, to be specific) that there have been only three people in the world who have really understood his music—thereby placing his life work in the esoteric class of Whitehead's symbolic logic and Einstein's theory of relativity. His reluctance to discuss his own work springs from life-long experience, which has taught him that the majority of those who come to him with idolatrous words on their lips reveal, when they flower into more elaborate conversation, an appalling ignorance of what he has tried to accomplish. If, however, Stravinsky feels that you possess an intelligent understanding of his scores, not only will he talk at length about his aims and ideals, but he will also have no hesitancy in telling you that his style has undergone a subtle and inevitable evolution, that his present neo-classical period is his most important phase and that the music world is not as yet sufficiently equipped to recognize the inherent greatness of his best works, among which he numbers *Œdipus Rex,* the *Symphonie des Psaumes* and *Perséphone.*

A musical conversation with Stravinsky is an invigorating experience if for no other reason than the unorthodoxy of his opinions. He esteems Donizetti and Bellini higher than he does Beethoven, Schubert, or Brahms. About Bellini he once said that the music world is still too immature to appreciate the real genius that created *Norma* and *La Sonnambula.* Wagner he detests instinctively and intellectually. His favorite composers include Mozart and Tchaikovsky. Among the moderns, he holds the highest esteem for Prokofieff, Hindemith and de Falla. None of the younger talents has made an impression upon him.

Stravinsky's world, however, does not consist entirely and completely of music. His intellectual horizon is sufficiently broad to include a keen appreciation of art and literature. Except for art, religion plays the most important rôle in his life. He is devoutly pious. In a corner of his study there hangs a painted icon over a lighted candle; in front of this Stravinsky prays each morning. He also attends the Russian Church in Paris regularly. By nature he is a mystic, believing firmly in his intuition and instincts and the power of heaven-sent inspiration. He is also morbidly superstitious.

There is nothing of the ascetic in Stravinsky. He is extraordinarily fond of good food and fine wines. Everything about him attests to his love for system and order. He dresses with the utmost neatness, his dress including spats, discreet jewelry, and a walking-stick. His daily life in Paris is systematically routinized to include not only his musical activities and his many appointments, but also his religious functions and even his regular gymnastic exercises before an open window. His desk is as neatly in shape after he has worked there for several hours as when he approaches it. A manuscript of his is the last word in precise and fastidious clarity; his calligraphy resembles fine print.

He detests theories concocted to explain his music. "A nose is not manufactured; a nose just is. Thus, too, my art," he once remarked to an interviewer. "For me, as a creative musician, composition is a daily function that I feel impelled to discharge," he wrote in his autobiography. "I compose because I am made for that and cannot do otherwise."

RICHARD STRAUSS

II

RICHARD STRAUSS

1.

"THIRTY years ago I was regarded a rebel," Richard Strauss once said about himself. "I have lived long enough to find myself a classic."

Other modern composers have had the satisfaction of seeing earlier bitterly attacked works assume, with the passage of time, unquestioned importance in the eyes of the music world. But Strauss is perhaps alone among modern composers in finding himself not only widely performed and enthusiastically accepted, but even stamped as a classical master—he who, only yesterday, was branded an outcast in music. In his own lifetime, Strauss has procured for himself a permanent and undebated niche in musical history.

This triumph, for all the gratification it brings to a composer, is not without a certain element of tragedy where Richard Strauss is concerned. Paradoxically enough, this, the greatest victory a composer can claim, has been for Strauss something of defeat as well. If Strauss has lived long enough to see himself become a classic, he has also lived long enough to know that artistically he has been dead a long time. If he has lived long enough to see his early symphonic-poems and operas assume prodigious importance in the eyes of his own age, he has also lived to discover that, despite his productivity, he has never equalled the quality of his early works, that, as a matter of fact, his immortality must rest implicitly with the productions of his youth.

The career of every significant artist has been marked by a slow and subtle evolution in which the growth, development and final maturity of the artist is reached in a series of successive stages. In the career of Richard Strauss, however, we have not an evolution but a slow and prolonged deterioration. If *Arabella, The Egyptian Helen* and *Tageszeiten*—Strauss' more recent works—had been composed during the early period of his artistic career, and if *Till Eulenspiegel* and *Salomé* had been the very latest fruits of his industry, that would have been a normal and healthy growth. As it is, Richard Strauss' musical development is upside down. He is greatest in his earliest and feeblest in his latest works. At the age of thirty, Strauss was the most individual, most strongly gifted and genuinely inspired composer of his time; he stood alone; his music, bursting from him in full-statured maturity like Minerva from the brain of Jupiter, was the utterance of undisputed genius. Today, Richard Strauss is still famous as a composer of those very works, and the undisturbed creative activity of forty years has added nothing to his stature. His later productions consist of music of effective technical skill; but gone are the heart, the imagination, the poetry, the dynamic force and inspiration of his early masterpieces. His later works represent an appalling decline.

Disintegration is always a pathetic spectacle. Richard Strauss, the greatest musical figure of his time, is, therefore, likewise the most tragic.

2.

Richard Strauss, the only son and elder of two children of Franz Strauss, famous horn player, and Josephine Pschorr Strauss, the daughter of the prosperous Bavarian brewer, was born in Munich on June 11, 1864.

Franz Strauss, who was employed as solo horn player in the court orchestra, was an eminent artist on his instrument. Von Bülow once referred to him as the "Joachim of the horn." The career of Franz Strauss assumes particular interest, in connection with that of his son, in that he was the leader in Munich of all cabals and intrigues against Richard Wagner. Franz Strauss hated Wagner's music with a lusty passion, expressing that hate unmistakably and unequivocally. Once, in the midst of a rehearsal under Wagner himself, Franz Strauss impudently rose from his seat and walked out of the orchestra-pit because he would not perform such music. On another occasion—when Strauss had played a Wagnerian horn passage with particularly beautiful tone and phrasing—Wagner openly suggested that a performer who could play in such a fashion could not possibly hate the music he was performing; to which Franz Strauss acidly and vehemently answered that his performance had absolutely nothing to do with his opinion of the music. Franz Strauss, it might be added, lived long enough to see his son Richard become one of the most devoted disciples of the Wagnerian music-drama. Wagner would have been the first to appreciate the irony of this situation.

Richard was a precocious child. At the age of four he began the study of the piano under the guidance of his mother, his progress rapidly attracting the admiration of his father. His sixth year found him attempting composition. He produced a rollicking polka, *Der Schneiderpolka*, and an art-song inspired by the song the children were singing round the Christmas tree. When he was sent to elementary school in Munich, his mother would wrap his books with music note-paper of which there was always an abundant supply in the Strauss household. It was soon discovered that, in class, little Richard was deaf to the instruction of his teachers; he was often busy filling his bookcovers with melodies and abortive compositions.

The father knew definitely that his son had an extraordinary musical instinct and formidable native talent. He knew also that his son was destined for greater achievements than those which lie in the hands of a virtuoso. To prepare him adequately for whatever future was destined,

Franz Strauss gave his son a comprehensive education. After four years of elementary school, Richard was sent to the Gymnasium where he remained until 1882. Music was, to be sure, followed industriously. The study of the piano and the violin was pursued with intensity under August Tombo and Benno Walter respectively. Likewise for five years young Strauss was given a comprehensive schooling in harmony, counterpoint and instrumentation by Kapellmeister F. W. Meyer.

The name of Richard Strauss soon asserted itself prominently in Munich's musical life. While he was still in the Gymnasium, a chorus for Sophocles' *Elektra* and a *Festival Chorus* were performed at a student concert of the Gymnasium. Shortly after this—Strauss had just seen his sixteenth birthday—a well-known singer, Frau Meysenheim, introduced into her program three songs of Strauss. One year later, Strauss made his creative industry felt even more strongly. On March 16, 1881, his violin teacher, Benno Walter, introduced the young composer's *String Quartet in A.* Two weeks later, the great Wagnerian conductor, Hermann Levi, performed Strauss' *Symphony in D-minor.* Thus, still in his apprenticeship, Strauss tasted the sweetness of success.

His youth, of course, had made him flexible to his father's peculiar penchants and prejudices. Hence, at first, Richard Strauss was a vehement anti-Wagnerite. *Tristan und Isolde,* when he first heard it, represented to him the incoherent jargon of a maniac. Hence, too, Strauss was powerfully influenced by the music of Johannes Brahms. Most of his early works show many of the characteristics of Brahms—the allegiance to classicism, the epical stature of form, the sensuous sweeps of melody, the elegiac tenderness of the meditative moments. Johannes Brahms was familiar with the music of young Strauss and was heartily pleased by the high flattery of imitation. After the performance of Strauss' first symphony, Brahms approached the young composer, patted him paternally on the shoulder, and exclaimed: "This is quite pretty music, young man!"

Between 1882 and 1883, Strauss continued his academic studies at the University of Munich. This was an eventful period, because at this time Strauss discovered Wagner for the first time. He attended performances of *Tristan* and *Walküre* when, to his amazement, the labyrinth of Wagner's music extricated itself and Strauss perceived the inevitable logic and truth of Wagner's art. He had already been deeply impressed by studying Wagner's scores; he now emerged a perfect Wagnerite. Eight years later, the conversion became complete when Strauss attended the Bayreuth festival to pay homage at the Wagnerian shrine.

Upon leaving the Munich University in 1883, Strauss came to Berlin for a short visit where the court orchestra, under Raedecke, presented his *Overture in C-minor*. While in Berlin, his publisher, Eugen Spitzweg—convinced of his enormous promise—sent a set of Strauss' piano pieces to Hans von Bülow, the great conductor of Meiningen. "I thoroughly dislike them," was von Bülow's opinion, "they are unripe." But that there was something in Strauss that impressed von Bülow strongly became apparent when, shortly afterwards, the conductor introduced the *Serenade for Thirteen Wind Instruments* in Meiningen, at the same time expressing his faith in the young composer in no uncertain vocabulary. Strauss was urged by von Bülow to compose other works for him, and in the year that followed he produced a *Concerto for Horn and Orchestra* and a *Suite* (also for thirteen Wind Instruments). The last-named work, Strauss himself conducted, and, as though to express his full faith in the young musician more emphatically, von Bülow compelled Strauss to direct the work without the benefit of a single rehearsal.

On October 1, 1885, von Bülow appointed Strauss as his assistant with the Meiningen orchestra at a salary of $360 a year—launching Strauss upon a career as conductor which

was eventually to become almost as preëminent as his creative life. The following year was one of intense activity
for Strauss. He appeared frequently at the Meiningen concerts in the rôles of conductor and concert pianist; in November, 1885, as a matter of fact, von Bülow passed on the
baton of the orchestra completely to Strauss. This activity,
however, did not interfere with his creative work. He
composed two new large works—a *Symphony in F-minor*
(which was given its world's première in America by Theodore Thomas on December 13, 1884) and a *Piano Quartet*
which won a prize offered by the Berlin Tonkunstlerverein
offered for outstanding new chamber music.

It was at this time that Strauss met and became a close
friend of Alexander Ritter, who was probably the greatest
single influence in his career. What Diaghilev was later to
be for Stravinsky, Ritter was now for Strauss. Both composers owe their sudden evolution to independent musical
writing and full freedom of expression and individuality of
style, to the outside influence of a strong, dominating and
integrated personality. Ritter, a violinist in the court
orchestra in Munich, husband of the niece of Richard Wagner, was not only an excellent musician, but a man of profound intellect, a student of philosophy. In endless
conversations on art, in extensive theorizing about the
æsthetic mission of music, Ritter unfolded new horizons for
Strauss, pointed out to him altogether new directions. "His
influence was in the nature of a storm wind," Strauss later
confessed. "He urged me on to the development of the
poetic, the expressive in music as exemplified in the works
of Liszt, Berlioz and Wagner." Through Ritter's advice,
Strauss was urged to abandon the constraining classicism of
Brahms—in which his fiery spirit was smothered—and to
adopt the more plastic form of Liszt's tone-poems. Richard
Wagner had recently died; Ritter urged Strauss to carry the
Wagnerian torch, to desert the creation of "pure" symphonic music and to turn to pungent dramatic expression.

RICHARD STRAUSS

Even more important, Ritter inspired in Strauss independent thinking, and gave him the moral courage to put down upon paper those original conceptions which Strauss had confided to him in moments of intimate conversation. As a result of Ritter's friendship, Strauss' music changed its character and personality almost overnight.

Early in 1886, Strauss traveled to Italy for a brief holiday. Upon his return he composed the first work to disclose a revolutionary metamorphosis in his style, *Aus Italien,* the first music in which Strauss permitted his flair for dramatic writing to assert itself. *Aus Italien,* in Strauss' own description, is "the connecting link between the old and the new." It cannot be said that von Bülow was able to follow the swift pace of his protegé. "Does my age make me so reactionary?" wrote von Bülow after seeing the score of *Aus Italien.* "I find that the clever composer has gone to the extreme limits of tonal possibilities (in the realm of beauty) and, in fact, has even gone beyond those limits without real necessity."

On August 1, 1886, Strauss was appointed third Kapellmeister of the Munich Opera under Levi and Fischer. The following March, he conducted *Aus Italien* for the first time. The audience, first apathetic to Strauss' new style, soon expressed its disapproval unequivocally. When the fourth movement of the work was being performed—in which, to express the abandon of Neapolitan life, Strauss for the first time unleashed his cacophony—hissing and catcalls were heard throughout the auditorium. Upon the conclusion of the performance, father Franz Strauss, who was in the audience, rushed backstage to give his son words of consolation. To his amazement he found Richard sitting on the edge of a table, his feet dangling cheerfully. The fiasco had evidently made no impression upon him; Strauss was now too sure of himself, and too sure of his direction.

3.

Between 1889 and 1894, Strauss officiated as court conductor in Weimar. Of greater importance is the fact that in that time he stepped into his full stride as a composer. He had already written an energetic violin sonata and several songs of great poignancy; he now began the composition of the first of those tone-poems which brought him world fame. In the fall of 1889, Hans von Bülow performed *Don Juan* at a concert of the Weimar Court Orchestra. *Don Juan* was not, strictly speaking, the first of Strauss' tone-poems—*Macbeth* having been composed a year earlier. But it was the first large work he wrote which is part of the modern concert-repertory.

Don Juan, for which Strauss never supplied any specific program material, was modeled after a poem of Nicolaus Lenau. "My *Don Juan*," explained the poet, "is no hot-blooded man eternally pursuing women. It is the longing in him to find a women who is to him incarnate womanhood, and to enjoy, in the one, all the women on earth, whom he cannot possess as individuals. Because he does not find her, although he reels from one to another, at last Disgust seizes hold of him, and this Disgust is the Devil that fetches him." This might very aptly serve as the brief for Strauss' music.

Don Juan was the harbinger of what was soon to follow. After *Don Juan* came the deluge—of masterpieces.

Death and Transfiguration was completed in 1889, and was introduced by Strauss himself in Eisenach on June 21, 1890. Strauss' friend, Alexander Ritter, wrote the poem which serves as the program for Strauss' music. "In the little room, dimly lighted by only a candle end, lies the sick man on his bed. But just now he has wrestled despairingly with Death. Now he has sunk exhausted in sleep. . . . But Death does not long grant sleep and dreams to his victim. Cruelly he shakes him awake, and the fight begins afresh.

Will to live and power of Death! What frightful wrestling! Neither bears off the victory, and all is silent once more! Sunk back tired of battle, sleepless, as in fever-frenzy the sick man now sees his life pass before his inner eye. . . . First the morning red of childhood. . . . Then the youth's saucier play—exerting and trying his strength—till he ripens to the man's fight, and now burns with hot lust after the higher prizes of life. The one high purpose that has led him through life was to shape all he saw transfigured into a still more transfigured form. Cold and sneering, the world set barrier upon barrier in the way of his achievement. . . . And so he pushes forward, so he climbs, desists not from his sacred purpose. What he has ever sought with his heart's deepest yearning, he still seeks in his death sweat. . . . Then clangs the last stroke of Death's iron hammer, breaks the earthly body in twain, covers the eye with the night of death. But from the heavenly spaces sounds mightily to greet him what he yearningly sought for here: deliverance from the world, transfiguration of the word." [1]

Death and Transfiguration was followed, five years later, by *Till Eulenspiegel's Merry Pranks, After the Old-Fashioned Roguish Manner*—first performed in Frankfurt, in September, 1895. *Till Eulenspiegel* was based upon a celebrated legend about a practical jokester who went through life, whistling nonchalantly, as he perpetrated one successful prank after another—some harmless, some excessively vulgar, some malicious. "It is impossible for me to furnish a programme to *Eulenspiegel*," Strauss wrote to Dr. Franz Wüllner, who conducted the second performance of the work (in Cologne). "Were I to put into words what I had in mind in composing the difficult parts, they would often sound queer, and might even give offense. Let me leave it, therefore, to my hearers to crack the hard nut which the Rogue has handed them. By the way of helping

[1] Translated by William Foster Apthorp.

them to a better understanding, it seems sufficient to point out the two 'Eulenspiegel' motives, which, in the most manifold disguises, moods, and situations, pervade the whole up to the catastrophe, when, after he has been condemned to death, Till is strung up a gibbet. For the rest, let them guess at the musical joke which a Rogue has offered them."

Incidentally, although Strauss mercilessly destroys Till at the gallows in his tone-poem, the legend was more merciful: the story originally had it that Till, by his sharp brain, escaped the doom to which his mischief had brought him.

Following in the footsteps of *Till Eulenspiegel* came *Thus Spake Zarathustra*, "freely after Friedrich Nietzsche," completed on August 24, 1896, and performed on November 27 of that year at Frankfort-on-the-Main by the composer. "I did not intend to write philosophical music or portray Nietzsche's great work musically. I meant to convey by means of music an idea of the development of the human race from its origin, through the various phases of evolution, religious as well as scientific, up to Nietzsche's idea of the Superman." And, in an interview, Strauss added that he desired in *Zarathustra*, "to embody the conflict between man's nature as it is and man's metaphysical attempts to lay hold of his nature with his intelligence—leading finally to the conquest of life by the release of laughter."

Two more great tone-poems were to emerge from Strauss' adventures with his new musical style. *Don Quixote, Fantastic Variations on a Theme of a Knightly Character*—built upon incidents from Cervantes' immortal novel—was composed in 1897, completed December 29, 1897, and was introduced on March 18, 1898, at the Gürzenich concerts of Cologne, under the baton of Franz Wüllner. Approximately one year later, on March 3, 1899, the Museumgesellschaft of Frankfort-on-the-Main introduced Strauss' autobiographical tone-poem, *Ein Heldenleben* (in the section describing the hero's soul, Strauss utilized thematic material from his principal works to date, thereby summing up his own spiritual development)—a depiction of the struggles of a hero with his many enemies.

These tone-poems, stunning as they did the musical intelligence of the late nineteenth century, made Strauss the storm-center of the music world. A few there were who proclaimed Strauss a prophetic voice in music, but these were sadly outnumbered by those who esteemed him a charlatan and his music charivari. To the majority, the subtle form of Strauss' tone-poems appeared episodic, rambling, incoherent, because the transition from one subject to the next was not so clearly defined as it was in Liszt, for example, and because Strauss introduced innumerable minor motives to describe the program he was following. Moreover, the dramatic intensity of Strauss' dissonances appeared to be only so much unbearable noise. *Till Eulenspiegel,* in the opinion of one writer, was "a vast and coruscating jumble of instrumental cackles about things unfit to be mentioned." Claude Debussy referred to a Strauss work as a piece "resembling 'An Hour of Music in an Asylum.'" Strauss' gargantuan orchestra, which included such singular instruments as a "wind machine" and a "watchman's rattle," inspired malicious satire. Strauss' dramatic realism in transferring his programmatic material into music—he even attempted to translate into tone the bleating of sheep, the galloping of horses, the posture of Till holding his nose, the babbling of wives in the market-place—was subject for robust hilarity. Strauss' egotism in identifying himself as the hero of his *Heldenleben* created bitter resentment.

Dissension and debate, resentment and hilarity, criticism and praise, all extravagant, combined to spread the name of Richard Strauss from one end of the music world to the other. Curiosity about his works inevitably brought performances in every important music center. By the dawn of the twentieth century, Richard Strauss was the most dominant figure in the world of contemporary music. There were those who detested him and who savagely attacked his works; but to be unfamiliar with them or to ignore them was impossible.

Time has elevated these tone-poems to that high position in musical literature they deserve. They are not without their faults, and frequently—with the exception only of *Till Eulenspiegel*—Strauss introduces material of banal quality. Yet who can deny today that they are works of genius? Here is a technical skill that seems almost innate, a prodigious mastery of the orchestra, an ability to cull from it qualities and effects it had never before produced. Here was an uncanny ability to etch character through the supple use of rhythm, an incredible talent at etching atmosphere and background in a few bars, an almost infallible touch in portraying every subtle shade of emotion. Here, finally, was a burst of sensuous melody which pours in never-ending abundance, as intoxicating as champagne, as luxuriously splendid as the sun that pours through the opening pages of Zarathustra's invocation. Within these tone-poems one meets with immortal phrases, imperishable lines, stretches of deathless tone which inspire and electrify with every hearing. The nervous quivering of the violins in *Till Eulenspiegel* at the close of the work (bringing the recapitulation of the opening theme to a culminating point and heralding the approach of the concluding explosion) sounds a pathos more heartbreaking than the extravagant tragedies of Tchaikovsky's glissandos—and this in a work that sparkles and glistens with malicious irony! Zarathustra's invocation to the sun bursts upon us with a magnificence that stuns and stupefies. *Don Juan* is full of the hot and restless blood of youth. Has musical literature many effects so electrifying as the energy that sweeps through the first four measures of this work like a hurricane? The opening of *Death and Transfiguration* paints with the first few bars an atmosphere of despair and frustration that permeate the entire work. Where else—with the exception of *Tristan*—can one dupli-

cate the magnificent passion and ecstasy of the *Heldenleben*
love music? And so on and on through the tone-
poems. . . .

4.

We have traveled so swiftly in our biographical narrative
that it is necessary to retrace our steps briefly.

In the spring of 1891, Strauss suffered congestion of the
lungs which, aggravated by a general nervous breakdown
brought on by overwork, became so acute that the doctors
despaired of his life. At one moment, Strauss—certain
that he was dying—expressed the sentiment that it was
difficult to die without having once conducted *Tristan*. Fortunately, the illness was gradually relieved. In the spring
of 1892, Strauss took a long voyage to the warmer climate
of Greece, Egypt and Sicily as a rest cure. In Cairo, as a
relief from the monotony of travel, Strauss began work
upon his first opera, built upon an original libretto. The
first act was completed in Luxor, the second in Sicily, the
third in Marquartstein, Upper Bavaria. On May 12, 1894,
Strauss himself conducted the first performance of his opera
Guntram in Weimar. Being modeled too closely upon the
Wagnerian music-drama, *Guntram* was a dismal failure, and
was given only one performance when produced again in
Munich, November 16, 1895.

One of the two featured singers in the cast of *Guntram*
in the Weimar production was Pauline de Ahna, daughter
of a military officer, and a singer of great talent. Strauss
had met her three years previously at Feldafing, a Bavarian
summer resort, and from that time on their friendship grew.

The friendship between Richard Strauss and Pauline de
Ahna was prolonged; but their courtship was brief. They
were married on September 10, 1894.

She made him a remarkable wife. A shrewd administrator, practical, clear-headed and supremely efficient, she

managed Strauss' affairs with a capable hand and a keen
intelligence. She arranged his social program, advised him
on all his business affairs, planned his day methodically.
She regulated his life with military precision. He soon
learned to depend implicitly upon her judgment, and he
permitted his life to be governed by it. Frequently, when
Strauss dallied too long in his garden or over a book, his
wife would call out to him: "Now, Richard, you had better
return to your composition!"—much in the manner of a
mother reminding her recalcitrant son that it was time for
the piano exercises. The extent to which Strauss was dominated by his wife is revealed by an amusing anecdote. The
Strausses were attending a social function at the Kaiser Bar
in Vienna, when a young lady begged Richard Strauss for
a dance. "I would love to," he answered, his face becoming
red as he directed furtive glances at his wife. "But I really
don't believe she would permit me."

In 1898, Richard Strauss was one of the founders of—
and one of the most vigorous protagonists for—the *Genossenschaft Deutscher Tondichter*. Strauss had for a long time
been bitterly opposed to the system then existing whereby
orchestras could perform the work of living composers without the payment of any royalty. As a remedy, Strauss
founded the *Genossenschaft* which, uniting the German composers into a strong and unified body, demanded that the
performance of every modern work be remunerated by the
orchestra performing it.

For this, a mountain of abuse and invective descended
upon Strauss. Orchestras objected violently to increasing
their already formidable expenditure; publishers and young
composers raised the cry that the orchestras would not perform new and unknown music of lesser composers if a
payment was necessary—thereby plunging the neglected
composer into still greater obscurity. Strauss was accused
of being mercenary, of attempting to convert art into a business. However, neither abuse nor criticism could drive

Strauss from the field of battle. Perhaps it is true that he was guided by personal considerations—Strauss, from the very first, was intensely materialistic; but it is absurd to deny that he was likewise motivated by the knowledge that with his victory composers throughout the world would profit enormously.

The battle was a bitter one, but it was Strauss and his *Genossenschaft* who emerged victorious. Today, principally because of their efforts—no modern work is performed anywhere by a symphony orchestra without the payment of a specific royalty to the composer.

Beginning with the turn of the century, Strauss divided his enormous energy equally between two major activities—conducting and composition. In both of these he prospered. After traveling across the face of Europe as a guest of the foremost orchestras, achieving an enormous reputation as interpreter not only of his own works but of the classical composers as well, he was appointed conductor of the Berlin Philharmonic. For a few years he officiated as a conductor of the Berlin Royal Opera. Then, royal favor being with him, he was elevated in 1898 to the position of general director, which he retained for twelve years.

As a composer, Strauss deserted the form of the symphonic-poem—which he strongly felt that he had exhausted —and turned more intensively to the song and the opera. With the exception of the *Symphonia Domestica*—which Strauss introduced during a visit to America on March 21, 1904—Strauss comparatively neglected orchestral music.

On November 21, 1901, Strauss' second opera, *Feuersnot* —a satire on Munich—was introduced at the Dresden Opera. Like *Guntram, Feuersnot* failed because Strauss was fumbling in a new medium. But on December 9, 1905, Strauss definitely assumed the same significance as an operatic composer that, a few years back, he had assumed as a creator of symphonic-poems. On that date, the Dres-

den Opera presented his *Salomé,* based upon the famous
play of Oscar Wilde.

In *Salomé,* Strauss finally succeeded in pouring into operatic mould that sensuous melody, that rich harmonization,
that subtlety of musical characterization, that spontaneous
passion and emotion which appear so abundantly in his best
tone-poems.   He had definitely found his sphere as an
operatic composer.

Salomé made Strauss once again the center of storms and
abuse.   In England, the censors forebade the production of
the opera on grounds of immorality.   In America, after the
first performance, such a tempest of protest arose over the
"licentious" theme of the opera that it was hurriedly
removed from the repertoire.   Strauss was vilified and slan-
dered by self-righteous Puritans.   Fortunately, Germany
and Austria adopted a saner and healthier attitude, and
with frequent performances it became apparent that *Salomé*
was neither carnal nor demoralizing.   When, in 1934, the
Metropolitan Opera House revived *Salomé,* for the first
time since the "scandal" of twenty years back, more than
one critic expressed amazement that so innocuous a subject
could have aroused such a tempest of moral indignation
(but this was largely because the horrors had been toned
down).

Elektra, which followed *Salomé* by four years, inaugurated the collaboration of Richard Strauss and the
distinguished Austrian poet and dramatist, Hugo von
Hofmannsthal.   Hugo von Hofmannsthal was, in more
respects than one, the ideal librettist.   He was not only a
master of his dramatic craft but, a musician in his own
right, he could fashion poetical plays that could lend themselves to musical treatment; he was also capable of—as he
did not hesitate in doing—giving the composer advice upon
his musical composition. Strauss and von Hofmannsthal did
not meet frequently.   Each worked in his own villa but,
through a prolific exchange of correspondence (which was

edited by Strauss' son and published in 1928), they succeeded in working hand in hand, each over his own assignment, each giving advice and criticism to the other. Strauss
(in his less contrary moments) frequently referred to von
Hofmannsthal as his "alter ego," and more than once expressed the sentiment that their collaboration had been
ordained by fate. "You are a born librettist," Strauss
wrote to him, "which is, in my opinion, the greatest compli-
ment, for I consider it far more difficult to write a good
operatic text than a fine drama." [2]

The collaboration of Richard Strauss and Hugo von
Hofmannsthal persisted for almost twenty-five years and
resulted in the following operas: *Elektra* (1909); *Der
Rosenkavalier* (1911), *Ariadne auf Naxos* (1912), the
ballet *Josephs Legende* (1914), *The Woman Without a
Shadow* (1919) and *The Egyptian Helen* (1928).

Of these operas, which range in quality from the sublime
to the ridiculous, the most personal and uniformly inspired
is *Der Rosenkavalier,* which, one might say without exaggerated enthusiasm, is one of the great contributions of the
twentieth century to the operatic stage. Strauss had for
some time been eager to compose a comic-opera in which
the rich ironic vein of his musical style might be given free
play. He was thinking of something in the nature of
Johann Strauss' *Der Fledermaus,* a work which he adored.
He aspired to produce an opera that would be playful,
satiric, pungently ironic, broadly farcical and, at other moments, tender and passionate. He conveyed his wishes to
his collaborator, Hugo von Hofmannsthal, and asked for
a suitable book. "I shall try," wrote the poet in reply, "to
put myself in sympathy with the requirements, possibilities,
and stylistic canons of comic opera. . . . If I succeed, as I
confidently hope to do, the result will be something which,
in its blending of the grotesque with the lyrical, will to a

[2] *Correspondence between Richard Strauss and Hugo von Hofmannsthal,*
edited by Franz Strauss.

certain extent correspond with your artistic individuality—
something which will be strong enough to keep its place in
the reportory for years, perhaps for decades."

The libretto which von Hofmannsthal prepared far sur-
passed the expectation of the composer both for its comic
and dramatic possibilities; and it inspired Strauss to write
his most consistently inspired score. In 1911, the Dresden
Opera introduced *Der Rosenkavalier,* with Carl Perron as
Baron Ochs. It was a triumph from the very first.

Der Rosenkavalier is, probably, the highest peak in
Strauss' operatic art. No libretto and music in operatic
history suit each other so well as Hugo von Hofmannsthal's
drama does Strauss' often sprightly, often profound music.
Strauss has never excelled the spontaneity of this music. It
is well-shaded; it has subtle contrasts; it has the warmth and
the pulse of the human heart-beat. It is alive and bright-
faced from the very first bar to the last. The character of
Baron Ochs, one of the most vitally alive in all of opera, is
etched in unforgettable strokes of broad satire not only in
the libretto but in the music as well. Strauss caught the
gusto and exuberance of the play with enviable felicitousness
in his music. But this opera was not merely a subtle play of
comedy and satire. At other moments, Strauss was swept
to an intensity of expression which produced music of incomparable depth. It is very doubtful if even Strauss himself
ever equalled the magnificent emotional intensity of the
Marschallin music of the first act.

After *Der Rosenkavalier* came the dusk of the god. It
almost seemed that with one final magnificent speech, a
genius had completely exhausted himself. The decline of
Strauss as a creative artist began in 1911 and continued
permanently. In the opera, Strauss produced *The Woman
Without a Shadow, Intermezzo, The Egyptian Helen, Arabella* where one could find hardly more than a supreme
technique and the ingenious resources of a trained intellect.
But here a heart has ceased to feel deeply, to respond sensi-

tively to beauty, to express itself in uncontrollable bursts of inspiration. In these works one no longer feels the freshness and charm which were always attributes of Strauss' style. The melodies are stilted, following obvious patterns; the harmonies, though ingeniously contrived, are dull to the ear. The waltzes of the *Intermezzo,* for example, are pathetically derivative from those of another, and fresher, Strauss. And, in *The Egyptian Helen,* does one actually perceive Richard Strauss copying fragments of a melodic line from Rimsky-Korsakoff?

Orchestrally, the fate of Richard Strauss was equally pathetic. The last tone-poem, *Ein Heldenleben,* was composed in 1899, *Symphonia Domestica,* with its petty musical setting of domestic bickerings marked the turning point; despite its occasional inspired flight of dramatic effect and melody, *Symphonia Domestica* clearly showed us the beginning of the decline of Strauss as a symphonic composer. The fat and vulgar *Military Marches* came in 1907, the *Festliches Praeludium* in 1913, the *Alpensinfonie* in 1915, *Schlagobers* in 1924 and *Tageszeiten* in 1928. Gone, completely, are the former electric energy, the former magnificent outbursts of passion, the former tenderness and sensitivity. Instead, we have a theoretician playing with harmonic rules, a technician who becomes unspeakably boring.

Even the song composer had exhausted himself. The ability to produce exquisite cameos of emotion had eluded his touch. One had merely to compare the charming and ingenious *Nichts* and *Allerseelen* (1882), and the profoundly moving *Traum durch die Dämmerung, Morgen* and *Ständchen* with such obviously manufactured morsels as *Gefunden* (1906) and the sterile expanses of the *Tageszeiten,* for men's chorus and orchestra, to realize that the technique may still be present, but the inspiration is dead. It was, therefore, somewhat sorrowfully that Ernest Newman wrote in 1934, on the occasion of the seventieth birthday of Richard Strauss, that "Strauss *was* a genius." The tense is accurate. Strauss was a genius more than twenty-five years ago. Today, he is hardly more than an experienced craftsman.

5.

Despite the decline, Richard Strauss remained the darling of the music-world, particularly of the German and Austrian music lovers, each of whom claimed him as their own. As long as the tone-poems were featured on symphony programs, and *Salomé, Elektra* and *Der Rosenkavalier* were permanent fixtures in the operatic repertoire, just so long did a music world feel grateful to the creator of such masterpieces. Thus Vienna gave him a gift of the magnificent grounds cut from the park of the Imperial Belvedere Palace if he consented to remain in that city for four months a year. Thus, too, when Strauss visited America again in 1921 he was given a royal reception. Pilgrimages were made by musicians throughout the world to his villa in Garmisch-Partenkirchen to pay homage to a master. And whenever Strauss conducted (Strauss served as conductor at the Vienna State Opera from 1919 to 1924, and since that time has been a guest conductor in Munich, Berlin, Vienna and Bayreuth), an audience would rise to its feet in respect to a great musical figure.

When, in 1933, the Nazi government assumed power in Germany and instituted an artistic creed which revolted the integrity of every artist—a creed which banished every artist of Jewish race, which viciously denounced any music constructed from an original matrix, and which elevated to the highest artistic standards Nazi musicians of negligible background and equipment as well as music pompously chauvinistic—an entire world waited to see what would be the attitude of Germany's greatest musician. Of all musicians in Germany, Strauss was in the strongest position to express his contempt of such a ruthless artistic policy as that which was adopted by the Nazi government. His world prestige protected him. He would have been welcomed with open arms by any country in the world, where he could easily have maintained his sovereign position in music, if he chose to rebel against the Nazi program.

To the amazement of the music world, Strauss first tacitly, then openly, supported the Nazi artistic creed. He expressed the opinion that a government had the right to dictate a country's artistic policy, and that it was the duty of every citizen to follow such a policy without question or vacillation. Thus, when the foremost Jewish musicians of Germany were banished, reducing Germany to a state of musical poverty it had not known for more than two centuries, Strauss remained silent. When it was forbidden to perform the "pernicious" music of such Jewish composers as Mendelssohn and Mahler, Strauss—who had previously loved Mendelssohn, and exerted herculean effort to bring recognition to the music of Mahler—quietly renounced these composers. And when æsthetic standards had changed to elevate to importance music of vulgarity, bombast and affectation, Strauss enthusiastically welcomed the change. On November 15, 1933, in gratitude for and acknowledgment of his position on Nazi music, the Kulturkammer appointed Richard Strauss president of the Third Reich Music Chamber.

It was not long before Strauss learned that it was not so easy to goose-step to the Nazi creed. In 1934, the Kulturkammer, eager to erase every memory of Mendelssohn, urged Strauss to compose new music to Shakespeare's *A Midsummer Night's Dream,* on the pattern of the Mendelssohn music, which might displace it permanently. Strauss, who could blind himself to sacrilege perpetrated by others, could not bring himself to commit it himself. He refused, and the Kulturkammer expressed its displeaure. In 1935, a much greater rupture arose between Strauss and the Nazi government. Strauss had asked Stefan Zweig, the celebrated Austrian writer—a Jew—to prepare a libretto for an opera. Zweig wrote a play, *The Silent Woman*, which Strauss set to music and which was produced at the Dresden Opera on June 24, 1935. On June 11, 1935, the Kulturkammer openly expressed indignation that Strauss should ally himself with a Jew, asking at the same time for Strauss' resignation as president of the Third Reich Music Chamber. A conciliation between Strauss and the Kulturkammer was attempted; but the Kulturkammer refused to renege on its anti-Jewish policy which demanded rigid punishment for all its violators. On July 13, 1935, therefore, Richard Strauss resigned his position, and secluded himself in his villa in Garmisch-Partenkirchen away from the limelight. He had already lost considerable caste in the eyes of half a music world because of his position in Nazi music. It was bitter for him to realize that he had now likewise lost caste in the eyes of his own country.

6.

Richard Strauss is tall and lean and, though his shoulders stoop slightly, his build is athletic. He appears much younger than his years. His step is brisk; when you shake his hand you feel a firm, strong clasp. His face, to be sure, is heavily lined, but it possesses almost the freshness of a man thirty years younger. It is a mobile face, with subtly varying expressions; and it is a curious blend of strength and weakness. Strength—in the high, majestic forehead, giving his head an appearance of exaggerated size. Weakness—in the soft, dreamy, philosophic eyes, and in the effeminacy of jaw and chin. A short, gray moustache abruptly separates his firm and uncompromising lip from a small upturned nose.

He is a pleasant companion, usually very spirited and in good humor, with an enormous capacity for enjoying life.

He is enormously fond of beer, delights in playing cards—particularly *Skat*—and indulges enthusiastically in many games of sport. The society of good friends affords him particular enjoyment. His conversation is fluent and brilliant (he speaks with a marked Bavarian accent), generously sprinkled with bright witticisms. At a dinner given in his honor, a speaker generously referred to Strauss as the "Buddha of modern music." "If I am the Buddha of modern music," whispered Strauss to his neighbor, "then this fellow is its Pesth!" This anecdote is characteristic of his tongue's glibness.

His intelligence is unusually expansive, embracing many fields: politics and science, literature and music, the arts and history. A good philosophic background gives unity to these many interests. A particularly important influence in his thinking has been Nietzsche; Strauss believes implicitly in the Superman and, at different periods, has identified the Superman with the Kaiser and with Hitler. He is also irremediably chauvinistic, has been so for more than fifty years. During the early part of the World War, he was one of the first German intellectuals to sign a manifesto expressing withering contempt for France. His union with the Nazis can probably be best explained by his great allegiance to his country. Germany, right or wrong has always been his political creed.

In all of his business dealings Strauss has been known to be shrewd, capable of driving a hard bargain, relentless whenever he knew he had the upper hand. He has always had an unhealthy lust for money, pursued it with unswerving devotion. In his youth, his explanation for his love of money was partly convincing. "A composer must be financially independent to do his best work. I am trying to make myself financially independent for life." But as his wealth increased by leaps and bounds without bringing with it relaxation from its pursuit, Strauss' one-time explanation no longer rang true. Many amusing anecdotes are told to illustrate Strauss' amazing avidity where money is concerned. At one time, shortly after a performance of his *Josephs Legende* by the Diaghilev Ballet in Paris, Strauss—who was already a wealthy man—invited the foremost musicians, writers and artists in Paris to a feast at Larue's. The feast was the last word in sumptuousness and good taste. There was only one flaw: At the end of the feast, each visitor received his own check for the meal he had just eaten!

In music, Strauss' greatest admiration is not Wagner but Mozart, whose structure and instrumentation have exerted a powerful influence upon his own musical writing. Frequently, when young musicians come to him begging to be accepted as pupils—in their hands scores full of unorthodox harmonies and rebellious counterpoint—Strauss firmly tells them to spend two years in studying the scores of Mozart and then to return to him for lessons.

Concerning his method of composition, he has left copious notes. "I compose everywhere . . . walking or driving, eating or drinking, at home or abroad, in noisy hotels, in my garden, in railway carriages. My sketch book never leaves me, and as soon as a motive strikes me I jot it down. One of the most important melodies for my . . . opera [*Rosenkavalier*], struck me while I was playing a Bavarian card game. . . . But before I improvise even the smallest sketch for an opera, I allow the texts to permeate my thoughts and mature in me for at least six months so that the situation and characters may be thoroughly assimilated. Then only do I let musical thoughts enter my mind. The sub-sketches then become sketches. They are copied out, worked out, arranged for the piano and rearranged as often as four times. This is the hard part of the work. The score I write in my study, straightway, without troubling, working at it twelve hours a day."

SIR EDWARD ELGAR

III

SIR EDWARD ELGAR

1.

WHEN, in 1904, Edward Elgar was knighted by King Edward VII for his services to English music, there were some critics who referred to him as the greatest English composer since Henry Purcell. Praise that brushed aside two centuries of musical development seemed, at first glance, absurdly extravagant. Yet a glance at English musical history discloses why Elgar's stature should have loomed so formidably, even in 1904. Thomas Arne, Thomas Attwood, Michael Balfe, John Field, John Stainer, Charles Villiers Stanford, C. Hubert Parry, Sterndale Bennett, Arthur Sullivan—respectable musicians all, but hardly creative giants. In such company, Elgar's stature inevitably assumed exaggerated height. English composers after Purcell had, at their best, produced music of some charm, considerable technical adroitness and occasional fluency of self-expression. Elgar, however, seemed to be the first since Purcell to free himself completely from the tight-lipped restraint of Anglo-Saxon temperament, to rise above academic formalism to achieve a musical expression which other countries, warmer in blood, might hear with pleasure and admiration. He freed English music from the constraining provincialism which had kept it in bondage for two centuries, thereby making it possible to stand beside the music of other countries. When, in 1928, an English gentleman, Leo Francis Howard Schuster by name, bequeathed to Elgar an inheritance of $35,000 because he "saved my country from the reproach of having produced no composer worthy to rank with the great masters," he was to a great extent expressing the sentiment felt by all England twenty-four years back when the distinction of knighthood was conferred upon Elgar.

However one may esteem Elgar today—whether one succumbs to the enchantment of his romanticism or becomes impatient with his failure to produce an unmistakably individual speech, whether one praises the high plane of beauty on which he poised his greatest works or accuses him for his failure to influence the direction of modern music—one cannot deny that, for all his shortcomings, he brought prestige to English music in the eyes of England and the rest of the world. He arrived at a time when, creatively at least, musical England was almost barren. He composed his major works at a period when it was strongly believed that an Englishman could never produce music of first importance. Elgar himself had said at the dawn of his career: "England is not a musical nation, and never will be. As soon as the country is musical it will cease to be English. England has not produced any music used at funerals. And nobody thinks he is properly married unless Mendelssohn's wedding march is played."

Paradoxically enough, it was Elgar's life work that was later to contradict at least a part of this statement.

2.

The birthplace of Sir Edward William Elgar was Worcester, where on June 2, 1857, he was born to a family already well burdened with offspring. The father of the family, W. H. Elgar, was organist at the Roman Catholic Church of St. George in Worcester. The income of organist being insufficient to supply the many demands of a prolific family. Mr. Elgar soon opened a music-shop in partnership with his brother. Whatever was required in Worcester of a musical nature, the music-shop of the Elgar brothers could supply. W. H. Elgar also played the violin in local orchestras.

Edward Elgar early disclosed an unusually keen mind and an extraordinary sensitivity to art. From his mother, Ann Greening Elgar, he acquired a profound love for literature. While still a boy, Elgar would withdraw from the well-cluttered stable-loft of the Elgar ménage the dusty volumes of Sir Philip Sydney's *Arcadia,* Shakespeare's tragedies and Drayton's *Polyolbion* which he perused avidly. His artistic temperament disclosed itself in other directions as well. He is said to have been moved strongly by mediæval carvings in the Worcester Cathedral. And he had a healthy appetite for music. He could spend tireless hours at the feet of his father in the organ-loft at the Cathedral, where the latter performed the organ master-pieces of Johann Sebastian Bach. He could pore in-defatigably over the musical scores he found at home; a piano arrangement of Beethoven's *First Symphony* excited and thrilled him when he was still very young. He could also find amusement in memorizing the rules and writing out the exercises in text-books on harmony, counterpoint and thorough bass.

His early schooling took place at a "ladies' school" whither Edward was sent as a child. There he received his first lessons on the piano, and also violin lessons, which he preferred even more. Subsequently, further instruction in academic studies was pursued at the Littleton House. Then—Edward was sent to London in his 16th year to enter the legal profession. For three years, he pursued the study of law in a solicitor's office. Then nostalgia for Worcester and its richly musical atmosphere proved too strong for him. He asked for, and received, the permission of his father to return home, help in the shop, and devote himself to such musical activity as he could find in the vicinity of Worcester.

Elgar literally plunged himself into every musical occupation or diversion that presented itself upon his return home. His father's shop being a haven for musical apparatus of all kind, he began the study of every instrument within reach. The organ, piano and violin—with which he was already acquainted—he studied with greater assiduity than before. Theory and thorough-bass books were still studied indefatigably during the dark hours of night. Was there a commission in the Elgar shop for the composition of an original tune, Elgar wrote it; was there an order for a small orchestra to perform at a special occasion, Edward was among the instrumentalists. He eagerly substituted for his father at the Cathedral organ when the old man felt need of recess. He joined an amateur wind quintet as a bassoon player. Every orchestra that assembled within several miles of his home had him for a member. At one time, the sudden absence of the concertmaster of one of these amateur orchestras, brought Elgar to the first desk, where he fulfilled his duties so efficiently that for the next few years he retained this position. He also gave solo performances on the violin at any and every provocation, soon achieving a formidable local reputation. He even became bell-ringer in the parish of Worcester every evening at curfew because he loved the sound of tolling bells. From this occupation, however, he was soon dismissed—when the entire town objected vehemently because the bell-ringer, in his absorption with the musical sounds, had prolonged curfew time each evening by some fifteen minutes.

At this time, his great aspiration was to become a virtuoso, a concert violinist. To bring this dream to realization he withdrew from his numerous activities in Worcester, returned to London in 1879 and became a pupil of Adolf Pollitzer, an admirable violin teacher about whom Elgar spoke highly in later life. Elgar began his violin study with his customary industry and thoroughness. When, at the second lesson, Pollitzer asked Elgar which exercise in the book he had studied for the lesson, Elgar answered with

SIR EDWARD ELGAR

surprise: "Why all of them, of course!"—and, to the amazement of his teacher, he began to perform the entire book of exercises from memory. At the same time, Elgar was an eager attendant at all the principal concerts in London, particularly those conducted by August Manns at the Crystal Palace.

The fascination of a virtuoso career soon began to pall for Elgar. After five lessons he decided definitely that his musical destiny rested elsewhere. Precisely where, he did not as yet know definitely—even though he pursued composition with some zest. He strongly suspected that it would be the organ.

Upon his return to Worcester, he was appointed pianist and conductor of the Worcester Glee Club, and bandmaster of the Worcester County Lunatic Asylum. These positions not only gave Elgar his initiation with the baton but they also released a veritable creative flood. For these two organizations, Elgar composed a copious supply of music in every vein—light and serious, religious, military and dance, instrumental and choral. Original quadrilles for the Worcester County Lunatic Asylum brought him one dollar and twenty-five cents a set. Minstrel songs were reimbursed with thirty-six cents a piece. No creative task appeared too menial for the young musician, nor any too ambitious.

In 1882, Elgar took a short holiday in Germany, visiting Leipzig (where, years back, his dreams had centered) to come into greater intimacy with the music of Robert Schumann whom he admired greatly. Three years after this, Elgar assumed the position of organist at the St. George Cathedral.

In 1889, Elgar was married to Caroline Alice Roberts, the daughter of a military officer. A girl of literary talent as well as of rich and well-rounded cultural background, Alice's influence upon Elgar was overwhelming, as he himself frequently confessed. She was not a musician, if by

the term we designate someone with a formal academic
training and a strict technical equipment. But if we are to
include among musicians those who, in spite of their lack
of formal training, possess a profound love for the art, an
instinctive feeling for the correct phrase and the proper
line, and an infallible critical sense which cannot tolerate
the trite or the stilted, then Alice was a musician among the
elect. |Throughout his life, Elgar leaned heavily upon her
critical judgment. He played for her each of his works in
the various stages of their growth, and depended implicity
upon her opinion. He confessed more than once his
amazement at her keen critical perception. "I play phrases
and tunes to her," Elgar confessed in later life, "because
she always likes to see what progress I have been making.
Well, she nods her head and says nothing, or just 'Oh,
Edward!'—but I know whether she approves or not, and
I always feel that there is something wrong with it if she
doesn't. . . . A few nights before . . . I played some of
the music I had written that day, and she nodded her head
appreciatively, except over one passage, at which she sat
up, rather grimly I thought. However I went to bed leaving it as it was; but I got up as soon as it was light and
went down to look over what I had written. I found it as
I had left it, except that there was a little piece of paper,
pinned over the offending bars on which was written, 'All
of it is beautiful and just right, except this ending. Don't
you think, dear Edward, that this end is just a little . . . ?'
Well, I scrapped the end. Not a word was ever said about
it; but I rewrote it; and as I heard no more I knew that it
was approved." [1]

The influence of Caroline Elgar made itself strongly felt
from the first. It was not mere accident that, shortly after
his marriage, Elgar suddenly decided to give up the playing
of the organ, to settle permanently in London where
musical life was more active, and to begin serious compo-

[1] *Elgar As I Knew Him,* by William H. Reed.

sition in larger and more ambitious forms. To earn his living, he gave music lessons. But the major part of his time belonged to concerts and creative work. Inspired by the enthusiasm and faith of his wife, Elgar began to work upon large canvases, which until now he had avoided, giving his talent full scope for expression for the first time.

Elgar soon decided that the disturbances of a large city were little conducive to concentration and creation. In 1891, he transferred his permanent home from London to Malvern. It was shortly after this that his first serious endeavors received performance. In 1893, the choral *Black Knight* was performed in Worcester. Three years later, the Worcester Festival of the Three Choirs featured Elgar's oratorio, *Lux Christi*. In 1897, a *Te Deum* and *Benedictus* were included in the Hereford Festival. Dignified compositions all, the work of a scholarly hand, impeccable taste and fertile imagination, but works which promised much more than they fulfilled.

Then, suddenly, the first of Elgar's great works uprooted musical England from its comfortable obscurity.

Early in 1899, Elgar completed a major orchestral work, a set of variations on an original theme, which he called *Enigma*. A London agent of Hans Richter caught a glimpse of this score and was sufficiently impressed to send it to the great conductor in Vienna. For a long time previous to this, Richter—because of his many engagements in England—had been eagerly searching for a talented orchestral work by an English composer which he might feature on his programs. Richter did not know Elgar, had never even heard of him. This set of variations on an original theme, however, impressed Richter immediately as the first modern English music in his knowledge which avoided pedantry and technical display, which was warmly emotional and tender, and possessed a strength of beauty all its own. Richter, therefore, decided to exploit the work fully. Through Richter's baton, not only the *Enigma Variations,* but Edward Elgar as well, became known throughout England.[2]   On February 7, 1901, the *Enigma Variations* was performed for the first time out of England, at a concert of the Städtische Musikverein in Düsseldorf, with Julius Buths conducting.

These variations—each of which is prefixed in the score by a set of initials—were designed by Elgar as tonal portraits of his personal friends.   The first variation, a highly eloquent and poetical movement, is a portrait of Elgar's wife; the last variation is a self-portrait.   "It is true," as Elgar confessed in an interview, "that I have sketched, for their amusement and mine, the idiosyncrasies of fourteen of my friends, not necessarily musicians; but this is a personal matter and need not have been mentioned publicly."   The reason why Elgar referred to this work as *Enigma* was, however, for a long time enshrouded in mystery.   "The *Enigma,*" Elgar insisted, "I shall not explain—its 'dark saying' must be left unguessed."

Actually the "Enigma" is a hidden theme which—Elgar said—though never played, *could* accompany every variation.   It may be said to be present as a "silent accompaniment."   The prominent New York critic, H. E. Krehbiel put forward the theory that this silent theme is the motto melody of Wagner's *Parsifal.*

If the orchestral variations, the *Enigma,* brought the limelight of recognition upon Elgar, his next work made him a national, even an international, figure.   In 1900, *The Dream of Gerontius* was performed in Birmingham. A choral composition, based upon a poem of Cardinal Newman, consisting of a series of lyric and dramatic episodes portraying the doctrine of purgatory as taught by the Catholic Church, *The Dream* was so suffused with mysti-

[2] Strictly speaking, the *Enigma Variations* as introduced by Hans Richter is not the same as that which is performed today.   After the first performance, Elgar revised some sections of the work, and added a coda.   In this new form, it was first introduced at the Worcester Festival with Elgar conducting.

cism and poetry, contained choral writing of such beauty, and orchestration of such effectiveness that (although the performance was a failure) some English music critics rubbed their ears with incredulity. Bernard Shaw confessed that he had always regarded English composers with suspicion, but that when he heard *The Dream* he was convinced that the first great English composer had definitely arrived. In December of 1901, *The Dream* was performed in Düsseldorf, Germany, where its success even exceeded that which it enjoyed in England. Several months later, it was repeated at the Lower Rhine Festival in what was probably the first occasion upon which a modern English composer was cheered in a foreign country. Richard Strauss, who was in the audience, made a public address at a banquet in Elgar's honor in which he referred to the work as a masterpiece. This praise—bringing with it the approval of one who was probably the most famous living composer—established Elgar's reputation throughout the world of music.

In 1901, Elgar composed his set of six chauvinistic military marches, entitled *Pomp and Circumstance,* which endeared him to the Crown. The first of these, the one in D-major, has become world-famous; it is this march which is referred to when *Pomp and Circumstance* is mentioned. When Edward VII first heard it, he exclaimed: "That tune will go round the world." It was a prophetic remark. *Pomp and Circumstance* has since become a second national anthem for England. It is as well known, probably—and is as strongly associated with Great Britain—as *God Save the King.*[3]

When, in 1902, Edward Elgar was selected to compose the Ode for the coronation of Edward VII, he was officially

[3] It will be recalled that in the monumental motion-picture about England, Noel Coward's *Cavalcade,* it was *Pomp and Circumstance* that was utilized as a sort of *leit-motif,* linking the various scenes.

being recognized by the Crown as the greatest living English composer.

In 1903, the Birmingham Festival featured a new Elgar oratorio, *The Apostles,* which added to his fame. Elgar had intended to construct a gargantuan trilogy of oratorios, of which *The Apostles* was to be the first, which would describe the founding of Christianity. Three years later, he was to compose a second part of the trilogy: *The Kingdom.* But the venture eventually lost its appeal for Elgar, and he never composed the concluding work.

The year of 1904 definitely established Elgar as a world figure in music. It was the year of his knighthood, but of even greater significance was it that at that time there took place a monumental three day festival of his music at Covent Garden, London. *The Dream of Gerontius, The Apostles* were among the important works featured, as well as a new orchestral composition, *In the South,* inspired by a recent visit to the Italian Riviera. And it was found by more than one critic that the quality of the music that was performed was sufficiently remarkable to place its composer in the front rank of English musical creators of all time.

3.

During the next ten years Elgar solidified his magisterial position in English music with the composition of a series of remarkable works. The *Introduction and Allegro,* for strings—in which Elgar brought to modern usage the concert-grosso form of old—came in 1905. The *First Symphony in A-flat* was so sensational when introduced by Hans Richter in Manchester in December, 1908, that it was given no less than a hundred performances during the next year. In 1910, Elgar produced his *Concerto for Violin and Orchestra,* dedicated to Fritz Kreisler, and introduced by him at Queen's Hall on November 10, of that year—the first violin concerto by an English composer to earn a permanent place in the virtuoso's repertory. The *Second Symphony* followed the *Concerto* by one year, partly inspired by Shelley's *Invocation,* and dedicated to the memory of His Majesty, Edward VII. With *Falstaff,* for orchestra (1913) this long line of distinguished music comes to an end.

The World War aroused Elgar's patriotic ardor. In August of 1914, he became a special constable in the Hampstead Division. The following February he resigned from this position, but soon afterwards joined the Hampstead Volunteer Reserve. At the same time, he enlisted his music under the English flag as well. Patriotism rang loud and clear in his works of this period. He set several war poems to music, including Emil Cammaerts' *Carillon*—which depicted the horrible tragedy of the German invasion of Belgium—Laurence Binyon's *The Spirit of England,* and a relatively mawkish work, *Le Drapeau belge.* He composed a symphonic prelude, *Polonia,* to help raise funds for relief in Poland, and he created the stirring if pompously chauvinistic scores to two war themes, *Fringes of the Fleet* (a set of songs) and *A Voice in the Desert.*

Following the War, Elgar turned to more poetical moods for his composition, creating a sonata for violin and piano, a string quartet, a piano quintet, and a violoncello concerto, all touched with the soft and tender sentiment, the sad brooding, and, at other moments, the virile strength which had long before this become the identifying traits of Elgar's works.

The major tragedy in Edward Elgar's life brought this productivity to an abrupt termination. On April 7, 1920, Lady Alice Elgar died. The funeral took place at St. Wulsten's Church in Little Malvern, where a performance of the slow movement of Elgar's string quartet was the only eulogy.

After the funeral, Elgar made a mental resolve that he

would never again compose a bar of music. His greatest
incentive for creation had passed away with his wife. Elgar's friends had always known what Lady Alice had
meant to him, realized that her death had been a terrible
blow to the composer. But this was their first recognition
of the dominant rôle she had played in his creative life.

They were to recognize this even more strongly as the
years passed. Whatever enthusiasm, whatever zest, what-
every industry Elgar had once had for musical creation
seemed to have died on the day they buried Lady Alice.
Frequently, his closest associates attempted to rekindle in
him his creative spark. They reminded him that he had
left his trilogy of oratorios unfinished, that *The Apostles*
and *The Kingdom* demanded a concluding work. They
spoke indefatigably of Sir Edward's one-time great ambition to produce an opera on Ben Jonson's play, *The Devil
Is An Ass,* from which Sir Barry Jackson had already prepared a suitable libretto. They begged for a third symphony. But to all of these entreaties Elgar turned a deaf
ear. Endlessly he repeated that he had put aside his pen
forever. When, in 1924, Elgar was appointed Master of
the King's Musick, it was hoped that this might be the
necessary impetus to drive the composer back to his music.
But this, as everything else, failed.

Elgar's patriotism, finally, succeeded in accomplishing
that which the entreaties of friends and associates had
failed to do. In 1929, King George V was stricken by a
serious illness, so serious that for a period the entire Kingdom figuratively held its breath. As a hymn of prayer for
the recovery of His Majesty, Sir Edward Elgar composed a
Christmas carol—his first composition in more than nine
years.

From that time, he slowly returned to creative work.
The major composition preoccupying him was the third
symphony. After the long idleness, composition came

slowly to Elgar. The progress of the new symphony developed at a snail's pace.

Meanwhile, in 1931, Elgar received from King George V the highest honor that the Crown could offer a composer—baronetcy. He had already, in previous years, been awarded the Grand Cross of the Victorian Order and appointed Knight Commander of the Victorian Order.

After two years of intensive work, Elgar had succeeded in producing profuse sketches for his new symphony. It now required only one concentrated period of work to bring the composition to final completion. In 1934, however, work on the symphony was permanently interrupted when Elgar's last illness brought him to bed. He had been suffering severely from sciatica. His physicians advised an operation which might relieve his pain—an operation which, at best, was only a temporary measure and of no value as an ultimate cure. After the operation, Sir Edward Elgar fought gallantly to regain his health. But he was a doomed man. His health degenerated markedly from week to week; he was soon a helpless invalid.

Three weeks before his death, Elgar assisted in recording one of his works, the march from *Caractacus*. A music-stand was ingeniously built upon his bed to enable Elgar to see the score from a propped-up position. Telephonic wires connected him to the Abbey Road Studios where the London Symphony Orchestra, under the direction of Lawrence Collingwood, rehearsed the work. By telephone, Sir Edward Elgar communicated his every wish as though he were in the very recording room itself.

Shortly before his death, Elgar extracted from his most intimate friends the promise that they would see to it that no one meddled with his sketches of the third symphony, that it remained permanently in fragments. This was his last request. On February 23, 1934, Sir Edward Elgar died at his home in Marl Bank.

4.

George Bernard Shaw once pithily described Sir Edward Elgar as a "typical English country gentleman." Like many English country gentlemen, Elgar was tall, erect and well-built, with well-proportioned features. His carriage possessed imperial dignity, his mannerisms were always well-poised and graceful. Characteristic of English country gentlemen, he was restrained, aloof, distant in the presence of strangers or mere acquaintances. He was almost suspicious of people he did not know well. Those who met him for the first time, often complained of his frigidity and found it difficult to believe that he was essentially warm and tender, generous to a fault, sympathetic to people in all walks of life. His fine sense of humor—he had an especially quick tongue for puns—his warm disposition, were known only to those who became his friends.

Elgar, moreover, had the English countryman's intense love of the outdoors. The greatest part of his life Elgar spent in the country. Dressed in the charming informality of rough outdoor clothing, he frequently indulged in long walking tours and bicycling. He had an extraordinary affection for flowers, woods, brooks, country paths. Chopping wood and clearing away brushwood delighted him as though it were a game. He also found pleasure in fishing; although it is said that he rarely caught anything, and when he did he always threw the fish back into the water.

Perhaps the outstanding trait of his personality was his keen and eclectic mind. He seemed to be interested in everything, know everything. His fund of information was the source of endless wonder and awe among his friends. His knowledge of science, architecture, woodcraft, for example, was more than a layman's. He was a chemist by avocation, had a chemical laboratory in which he spent many tireless hours of experimentation. His prodigious memory enabled him to retain tenaciously whatever he read, heard or saw: thus he was well versed in law (which he had studied in his youth), knew history with the thoroughness of a scholar, was formidably acquainted with literature. He is said to have known the great English poets —particularly Shakespeare—remarkably well. He was, therefore, at ease in any and every circle, was often the most fluent conversationalist in whatever group he joined.

There was something charmingly boyish about him until the end of his life. A part of him, at least—a part known only to his closest friends—never passed beyond adolescence. He had, for example, a robust enthusiasm for games of all kind. Cribbage excited him. When cross-word puzzles first came to popularity, he was one of the most passionate victims of the fad. He liked billiards, played it with the utmost of concentration—mathematically computing each and every shot and strategically planning his position not only for the next shot but for the one after that as well. He had a schoolboy's taste for mischief, pranks, little tricks perpetrated upon unsuspecting friends. He even, at certain times, found singular delight in playing (and winning at) "Beaver": the game in which, while strolling the street, one shouts the word "Beaver" each time one sees a man with a beard, a black beard earning for the first caller of "Beaver" one point, a red beard, three.

His musical taste was as eclectic as his intellectual interests. Generally speaking, he liked everything in music that was good, though he preferred the Romantic School and cared little for the Elizabethan composers. He adored Schumann, loved Bach and Purcell, and numbered Handel, Berlioz, Stravinsky, Mendelssohn, Rossini, Meyerbeer, Puccini, Beethoven, Haydn, Mozart, Liszt and Richard Strauss among his favorite composers. He even manifested a keen interest in jazz. At one time he sent an urgent telegram to Bernard Shaw urging him to buy the phonograph record of *Oh Mo' nah!,* a fox-trot, the rhythm of which had thrilled him.

As a composer, he had no favorite method of working. He conceived music at all times, while walking, during play, in the middle of the night, or during conversation with his friends. He was always scribbling ideas on scraps of paper. These he guarded carefully, referred to them periodically, and developed them into his major works. He worked easily and swiftly. Creation seemed to come as naturally to him as breathing or speaking. Frequently, he wrote his music as effortlessly as other people write letters.

Where his own music was concerned he was charmingly modest. He liked what he composed, felt that some of it was of importance; but he never lost his perspective. It is for this reason that, when confronted with the profuse praise of a mawkish admirer, he could frequently become stingingly acid. He knew his own strength and his own weakness. In a career studded with honor, adulation and glory he succeeded—with singular consistency—in keeping his head.

5.

Of the composers of our time, Edward Elgar will probably age the most quickly. Already his music is beginning to wear thin. What charmed us most upon first and second hearing, becomes somewhat boring with intimacy. For all their fine qualities, the *Concerto for Violin and Orchestra,* the *Engima Variations* and the *Dream of Gerontius* appear more and more old-fashioned each time we hear them. Their day, for all its brilliance, will be brief.

It is, of course, irrefutable that, at his best, Elgar had many admirable qualities as a composer. There was in him a sensitive feeling for mysticism and poetry which led him, particularly in his oratorios, to open sluices of melody and fluid counterpoint. His musical writing could be crystal-

line, pure and clean. It always bore the stamp of good
taste and breeding. He was not afraid of emotional display, filling his music with an intensity of feeling that, at
first, moves the hearer profoundly. Moreover, he had an
infallible sense for orchestration, an instinct for building
dramatic sequences, and could voice pageantry and glamour
with a magnificently rich tonal speech.

However, Elgar is not an immortal because he had every
virtue except that of originality. He failed to produce an
idiom distinctly his own. Much of his speech is derived
from Schumann, some of it from Wagner. He borrowed
liberally; there are always betraying fingerprints on his
music. Even his greatest works lack a strong spine of
their own. Truth to tell, Elgar was too little the experi-
menter, too little the adventurer, too little the pioneer. He
was never interested in exploring new avenues of expression. In consequence, his music cannot quite free itself
from the faint aroma of stagnancy.

His language was sometimes one of beauty, of which the
sixth variation, marked *Andantino,* of the *Engima Variations* is an eloquent example. But if this beauty palls upon
us with intimacy it is only because it fails to have a truly
personal or individual character. His musical thinking
often takes ingenious turns; it was, for example, a charming device in the *Concerto for Violin and Orchestra* to
permit the solo violin to play the concluding bars of the
orchestral introduction to the first movement, or to write
an *accompanied* cadenza for the third movement. But this
ingenuity is too often merely superficial trickery, lacking
artistic genuineness. The charm of his harmonic and contrapuntal writing, the brilliancy of his orchestration, and
the warm heart-beat of his best melodies even today inspire
respect and admiration when we listen to the *Second Symphony,* the *Enigma Variations,* the *Violin Concerto* or the
best oratorios. But these, after all, are unsatisfying sub-
stitutes for profundity and originality.

JAN SIBELIUS

IV

JAN SIBELIUS

1.

JAN SIBELIUS represents to Finland something more than merely its greatest composer. In Finland, Sibelius is a national hero, an "uncrowned king" as the Finns frequently refer to him, Finland's most significant and eloquent "ambassador of good will," to the rest of the civilized world. Sibelius has done more to bring prestige to his country, to explain and interpret it to the outside world than any other man living or dead, and for this his countrymen honor him as a national hero. To the children, the name of Sibelius has a magic aura of glamour as though its owner brandished a sword instead of a creative pen, as though its owner were some world-famous athlete like Nurmi instead of a composer of great symphonies. The older people frequently toast him in the taverns of Finland, just as they would a political figure who held the fate of their country in his hands.

To such nationwide adulation and respect, Sibelius responds with that charming modesty which is frequently a characteristic trait of the truly great. He does not minimize the value of his music, but neither the extravagant praise nor the glory which he has received has succeeded in stripping him of frequent doubts whether his music is worthy of all the rhapsodic evaluations it has received. Two anecdotes, quoted in a recent magazine article, neatly illustrate his sincere modesty. At one time he visited a museum of primitive tools with a friend. "The man who invented the harrow," commented the friend playfully, "is far greater than the man who invented Sibelius' symphonies." "That's perfectly true," Sibelius answered simply and forcefully. At another time, a violinist of no particular renown visited him and expressed his profound admiration for the master's music. When the violinist left, Sibelius exclaimed excitedly: "I do think that he was really interested in my music!"

For a national figure, Sibelius is surprisingly aloof from all ceremony. He lives far from the madding crowd in a picturesque village called Järvenpää, surrounded by the bleak austerity of Scandinavian forests, thirty miles north of Helsingfors. Trains do not generally stop at Järvenpää, which is too insignificant a spot for a permanent place upon the timetable. But one has merely to inform the conductor of any northbound express train that a visit to Sibelius is contemplated when the train will make Järvenpää a halting station. From here it is only a short distance on a dirt road to Villa Ainola, Sibelius' log-house. Of modern composers, Sibelius is among the most inaccessible. However, a discreet and carefully worded note will frequently be more efficacious than elaborate and important letters of introduction in eliciting from the composer an invitation to spend a few hours with him and his wife (his five daughters, all of whom are married, no longer live with him) at their home.

In shaking his powerful hand and in looking at his massive frame which literally towers over the visitor it becomes difficult to remember that this is a sensitive creative artist. No man ever looked less his part. In build, Sibelius is more the athlete; now that he is entirely bald he gives the appearance of a professional wrestler. He is almost six feet of strength and muscle. His frame is enormous, but each of his features is in harmony with the other. His head has a majestic dignity and power, with his deep-set eyes burning intensely under a high and impressive forehead, and his square jaw, firm lips and assertive chin give a strong suggestion of latent power.

Photographs give him an almost stark austerity which has tempted more than one writer to describe him as possessing the dark and sombre melancholy of a Scandinavian forest-scene. There is, however, no veil of gloom enveloping Sibelius. Those who have met him know that he is jovial, gregarious, full of healthy spirits, capable of a fleet witticism; his disposition is as ruddy as his health. He is hardly an ascetic. He is a connoisseur of good foods, enjoys liquor and insists upon smoking only the most expensive cigars. Conversation with friends is probably his favorite pastime; he is a voluble and enthusiastic talker on many subjects.

Formerly a prolific traveler, Sibelius today rarely leaves his villa, except for an occasional visit to Helsingfors to attend some important performance of his music. These periodic thirty-mile trips to Helsingfors require more effort of him today than did his transcontinental voyages when he was a few years younger. He detests the festivities that always await him in the Finnish capital, and always looks forward impatiently to the moment when he can return home. Truth to tell, life for him is singularly complete at Järvenpää. He is surrounded by the natural beauty of the Finnish countryside which always exhilarates and inspires him. By nature a mystic, he feels himself in direct communion with the great infinite in Järvenpää. At his home, too, he has his many books (he reads biography and history extensively, as well as Latin and Greek masters in the original), valuable paintings, and scores of musical masterpieces all of which satisfy him spiritually as completely as his liquors, good food and excellent cigars appease his appetite. He likes solitude, but is by no means a recluse. He can frequently be found in the village tavern, surrounded by the natives of Järvenpää, indulging heartily in both the *schnapps* and the loud-voiced conversation.

He dislikes to discuss his own music; when asked to do so he stammers and stumbles like an embarrassed schoolboy. He is particularly reticent when talking about a composition in progress. But when the conversation turns to the works of other composers he becomes singularly loquacious, expressing his likes and dislikes forcefully and unequivocally. His musical tastes are eclectic, ranging from the polyphonic music of Victoria and Palestrina to the waltzes of Johann Strauss, embracing such composers as Bach, Mozart, Beethoven, Brahms and Verdi. He finds little sympathy with the Wagnerian music-drama, and interests himself only casually with modern musical tendencies.

He still expends enormous energy in composition. Writing music does not come easily to him, even though he has produced more than one hundred and fifty works. He generally works at night, two tall candles at his elbow lighting the paper in front of him. Frequently, the fruits of many hours will consist of no more than a page or two. He has a severe conscience which will never permit him to consider a work completed unless he is satisfied with it thoroughly. Each of his symphonies has taken him several years to perfect. He celebrated his fiftieth birthday with the *Fifth Symphony* and did not complete his *Seventh Symphony* until his sixtieth birthday. Thus, too, although he had been working on his *Eighth Symphony* for some six years, he remained deaf to the pleas of an entire music world that begged him to complete it in time to help celebrate his seventieth birthday, and refused to permit the score to leave his hands because he was not entirely satisfied with it.

2.

Jan Julius Christian Sibelius was born in a small town in the interior of Finland, Tavastehus, on December 8, 1865, the son of a regimental doctor. The atmosphere in the Sibelius home was one of serenity and culture, which young Sibelius imbibed freely. He was a sensitive boy, responding to beauty in every form as magnetically as a leaf is attracted to the sun. The love of Nature and music were his two predominating passions as a child—and both were strongly encouraged by his intelligent parents. Books, particularly poetry, likewise assumed an important position among his interests.

In his fifth year, Jan began to derive pleasure and amusement from exploring consonant harmonies on the family piano. Four years later he began to study the piano seriously, it being noted from the very first that he expended much more diligence on his improvisations than on his finger exercises. By his tenth birthday, he was already the proud composer of a piece of music, entitled *Drops of Water*, a duet for violin and violoncello consisting entirely of *pizzicati*.

In his eleventh year, Sibelius entered the Finnish Model Lyceum for his first intensive academic education. He was well-liked by his fellow pupils because of his warm, lovable and witty disposition. He indulged freely in all childish games of which he was always the leader and participated in every cultural activity offered by the school—principally acting and the conducting of a small boys' orchestra. He was, however, not a distinguished pupil. Moody and introspective from earliest childhood, he permitted his mind to stray into distant pastures while he was still in class. "Jan found it difficult to sit still during lessons and listen to things that did not interest him," we learn from a fellow student. "He sat, buried in thought, and would be quite absent minded, when questioned suddenly. On such occasions our beloved head master, Gabriel Geitlin, would look at him reproachfully and say with a deep sigh: 'Good gracious, again Sibelius is in another world!' "

Music began to absorb his interest once again when, in his fifteenth year, he became a student of the violin of Gustav Levander, a conductor of a military band. The violin fascinated Sibelius as the piano had never succeeded in doing. He studied industriously, spurred on by the driving force of an ambition to become a celebrated virtuoso. During hours free from a school or violin lessons he would wander into the woods skirting Tavastehus, violin in hand and, like some modern Orpheus, serenade the trees and flowers with original tunes that burst from him spontaneously. The joy of such creation determined Sibelius to study composition more seriously. He hungrily devoured such theoretical books on harmony and counterpoint as he could find in the school library. These books gave his growing imagination the necessary equipment: while still in early adolescence he composed a trio and a piano quartet.

In 1885, having graduated from the Lyceum, Sibelius was sent to the University of Helsingfors to begin the study of law. His gifts as a musician had been praised and appreciated by his mother and grandmother, but both of them felt that the musical profession offered a sorry future. They contemplated a government post for Jan, for which a legal preparation was essential. Law, however, held but small appeal for Sibelius. He deliberately negected its study, entered the Musical Academy of Helsingfors for a more thorough training in violin and composition, and devoted those hours prescribed for legal study to the pursuit of musical pastimes. After one year, Sibelius' family recognized the futility of keeping the boy from music. They permitted him to give up law completely and turn to the study of the art he loved. Sibelius could now immerse himself deeply and completely in his favorite study. Under the guidance of such sympathetic and uniquely appreciative teachers as Martin Wegelius and Ferruccio Busoni (who though still very young was already a piano teacher at the academy) Sibelius made broad strides towards maturity.

Adolf Paul, Swedish-German novelist and playwright, who was a fellow pupil of Sibelius at the Musical Academy, wrote of young Sibelius as follows: "He did not seem to dwell on this earth. His was a delicate, impressionable nature, with a sensitive imagination which found outlet in music at the slightest incitement. His thoughts always strayed, his head was always in the clouds, and he continually expressed such original and bizarre ideas that his friend and most faithful protagonist, Kajanus, said pointedly that in his normal mood he was 'like the rest of us when drunk.' "

Completing his course of study at the Musical Academy, Sibelius was enabled by a scholarship (followed later by a government grant) to go to Berlin in 1889 to continue his music study. The Berlin period was of inestimable importance to Sibelius' musical growth. His lessons from Albert Becker gave him a rigorous classical training which solidified his technique and gave him a consummate knowledge of form. Moreover, the active concert life of Berlin enabled him to hear a great quantity of music formerly unknown to him. Symphonic music particularly—for which he now manifested an unusual interest for the first time. It is of interest to note that in Berlin Sibelius heard a symphony called *Aino* (inspired by the Finnish national epic, *Kalevala*), the work of a compatriot, Robert Kajanus, who at the time was also in Berlin. This performance was of double importance to Sibelius: it turned his thoughts to Finnish national music as a basis for his composition and it brought him into direct contact with the composer who was to become his life-long friend and, as a conductor, the staunchest advocate of his music.

After a short holiday in Finland—where, in 1890, he became betrothed to Aino Järnefelt, the charming daughter of a general—Sibelius came to Vienna to put the final touches on his musical education. He came heavily equipped with letters of introduction. He contacted Brahms, but when the meeting was finally consummated it proved to be very uninspiring; it cannot be said that Brahms recognized in Sibelius genius in the raw. Other musicians, however, were more useful to Sibelius in their advice and encouragement—Hans Richter, for example, and Karl Goldmark.

After bringing his music study to a close in Vienna under Karl Goldmark and Robert Fuchs, Sibelius produced an orchestral overture (which was performed the year of its composition in Helsingfors) and an octet, in both of which a music student revealed that he was slowly evolving into an artist.

In the summer of 1891 Sibelius was back in his native country. His student days were over. The tools of composition were now at his command. In his composition he was still the immature voice uncertain and hesitant in his speech. His style, for want of personalization, still aped the romanticism of the German composers of his day. Individuality, a definite artistic direction, a strongly motivated message—these were sadly lacking in his music.

But—now that his apprentice years were over—these were not slow in arriving.

3.

At the time of Sibelius' return to Finland, a fever of patriotism—inspired by the Russian suppression of Finnish laws and privileges—attacked the country in a relentless wave. It was impossible for Sibelius not to feel it keenly and to react to it. He eagerly joined several groups which had been founded for the purpose of fostering chauvinistic ideals, and passionately joined in their discussions. This intense national feeling influenced his creative work vitally. He began to feel strongly that it was his duty and privilege to express his profound love for his country in his composition.

His first important work after his return home was a symphonic poem in five movements for large orchestra, chorus and soloists, *Kullervo*, a work glowing with revo-

JAN SIBELIUS

lutionary ardor and suffused with nationalistic spirit. Performed for the first time under the baton of the composer in Helsingfors on April 28, 1892, *Kullervo* received a phenomenal ovation. It is, probably, exaggerated enthusiasm to believe that the heroic strength of Sibelius' music overpowered the audience in spite of the comparative unfamiliarity of Sibelius' style of composition; undoubtedly, it would be much more accurate to say that the extraordinary success of *Kullervo* was caused by the fact that the music translated into tone what the audience was, at the time, feeling so strongly.

In any case, *Kullervo* brought nationwide fame to its composer, and there were already some critics to esteem him the most important musical voice in Finland. His position as a composer established, Sibelius was able to marry his beloved, Aino Järnefelt, on June 10, 1892. Their honeymoon was spent in Karelia, a section of Finland which Sibelius was later to immortalize in one of his orchestral works.

After the honeymoon, Sibelius made Helsingfors his home, engaging upon an active professional life as a musician. He became a professor of theory at the Musical Academy, a violinist of the Academy String Quartet and an instructor of theory at the orchestral school of the Philharmonic Society. His pedagogical duties were time-absorbing, leaving little opportunity for creative work. But Sibelius, the composer, was not altogether idle. Shortly after the emphatic success of *Kullervo,* Sibelius produced two more works for orchestra which increased his importance as a national composer. *En Saga* was composed in 1892, followed one year later by the *Karelia Suite.*

Commenting upon the origin of *En Saga,* Sibelius has said: "Robert Kajanus once pointed out to me how desirable it was to have a piece by me in the regular repertory of the orchestra, written for the general public and not making too great demands on their powers of concentration and comprehension. This would be an advantage both for the orchestra and for my popularity as a composer, Kajanus said. I was not at all disinclined to write a piece in a more popular style. When I got to work, I found that some notes I had made in Vienna were suitable for adaptation. In this way, *En Saga* appeared." Sibelius, despite his intention, had not produced a work of a popular vein. Its themes were fashioned upon designs too unorthodox, and the construction of the work was too subtly skilful, for the composition ever to achieve Promenade-concert appeal. It was, however, music of Finnish temperament and character, and as such made a powerful impression at its first performances.

The *Karelia Suite* was commissioned by the Viborg Student Society which desired music for a series of historical tableaux to be performed at a special concert held to produce funds for national education in Eastern Finland. The assignment pleased Sibelius considerably, for it enabled him to give expression to a different facet of Finnish temperament than he had done until now. The inhabitants of Karelia (southeastern province of Finland) were more amiable, livelier and more robustly exuberant a folk than their compatriots of Helsingfors. Sibelius could, therefore, produce music in a lighter vein, more buoyantly free-hearted than the more sombre pages of *En Saga* and *Kullervo*.

In 1894, Sibelius produced the most famous of his nationalistic works, *Finlandia*. This orchestral tone-poem is not, as was for a long time believed by the rest of Europe, an orchestral synthesis of authentic folk-melodies. Sibelius' themes are entirely his own, but they express the character and personality of Finland so admirably that they seem to possess indigenous qualities. *Finlandia* expresses the impressions of an exile's return to his native land with such flaming vividness and moving eloquence that it literally transported Finnish audiences into intoxicated ardor. As a matter of fact, *Finlandia* inspired such chauvinistic pride that, after a while, Russia banned its performances. In 1904, Sibelius was able to conduct *Finlandia* at a symphony concert in Riga only by changing the title to *Impromptu!*

With the performance of one more major work, the *Lemminkäi-nen Suite,* in 1896 (one of the movements of which has become famous in symphony concerts everywhere as *The Swan of Tuonela*) Sibelius' position as the leading composer of Finland became so definitely accepted that, in 1897, the Senate voted Sibelius an annual grant, the first Finnish composer to be thus honored. The importance of this grant can be judged by the fact that it enabled Sibelius to surrender many of his pedagogical duties and devote himself more earnestly to creation. The products of this leisure soon became apparent, proving eloquently that rarely has a government grant served its purpose so handsomely. In 1898, Sibelius produced his incidental music to *King Christian II,* a play by Adolf Paul. One year later, the greatest symphonist of our day made his official appearance when the *First Symphony* was performed under the direction of the composer in Helsingfors. It was a first symphony only in that the remarkable economy and compression of his later orchestral works, and his extraordinarily effective architectonic construction are suggested rather than achieved. But for a first symphony it was an unusually cohesive composition, maturely conceived and developed with a hand that was sure of itself, a highly personal expression.

During the next fifteen years, Sibelius pursued a less sedentary existence, traveling frequently out of Finland to the leading countries of Europe. The first of these extensive voyages took place in 1900. In Berlin, he was welcomed with open arms by such celebrated musicians as Felix Weingartner, the conductor, and Richard Strauss, and was informed that his music would be represented at the forthcoming musical festival of the Allgemeiner Deutscher Musikverein held at Heidelberg—a rare honor for a non-

German composer. From Germany, Sibelius went on to
Italy, settling in Rapallo, where—in a room overlooking a
beautiful garden of camellias, roses, almond trees, mag-
nolias, cypresses and palms—he composed the *Second Symphony.* The symphony brought to completion, Sibelius arrived at Heidelberg to conduct his *Swan of Tuonela* and
The Return of Lemminkäi-nen for the Allgemeiner Deutscher Musikverein. "My position as a foreigner among a
crowd of German composers with big names and influence
was no easy one," Sibelius recorded. However, the Sibelius
triumph was decisive and unmistakable. "The audience was
moved by the poetic beauty of both the legends and readily
became enthusiastic," commented Adolf Paul who was present. "Sibelius was recalled several times by tumultuous
applause and was complimented *coram publico* and behind
the scenes by a great number of celebrities. . . . Hermann
Wolff at once fixed a date for a Sibelius concert in Berlin.
In short, people's eyes were opened to the fact that this new
man was indeed a great figure and that the name of Sibelius
was one of the few round which the greatest hopes of the
music of the future would center."

In 1901, a serious ailment afflicted Sibelius—a disease of
the ears which threatened deafness. The terror of perpetual silence brought on a mental depression which enveloped Sibelius so completely that, for several years, he was
able to see the sunshine of hope only at far-distant intervals.
During this period of trial, Sibelius composed two famous
works, the *Valse Triste*—which gives us, perhaps, a particularly illuminating insight into his mental state at the
time—and the *Concerto for Violin and Orchestra,* both of
which were written in 1903. One of the few sources of
pleasure that Sibelius experienced during this dismal period
was the realization of a life-long dream: A new home was
built for him in Järvenpää, the Villa Ainola, in a setting of
peace and rustic simplicity most conducive to creative work.

In 1905, Sibelius' aural ailment was completely cured.

His spirits became revitalized with his health. He was now to have the additional pleasure of seeing his music acquire international prestige. In Berlin, his *Second Symphony*—conducted by him personally at the Busoni concerts—was received with unprecedented enthusiasm for a modern foreign work. This was followed shortly afterwards by a successful performance of the *Violin Concerto*. In Liverpool and Birmingham, Granville Bantock conducted two of Sibelius' works, while in Manchester Hans Richter presented the first two symphonies. In Milan, a young conductor—Arturo Toscanini, by name—introduced the *Swan of Tuonela* to Italian music audiences. In Paris, performances of Sibelius' music became a frequent event, particularly by Chevillard at the Lamoureux concerts. And, in 1908, Sibelius conducted his *Third Symphony* in London at the concerts of the Royal Philharmonic Orchestra.

The spring of 1908 found Sibelius once again immersed in depression. A malignant growth in the throat was feared to be a cancer. One operation, which took place in Helsingfors, failed completely to relieve Sibelius of his torturing pains. Sibelius left for Berlin to place himself in the hands of specialists. Thirteen operations followed, all equally painful, until the cause of Sibelius' pain—a tumour—was removed.

Following this experience, Sibelius composed two important works, a string-quartet which he called *Voces intimae,* and the epical *Fourth Symphony*.

At the invitation of a wealthy patron, Carl Stoeckel, Sibelius was brought to America in 1914 to participate in the Norfolk Festival of Music. The pomp and ceremony with which Sibelius was welcomed into the new world bewildered Sibelius, who could not believe that his art was so well known here. The press sang his praises in elaborately rhapsodic columns. Yale University honored him with a degree. This tribute to a great composer became even more effusive during the concert in which Sibelius conducted an entire program of his works. As he entered, an audience of two thousand music lovers rose to its feet in honor of a master. "During the last fifteen years I have felt three times that I was confronted with a world genius," wrote the New York music critic, Henry E. Krehbiel, in discussing this concert. "When Richard Strauss, first with the New York Philharmonic and later with the Boston Symphony Orchestra, performed his own compositions; when Arturo Toscanini in 1910 in the Boston Opera House directed an unforgettable performance of *Tristan und Isolde;* and lastly when by the courtesy of Mr. Carl Stoeckel I had the privilege of hearing Jan Sibelius from Finland direct nine of his old and new compositions on June 4, 1914."

The reception Sibelius received in this country moved him so deeply that he promised he would return to the country the following year to conduct more of his works with leading symphony orchestras. He was never able to keep that promise. While Sibelius was crossing the Atlantic on his journey homewards, the news electrified the world that the Archduke Francis Ferdinand had been assassinated in Sarajevo.

4.

The World War was a blow to Sibelius on many vulnerable spots. His sensitivity as an artist rebelled against a world suddenly plunging into madness. His intense need for tranquillity and repose could find little satisfaction in an age that dripped with blood. Moreover, he suffered materially almost as keenly as spiritually. The bulk of his income—which consisted of royalties from performances of his music in the rest of Europe, and from the publication of his works in Germany—was curtly intercepted, leaving him in a critical financial condition.

After the outbreak of the Russian Revolution, Sibelius' situation became even more trying. Shortly following the declaration of Finland's independence of Russia's domination, civil war broke out between the so-called "Red Guard" revolutionists and the "White Guard." Wholesale killing (of which Sibelius' own brother, a physician, was almost a victim), hooliganism, plunder spread throughout Finland. Suspense and uncertainty made the air tense. The authorities forebade Sibelius to leave his villa; but even there the composer was not altogether safe. Upon two different occasions, the Red Guards descended upon his home, subjected it to an intense search and threw the entire household into an uproar. Sibelius was seriously afraid of his life. Only when Germany sent troops across the border did the confusion in Finland resolve itself into harmony.

From such chaos, music provided the only possible escape. We have descriptions of Sibelius playing quietly upon the piano to soothe his startled children when the Red Guards stormed into his house. We also have verbal portraits of the composer, with disaster at his very door, plunging into the production of great music. During these difficult months, Sibelius created a great number of works.

With the War over, Sibelius set out upon extensive concert tours throughout Europe, which brought him to Norway, Sweden, England and Italy. Wherever he came he was greeted with ceremonious adulation. On the occasion of his sixtieth birthday, Sibelius conducted the first performance of his *Seventh Symphony* in Helsingfors.

In December of 1935, the entire world of music spontaneously rose to its feet to honor one of its great creative masters on the occasion of his seventieth birthday. The celebration was world-wide. In Finland, it was in the form of a national holiday, followed by a cycle of symphony performances that included Sibelius' most representative works. In Paris, London, Vienna, Berlin, Rome, Helsingfors, New York, Boston, Philadelphia there were programs devoted to Sibelius' music—eloquent testimony of the formidable stature of the composer, of his regal position among living composers.

But the most moving tribute of all, perhaps, came from America. At that time, the New York Philharmonic Symphony Society held a poll among radio listeners throughout the entire country for favorite symphonic music to be featured on an all-request program. When the votes were collected and counted, it was discovered that the name of Jan Sibelius headed the list of all living composers. He would not have been human if he had not been sensitively touched by this spontaneously affectionate response and sincere admiration of an entire country towards his life work.

5.

Obviously, the outstanding trait of Sibelius' music is its intense nationalism. His works—both such obviously national expressions as *Finlandia, Kalevala* or *Karelia,* and the more absolute creations as the symphonies—stem from autochthonous sources. One would be at a loss to enumerate those technical features in Sibelius' musical writing which are essentially Finnish. Sibelius never borrows directly from folk material, nor even closely apes melodic and rhythmic patterns of his country's folk-songs. And yet his works assume an unmistakable Scandinavian physiognomy. They have the gray, melancholy landscape of a Scandinavian countryside; they are drenched with the brooding elegiac tenderness and cold beauty of a Norse saga. Sibelius' melody has the broad expanse of the North country; like the North country, his melody is only gently touched by a soft sun. His harmonic colors are subdued by Northern restraint. At moments, his music possesses the strength and heroism of the Scandinavian heroes of the sagas; at other moments, a quiet introspection. Sibelius' music comes not only from a Finnish heart, but from the heart of Finland as well.

Except for its nationalism, the music of Sibelius is not easy to characterize. It falls into too many conflicting categories. It is guided by a strong classicism, and yet who can deny its frequent warm flush of romanticism? It is, at different times, strongly personal and individual, as in the later symphonies, and effetely characterless as in his march from the *Karelia Suite*. It sounds the vibrant note of tragedy, as in the plangent *Andante* of the *Second Symphony* or the restrained lament of the *Largo* of the *Fourth Symphony*. Yet the tread of futility and pessimism does not stride through the pages of Sibelius' music as it does, for example, in the later symphonies of Tchaikovsky. While Sibelius' works are suffused with a soft melancholy as gray and bleak as a winter sky in Scandinavia, his music at times bursts into a soft ripple of laughter, like the chuckle of a bright-faced child—the *Third Symphony,* for example, and portions of the *Karelia Suite*.

The one persistent note that Sibelius sounds in his greater works, particularly in the symphonies from the fourth to the seventh, is that of grandeur; he achieves majestic images which are uniquely his own. His music often rises to a plane of sublimity—the closing of the *Fourth Symphony* is an apt illustration—which appears to be other-worldly. Like some religious ritual, the best pages of Sibelius' later symphonies gives the listener the feeling of being spiritually purged.

Sibelius composes his works as though he were living in the nineteenth and not the twentieth century. He writes in an idiom as though Stravinsky, Schönberg or Ravel had never lived. Certain qualities of instrumentation, certain harmonic colors he has derived from the experiments of modern composers. But except for these negligible qualities, his music—even so late a work as the *Seventh Symphony*—is untouched by modern influence. Experimentation as such finds little favor with Sibelius. He is not for striking ground in radically new directions. He continues musical development from the point where Brahms left off, along the path of romanticism—a romanticism, to be sure, slightly cooled by Northern temperament. The symphonic form of Brahms is supple enough for his purposes; the long accepted conventions of harmony and melody are adequate for him. If he has succeeded in proving nothing else, he has convinced us that no form of music is ever outmoded for the composer who has sufficient imagination and talent to pour into it new ideas and sentiments.

And he has forcefully proved that originality as a composer need not consist in smashing traditions and constructing an entirely new vocabulary. Sibelius has evolved as personal and individual a speech as though he had twisted musical forms into distorted shapes and sizes. There is no mistaking the authorship of his windswept melodies, fresh, healthy, strong. There is no mistaking the hand that constructed the subtly built cathedrals of his symphonies, idea by idea, theme by theme, into a gargantuan and inextricable structure of sound. There is no mistaking the heart that felt and expressed the moving beauty and sadness of the slow movements. Sibelius' symphonies—for it is here that Sibelius expressed himself most successfully—are not only the proud utterances of a great nation. They are more especially the high-minded expression of a great man.

MAURICE RAVEL

V

MAURICE RAVEL

1.

THE French-Basque town of Ciboure slopes gently from
St.-Jean-de-Luz to which it is connected by a narrow
bridge. Only a stone's throw separates it from the border
of Spain. Being virtually a border town, Ciboure is a rich
pattern of two temperaments: Spanish color blends freely
with French refinement. Together with the poignant
nursery songs of French heritage; the children of Ciboure
are raised to the sinuous throb of Spanish folk-melodies.
Together with the studied elegance of French dances, they
hurl their bodies into the simian restlessness of a *fandango,*
which their parents had seen and brought back with them
from across the border.

It was in this miniature half-French, half-Spanish town
that Maurice Ravel was born. His mother was a native
Basque who spent several years of her youth in Spain.
There she met her future husband, who was of Swiss origin.
After marriage, they settled across the border in France
where, on March 7, 1875, Maurice Joseph was born. Spanish culture was Maurice Ravel's spiritual wet-nurse. He
was frequently lulled to sleep to Spanish songs which his
mother had learned to love in her youth.

Although Maurice Ravel was still a child when he was
plucked from Ciboure and transplanted in Paris, he never
lost the imprint which his border town birthplace had in-
delibly stamped upon his intellect. Across his musical lifework there stretches a border line which splits his creative
efforts into two distinct categories, just as it divided the
Pyrenees into France and Spain. On the one side of the

border lies his French music steeped in French tradition, the *Daphnis et Chloé*, the *Concerto for Piano and Orchestra, La Valse;* on the other lies his Spanish music, the *Rhapsodie espagnole*, the *Alborada del Gracioso, L'Heure espagnole,* etc. Ravel's entire artistic career has been marked by a continual transmigration across the French-Spanish border.

In his twelfth year, Maurice Ravel was brought by his parents to Paris where his study of music was launched. Truth to tell, Ravel was not unusually precocious, but his father—a devoted musical amateur—insisted that his son be trained in the art. Ravel's first teacher was Henri Ghis, something of a composer in his own right, who taught the boy the elements of piano playing. Charles René was soon afterwards enlisted to impart into Ravel the rules of harmony. Then, in 1889, Ravel was admitted into the Paris Conservatory. He entered the preparatory piano class of Anthiome, won the first prize for piano playing, and then passed on into the class of Charles de Bériot, where his fellow pupil was Ricardo Viñes, later to become a virtuoso pianist famous for his performances of Ravel's music.

At the time that Ravel was a student at the Conservatory, revolt against tradition in music was in the air in Paris. A group of fearless composers was already pronouncing an individual speech. In Montmartre, Erik Satie had already put to paper the brazen audacities of his *Sarabandes, Ogives* and *Gymnopédies;* in Italy, a Prix de Rome winner, Claude Debussy, had fashioned the fragile outlines of his *La Damoiselle Élue.* César Franck had already composed the *Quartet in D-major,* Gabriel Fauré his *Requiem,* Chausson was writing his *Concerto for Piano, Violin and String Quartet.*

The spirit of rebellion made the musical atmosphere of Paris pungent. It was impossible for Ravel—himself a hot head—not to sense it and react to it keenly. And so, he frequently startled his professor in harmony—the eminent

Émile Pessard—by bringing him exercises in which, from time to time, he sublimely disregarded the rules that had just been inculcated into him—rules which, the young student felt, prevented him from achieving those effects for which he groped instinctively. And in the classroom, while awaiting the arrival of the professor, he would inspire snickers of astonishment among his fellow pupils by playing for them a morsel of Erik Satie or one of the *Pièces pittoresques* of Chabrier which had strongly struck his fancy with the originality of their thought and the freedom of their treatment.

What was probably the turning point in Ravel's period as a student took place in 1897 when he entered the composition class of Gabriel Fauré. While Ravel had been a brilliant pupil under Émile Pessard and André Gédalge (André Gédalge later put to paper the opinion that Ravel was the most brilliant student of counterpoint he ever had), his teachers were too often at a loss to understand and to cope with his restlessness and impatience with academic principles. It was not until Ravel came to Fauré's class that he found a teacher of sympathy and understanding, a teacher who could encourage independent thinking and direct it into the proper channels, a teacher who knew that a free spirit like Ravel must be permitted full freedom of self-expression and allowed to evolve in his own unique manner. Fauré strongly encouraged Ravel's enthusiasm for modern music, and brought him into direct contact with the best modern scores of France and Russia. Thus, under Fauré, Ravel began his first intensive attempts at composition, utilizing his personal idiom unrestrainedly. His first piano pieces, composed at this time, already disclosed the distinct idiosyncrasies of his later style.

On May 27, 1899, Ravel introduced his first pretentious work to the public, the overture, *Shéhérazade,* at the concerts of the Société Nationale. It was received contemptuously by a public that felt that it had made too conscious and affected an effort at being original. Ravel had attempted to speak in a more elastic harmonic language than was prescribed in the text-books, and he refused to be throttled by a too rigid form. To the critics, this represented nothing more than a defiant gesture of youth; they, therefore, casually dismissed the work and its composer.

This first disappointment did not discourage the young composer. In 1901, he made a gesture for the much-desired Prix de Rome with a cantata *Myrrha,* which curiously foreshadowed Ravel's later gift at penning music crisp with irony. *Myrrha* received the second prize— shabby consolation for a young composer who dreamt of Rome and a creative life at the Villa Medici! For the next two years, Ravel continued to enter the Prix de Rome competitions, but with even less success than his initial attempt. In 1905—still undismayed!—he once again presented himself as a candidate. This time, the officials of the Conservatory, impatient with Ravel's failure to produce music more in line with their teachings, refused to give him even the opportunity of applying for the award. They attached to Ravel the label of "revolutionary" and perfunctorily dismissed him from the competition.

The directors of the Conservatory, however, had not reckoned with Ravel's bulging reputation as a composer. By this time Ravel had composed a series of unusual works which brought him, together with a certain degree of notoriety, considerable attention and admiration. In 1902, the pianist Ricardo Viñes introduced into his programs two notable pianistic pieces by Ravel, the *Jeux d'eau* and the *Pavane pour une infante défunte.* Two years later, the elusive beauty of the *Quartet in F-major* had made a marked impression upon the Parisian music public. There were a number of musicians in Paris, amazed that works of such full-grown maturity should have sprung from a composer of comparative inexperience and youth—were shocked that Ravel should be denied an opportunity of applying for a

MAURICE RAVEL

prize that he deserved only too well. There followed a veritable scandal. Newspapers joined prominent critics in viciously denouncing the reactionary leadership of the Conservatory. The storm grew in intensity until Théodore Dubois was compelled to resign as director of the institution, his post passing on to the more liberal and tolerant hands of Gabriel Fauré.

But the storm clouds that had settled over Ravel's head were not completely dissipated with the revolution over the Conservatory "scandal." In 1907, they once again burst into thunder and lightning. The occasion was the first performance of a new Ravel work for voice and piano, the *Histoires naturelles*. Inspired by the Impressionism of Claude Debussy, the *Histoires naturelles* appeared to more than one critic an effete imitation of the style of *Pelléas et Mélisande*. There then followed vicious denunciations of Ravel in which it was maintained that Ravel achieved his meteoric reputation through the elementary process of copying a fashionable composer's mannerisms. Pierre Lalo, the well-known critic, went so far as to accuse Ravel of shameless plagiarism.

A handful of critics, headed by the ever astute M. D. Calvocoressi, were however much more penetrating. Denouncing these calumnies, they pointed to features in Ravel's works to prove that small analogy existed between Debussy and Ravel, that those technical features which assert and reassert themselves in Debussy's work (principally the use of the whole-tone scale) almost never make their presence felt in the music of Ravel, that, moreover, Ravel's music was in temper and spirit directly antithetical to that of Debussy.

It was true that Ravel had been strongly influenced by Debussy whom he admired more considerably than any other contemporary composer. This admiration tempted him to compose a *Miroirs* for piano, just as Debussy had composed an *Images* for the same instrument, to produce

Un Barque sur l'océan just as Debussy had created *La Mer,* to match Debussy's *Iberia* with the *Rhapsodie espagnole.* The similarity in the subject of compositions is, to be sure, striking; but this strong similarity ceases when the quality of the music itself is subject to comparison. Ravel is more virile; in Ravel there is a greater variety of color, a richer depth and a greater intensity of expression.

Ravel's music, as a matter of fact, has shown less derivative influences than the music of most modern composers. Except for the lucidity of his form and the clarity of his structure, which he derived to a great degree from such early French masters as Couperin, and certain spiritual affinities with Debussy, Ravel's music is his own. His early music, even the earliest, reveals that individual strength, that firmness and poise, that intuitive feeling for form, that taste in development of subject matter that characterize the later works. As a matter of fact, Ravel's early teacher, Charles René, once remarked that even in the creative exercises which Ravel submitted as a boy, there were discernible fingerprints of the later mature composer! Certainly there is no mistaking the hand that shaped the *Quartet in F-major,* the *Pavane pour une infante défunte* and the *Jeux d'eau.* The touch may, at infrequent intervals, be the touch of Debussy, but the hand is unmistakably that of Ravel.

From the bitter brawl of 1907, Ravel emerged fully victorious when, during the next three years, he produced a series of remarkable works in which he more firmly established his own personality. In March, 1908, the Colonne concerts in Paris introduced the *Rhapsodie espagnole* which, in its sharpness and strong-muscled masculinity, was a far cry from Debussy's *Iberia. Rhapsodie espagnole,* echoing the Spanish impressions which Ravel had received as a child and never forgot, was vividly appealing to French music-lovers. Shortly after this, Ricardo Viñes received the enthusiastic cheers of an audience for the first performance of *Gaspard de la Nuit.* On April 20, 1910, the fragilely constructed and charmingly unpretentious *Mother Goose Suite* for four hands [1]—written, as Ravel noted in the score "for the pleasure of children"—was introduced at Salle Gaveau by Christine Verger, aged six, and Germaine Duramy, ten years old, to generous acclaim. And on May 19, 1911, the Opéra Comique presented Ravel's sparkling one-act opera, *L'Heure espagnole*. With this work Ravel had vindicated himself.

It is true that it was the publicity of the storms of 1905 and 1907 that had swept Ravel's name to prominence. But it was the works of 1908 to 1910 that solidified that fame and made it permanent.

2.

In 1910, Serge Diaghilev of the Ballet Russe—scenting greatness in a composer who could produce the *Quartet in F-major* and the *Rhapsodie espagnole*—commissioned Ravel to prepare a ballet on the theme of Daphnis and Chloé for the following season. During the entire year of 1910 Ravel worked assiduously on his new score. "I remember," wrote Walter Nouvel, "that the composer lived near Fontainebleau, in a small cottage. The floods were very heavy that year and, as we sat down to listen to what was ready of *Daphnis,* I noticed that the floorboards were curved by the waters pushing up underneath." [2]

When Diaghilev first heard the complete score of *Daphnis* on the piano he was excessively disappointed in it, and for a while seriously considered dropping the project from his plans. As the publisher, Durand, has noted: "In the Spring of 1912, with everything ready to put the work into rehearsal at the Châtelet, they announced in my office the arrival of Monsieur Diaghilev . . . Monsieur Diaghilev

[1] Later orchestrated by Ravel, and better known in this version.
[2] *Diaghileff: His Artistic and Private Life,* by Arnold L. Haskell (in collaboration with Walter Nouvel).

immediately led me to understand that the work did not afford him complete satisfaction, and that he hesitated to follow out the project. I employed my dialectic ability to bring back to Diaghilev his former enthusiasm for the plan. . . . Finally, after having reflected considerably, Diaghilev said simply: 'I will present *Daphnis.*' " [3]

Before it reached performance, *Daphnis et Chloé* confronted other obstacles than the first lack of enthusiasm in Diaghilev. Questions about the choreography brought about a rupture between Diaghilev and Fokine, the ballet-master, a rupture which became definite at the end of the season. There followed several delays and postponements; for a while the fate of *Daphnis* hung on a mere hair. Finally, *Daphnis* was magnificently performed at the Châtelet on June 8, 1912. Nijinsky was Daphnis, and Karsavina was Chloé. The scenery and costumes were designed by Léon Bakst. Pierre Monteux conducted. This, however, was not Paris' initiation to Ravel's masterpiece. A concert suite drawn from the music of *Daphnis* had been presented one year before this—on April 2, 1911—at a Châtelet concert by Gabriel Pierné.

The score contains the following summary of the action: "Daphnis lies stretched before the grotto of the nymphs. . . . Herdsmen enter, seeking Daphnis and Chloé. They find Daphnis and awaken him. In anguish, he looks for Chloé. She at last appears, encircled by shepherdesses. The two rush into each other's arms. Daphnis observes Chloé's crown. His dream was a prophetic vision: the intervention of Pan is manifest. The old shepherd Lammon explains that Pan saved Chloé, in remembrance of the nymph Syrinx, whom the god loved.

"Daphnis and Chloé mime the story of Pan and Syrinx. Chloé impersonates the young nymph wandering over the

[3] For this initial lack of enthusiasm for an unquestioned masterpiece, Diaghilev can, to a great extent, be pardoned, because he heard the work in a piano arrangement; and *Daphnis*—robbed of its gorgeous orchestral garb —loses much of its brilliance.

meadow. Daphnis as Pan appears and declares his love
for her. The nymph repulses him; the god becomes more
insistent. She disappears among the reeds. In desperation,
he plucks some stalks, fashions a flute, and on it plays a
melancholy tune. Chloé comes out and imitates the accents
of the flute by her dance.

"The dance grows more and more animated. In mad
whirlings, Chloé falls into the arms of Daphnis. Before
the altar of the nymphs he swears on two sheep his fidelity.
Young girls enter; they are dressed as Bacchantes and
shake their tambourines. Daphnis and Chloé embrace
tenderly. A group of young men come on the stage. Joyous
tumult. A general dance."

Daphnis et Chloé—partially because of the superb presentation of the Ballet Russe, but more especially because
the great score, now being heard a second time, could be
fully understood—was greeted with unquestioned warmth
and enthusiasm. The audience rose to cheer. However,
the music-critics were divided into two conflicting forces.
Emile Vuillermoz spoke of the "irresistible force" of the
dances, "the spontaneity of the harmonic language," the
"freshness of the ideas" and the "exceptional colors of the
orchestration," while Gaston Carraud was of the opinion
that the rhythmic element disclosed an extreme feebleness;
Robert Brussel was of the opinion that *Daphnis* was "the
most accomplished, the most poetic enterprise that Serge
Diaghilev has given us," but Pierre Lalo denied that
Daphnis was ballet-music of first quality. In striking contrast is this divergence of opinion to the unanimity with
which *Daphnis et Chloé* is today considered not only as
Ravel's masterpiece but as one of the half-dozen epochal
works of music in our time!

Daphnis et Chloé is most familiar to music lovers in the
form of two concert suites which have been drawn from the
score of the ballet and presented in symphony concerts
throughout the world of music. The first suite consists of

a *Nocturne, Interlude* and *Danse Guerrière;* the second suite
includes the *Daybreak, Pantomime* and the *Danse Generale.*

3.

The outbreak of the World War interrupted Ravel's
creative work. Fired by patriotism, Ravel enlisted in the
army and was assigned as motorist to the ambulance corps.

One of the first works to inflame his enthusiasm upon
his return from the battlefront was completing a series of
six piano pieces (begun in 1914)—dedicated to those of
his friends who had fallen in the war—entitled *Le Tombeau
de Couperin.* Later, Ravel orchestrated four of these six
pieces—the *Prelude, Forlane, Menuet* and *Rigaudon*—and
in this form it achieved its great prominence, being first
performed in 1920.

Shortly after the War, Ravel bought a beautiful villa,
the Belvédère, in Montfort l'Amaury, situated in the Île-de-
France section of France. Soon after settling there, Ravel
began to work intensively upon a composition whose theme
had been obsessing him for almost fifteen years, a musical
expression of the "apotheosis of the waltz." *La Valse* was
first performed by Camille Chevillard near the close of
1919 at the Lamoureaux concerts with overwhelming success, a success it has retained tenaciously to this day.

Ravel's next important work did not come until 1925. It
was a ballet, *L'Enfant et les Sortilèges,* to a scenario of
Colette, commissioned by Raoul Gunsbourg for the theatre
at Monte Carlo. The work was introduced at Monte Carlo
on March 29, 1925, under the baton of Vittorio de Sabata
with such an enthusiastic response that, on February 1,
1926, it was performed in Paris at the Opéra Comique
under the direction of Albert Wolff.

In 1928, Ida Rubinstein, the dancer, commissioned Ravel
to compose a work expressly for her. *Bolero*—dedicated to
Ida Rubinstein—took the music world by storm. Built

upon a single theme (which, truth to tell, was not in strict bolero rhythm),[4] repeated again and again, each time in a different instrumental dress, to an ever-increasing *crescendo* until, finally, the principal melody emerged into a magnificently stirring climax, *Bolero* literally swept the audiences off their feet. When Ida Rubinstein introduced the work in Paris in November of 1928, she had the Parisian music public at her feet. In New York, each time Stokowski, Toscanini or Koussevitzky performed the work (which was introduced by Arturo Toscanini in New York on November 14, 1929) they were greeted with intoxicated cheering.

Ravel's *Bolero* became in America a fashion and a fad. It was performed endlessly in movie-houses, concert-halls, on the radio. Six different recordings of the work appeared almost simultaneously. It was arranged for jazz-band, for two pianos, for solo piano, for various combinations of solo instruments. It was introduced into a popular musical revue on Broadway. Hollywood bought the title for a motion-picture. For one year at least America throbbed to bolero rhythm. Never before in musical history was there another example of a serious musical work, from the pen of one of the great living composers, achieving overnight the formidable and contagious popularity of a best-seller novel or a popular-song success.

During 1930 and 1931, Ravel devoted himself to the composition of a work which he felt was his fullest expression as a creative artist—a concerto for piano and orchestra. He worked, at times, ten to twelve hours consecutively a day, attempting to achieve the greatest economy of expression and the leanest of possible forms. The *Concerto* was completed in January, 1932, and was introduced in Paris by Marguerite Long. While not the most consist-

---

[4] As a matter of fact, the Spanish conductor, Enrique Fernández Arbós, was for a long time afraid to introduce *Bolero* in Spain because he feared that Spanish audiences, recognizing that the work was not in the strictest sense a bolero, might deem it a fraud.

ently inspired of Ravel's music, the *Concerto* possesses a pungent effectiveness and inexhaustible vitality as well as a remarkable concentration of expression.

Following the composition of the *Concerto,* Maurice Ravel suffered physical collapse brought on by the strain of overwork. For the past two years, Ravel has been under the vigilant eye of physicians and nurses, both at his own home and at a private sanitarium. Composition has, of course, been impossible. Only the most intimate friends have had access to him. It is believed that with rest and quiet, his health will be restored sufficiently to enable him to continue his creative work where it had been interrupted.

4.

Most of Ravel's greatest works divide themselves into two categories.[5] The first of these is his humorous music. Here the influence of Mozart can to a great extent be traced. Like Mozart, Ravel has attempted to make tones speak flippantly, often facetiously, often with irony and malice. Many of Ravel's compositions are primarily the works of a wit. *Myrrha* is a pungent ironical gem that laughs with each bar. *Histoires naturelles* is one of the high points of his humorous music. The accompaniment is subtle and deft; the harmony exotic; the melodies full of the twist and curve that give them a strange and haunting ironic color. The rhythms frequently play coyly and face-tiously. The music sparkles with bright-faced humor. But, perhaps, the most outstanding of his humorous works is that delicious opera, *L'Heure espagnole,* in which a mis-chievous book is wedded to an equally impudent musical score. All of the different shades of humor (ranging from broad burlesque and clowning to the most sophisticated wit), all the naïvete and impertinence of the comedy are

---

[5] There are of course, important works like the *Quartet* and the *Trio* which belong to neither one of these two categories.

reproduced, with a hand exquisitely poised, in this delicately tinted music. In more respects than one is *L'Heure espagnole* one of the most Mozartean of Ravel's creations.

The second category into which Ravel's greatest works divide themselves is his music for the dance. In this category come those works which have found the most popular appeal among audiences everywhere. The music to *Daphnis et Chloé* deserves first consideration. It proved to be the very culmination of Ravel's creations up to the time of its composition; nor has he ever since equalled the sheer burst of genius of this music. This is his most passionately sincere expression—an expression which must have burst from him in one outpouring of inspiration. This is his largest canvas, and upon it he spread the brilliance of color which dazzles and stupefies each time we come into contact with it. *Daphnis et Chloé* must inevitably rank with Stravinsky's *Le Sacre du Printemps* as the outstanding music of our day produced in France. A work fashioned with the utmost technical dexterity, a work which is volcanic in its energy, a work which now is exquisitely tender and poignant and now erupts into tonal ecstasy, a work whose many varying moods are painted subtly with a brush of many colors—this work is quite unparalleled in our time for sheer spontaneity of inspiration.

In his subsequent works for the dance—*La Valse* and *Bolero*—Maurice Ravel proved himself to be more the showman than the genius. Much of the fascination of these works—a fascination which has made them world-famous almost with the first hearing—is due to the fact that Ravel is a supreme technician who can create music of overpowering force and effectiveness even with trite material. It does not require much acumen to discover considerable superficiality in both of these works. And yet who will deny their appeal? *La Valse* is a study in the development of a theme —a theme which grows and twists and evolves and finally erupts into a colossal and breath-taking climax. *Bolero* is a study in instrumentation. From a hand less cunning and less consummate than Ravel's both these works would have proved to be intolerably banal. Ravel—omnipotent as he is with his musical tools—is able to make the music forcefully effective. Both *La Valse* and *Bolero* are decidedly the triumphs of a master technician. The man of genius speaks, rather, in *Daphnis et Chloé*, in *L'Heure espagnole* and in the *Quartet in F-major*.

5.

Maurice Ravel's villa is situated atop a long, sloping hill. From its terrace can be seen a panoramic view of the Île-de-France countryside extending for miles until it fades into the haze of the distant horizon. One of the windows of Ravel's villa looks out upon the historic church of the town. Le Belvédère is permeated with a spirit of repose and contemplation which Ravel has always considered indispensable for his composition.

Ravel's studio is, by far, the most interesting room in the house. Not only books, music, pictures and a grand piano, but innumerable trinkets, bibelots, objets d'art, antique furniture clutter the place to give it an atmosphere uniquely its own. One's first impression upon entering it is its resemblance to an overcrowded museum-room.

In this strange studio of curiosities, Ravel harmonizes picturesquely. He is usually dressed unconventionally: an affection for waistcoats of garish color and for startlingly colored ensembles of socks and handkerchiefs motivates his costume. Spats, and an ivory cigarette holder quivering at the end of his lips, complete the picture.

When he enters or leaves the room, his body moves with lightning and impulsive swiftness; when seated, his gestures are frequent and nervously agitated. He is short and slim, his build is slight, his cheeks have an emaciated hollowness. His eyes, electrically alive and restless, are the most attractive feature of his appearance. His thin lips curl in a Mephistophelean irony.

His intellectual range is not wide. The only language he speaks besides French is Basque, which he learned as a child. Poetry appeals to him strongly, but he is singularly disinterested in politics, science or history. His tastes frequently approach the simple: He adores dance music, visits night-clubs frequently to hear it, and at one time attempted to incorporate "blues" music and jazz into his own creative work. In 1928 when Ravel visited America, this writer asked him what impressed him most in this country. Ravel's answer was characteristic of him: Negro dance-music which he had heard in a Harlem night club, and the tap-dancers he had seen in one of the leading cinema houses.

A keen sense of fun is one of the predominant traits of his character. Frequently he indulges in the playful pastimes of a schoolboy. A writer-friend of Ravel, Charles Alvar-Harding, has noted that Ravel often convulses his friends with an explosive trick called the "seasick Chinaman," performed with a napkin and an orange. At one time, Mr. Alvar-Harding joined Ravel in a "water war" in which, dressed in raincoats, they threw heavy water sponges at each other. Once being caught at this pastime, Ravel explained to the intruder that they were merely enacting his composition, *Jeux d'eau.*

There remains to speak of Ravel's inherent modesty. Publicity he avoids as though it were a plague, and public appearances are a trial and an abomination to him. He likewise shrinks from all public recognition: upon two occasions he was offered the Legion of Honor which he twice refused. He derives greatest satisfaction from the complete seclusion and tranquillity which he finds at his home.

SERGE PROKOFIEFF

VI

SERGE PROKOFIEFF

1.

IF—AS in the descriptive phrase of the poet—music is the "heavenly maid," then one is strongly tempted to say that with Serge Prokofieff she has lost her virginity. In Prokofieff's works the musical art emerges from the temple and enters the market-place. Music, to Prokofieff, is not hallowed ground to which one must approach with genuflections and with sublime utterances on the lips. There is neither reverence nor humility in his compositions. Music, in Prokofieff's works, abandoned its halo of spirituality and assumed a rakish pose. Irony, sardonic mockery, insolence and irreverence form the well-known "Prokofieff manner" of composition, which during the past two decades has so often been imitated by lesser composers.

True, irony and wit are no strangers to musical expression in general, and certainly not to modern music in particular. But with Prokofieff, satire and wit have achieved their most felicitous and needle-pointed expression. Even more than Erik Satie or the members of the French "Six," Prokofieff has given voice to an impudence that is as infectious as it is disconcerting. He uses dissonance not to unleash tempests of sound, overwhelming the listener with a thunder of sonority, but sparingly, to inject acidity into his thought. His frugal polytonality is as sharp as a razor-blade. His melodies—characterized by a tripping, mocking figure for reeds which he employs frequently—seem to give tonal expression to the gesture of nose-thumbing.

In a recent interview, Prokofieff lamented the fact that critics insisted upon labeling him a satirist without realizing that his works have other and greater qualities. However, despite this protestation, it is as satire that his music must stand or fall. Sublimity or pure poetry are not to be found in Prokofieff. He seems ill-at-ease in his slow movements, as though incapable of concentrated thought; and he has never fully succeeded in producing a sustainedly beautiful page of music. It is almost as if he is incapable of taking himself seriously for too long a time. Even in a work like the *Classical Symphony*—which is a serious attempt to reproduce a Mozart symphony from a modern point-of-view—there gleams the unmistakable twinkle of a mischievous smile. Even in so deeply felt and intricately conceived a work as the *First Violin Concerto*, Prokofieff is not beyond striking a sardonic note—the third movement *(Moderato)*. Sentiment is rare with him; emotion as well.

He is, therefore, most himself when he strikes a malicious posture. Then he possesses an extraordinary gift at carving themes of an intensity and pungency that slash through his music like sharpened knives. His dynamics become brilliantly shaded and contrasted. The outlines of his forms are healthy and broad-chested. His rhythms leap nimbly with athletic muscles. His music sparkles and coruscates—avoiding banal subjects, oversentimentality, and platitudinous ideas. Whatever may be the fault of his music—and its severest shortcoming is that it never inspires the listener or moves him profoundly—it cannot be said that his music ever lacks originality, vitality or youth.

2.

Serge Prokofieff is in the vanguard of radical modern composers in his bold avoidance of consonant harmonies and in his preference for melodies that assume angular, often distorted, lines. What is particularly interesting to note is the fact that he did not arrive at revolt through subtle stages of evolution, as so many other modern com-

SERGE PROKOFIEFF

posers did, but was literally born to it. From his earliest years, his music smashed every accepted law of the harmony text-book—and at a time when rebellion was not the fashion. His restless temperament and his strong individuality compelled him to avoid scrupulously those paths which other composers before his time had traversed.

Serge Prokofieff was born on April 23, 1891, in the South of Russia, on the Sontzovka estate in the government of Ekaterinoslav. His earliest years were, therefore, spent on the steppes of Ukrania. There his mother, an excellent pianist, first introduced him to music by playing for him from the works of Beethoven and Chopin. His intelligent response to music and his abnormal interest in it tempted his mother to begin teaching him the piano at an early age.

He began composition equally early. When he was five years old he heard his parents and their friends discuss, at the tea table, a famine which at that time was devastating India. This conversation inspired Prokofieff to compose a *Galop Hindou* for piano, which depicts programatically the young composer galloping on horseback to bring food to the sufferers. This piece, though written in the key of F-major, brazenly dispenses with the note of B-flat. It may be that Prokofieff had not as yet learned his F-major scale. Or, as is equally probable, young though he was, he was already thumbing his nose at musical tradition!

When he was seven years old, his father took him for a short visit to Moscow where he attended performances of two operas, *Faust* and *Prince Igor*. How these operas moved him can best be judged by the fact that upon his return home he composed an opera of his own, *The Giant*, after an original libretto. *The Giant* was performed by his cousins at the estate of an uncle. "When your operas are given at the Theatre Imperial," the uncle told the boy laughingly, "do not forget that your first presentation took place in my house."

Three years later, Prokofieff—manuscripts in hand—was

taken to Taneiev, the celebrated teacher and composer.
The composer looked through the bundle of original pieces,
finding in some of them talent. "You have to develop a
more interesting harmony," was Taneiev's principal criticism. "Too much of your music employs the tonic, dominant and subdominant."

An interesting harmony! . . . It is amusing to mention
that eleven years after this Prokofieff had a second interview
with Taneiev, bringing with him another bundle of original
compositions. This time, Taneiev was horrified by Prokofieff's dissonant harmonies and audacious tonal experiments. "I have merely followed your advice, master,"
Prokofieff said, unable to restrain a smile. "When I was a
child you told me to develop a more interesting harmony
—which I proceeded to do without delay."

Meanwhile, upon the advice of Taneiev, Prokofieff
became a pupil of Glière. The study of composition un-
loosed in Prokofieff an oceanic surge of musical productivity.
During his first few months with Glière he composed a
symphony, two small operas and two sonatas for piano. In
these works, we are informed by Prokofieff, there was an
instinctive dissatisfaction with the existing rules of music.
He was guided principally by a driving force to express
himself individually and with originality. Time and again,
he destroyed a work impatiently because—though it contained good music—it sounded like the work of some other
composer. And his greatest satisfaction was achieved when
he had put to paper a thought or a motif which he knew
was entirely his own.

Glière brought his talented pupil to the notice of Glazunov who, in turn, urged the boy to enter the Conservatory
of St. Petersburg for an intensive musical training. At the
age of thirteen, therefore, Prokofieff was enrolled in the
Conservatory, where he was to remain for ten years. There
his masters—including Rimsky-Korsakoff, Liadov and
Tcherepnine—were at a loss to understand his temperament

and aspirations. However, neither the dissatisfaction of his teachers nor their bitter criticisms could swerve Prokofieff from his direction. A certain amount of inspiration and encouragement he drew from the musical scores of Scriabin and Max Reger. With these works as beacons lighting his path, Prokofieff composed a symphony, two operas, six sonatas and about a hundred piano pieces. The symphony was performed at a concert of the Conservatory but, because it defied all the teachings of the Conservatory, was badly received. Glazunov, the director (who had generously arranged the performance) was greatly disappointed. But Prokofieff—hearing his imaginative conceptions translated into sound—was convinced in the truth and importance of his direction.

While he was still a student at the Conservatory, Prokofieff's penchant for modernism found stout support in a society devoted to contemporary music, functioning in St. Petersburg. It was at these concerts that Prokofieff's music first received the appreciation it deserved—particularly the first two piano concertos, in which the "Prokofieff manner" is first clearly and unmistakably recognizable. At this time, too, an adventurous publisher, Jurgenson, accepted several of Prokofieff's works for publication.

In 1914, Prokofieff brought his studies at the Conservatory to a close—receiving three diplomas (in composition, piano and conducting) as well as the Rubinstein prize for piano-playing. Shortly after his graduation, he took a holiday trip to London where he was introduced to that celebrated impresario of the ballet, Serge de Diaghilev. Once again Diaghilev recognized genius in the raw; he, therefore, commissioned Prokofieff to prepare a ballet for the Ballet Russe.

Exhilarated by an assignment which Prokofieff felt would bring him widespread fame throughout Europe, he returned to Russia to fulfill his contract for Diaghilev. Shortly after his return, the World War, like a bolt of lightning, struck Russia and set it aflame.

3.

Fortunately, because Prokofieff was the only son of a widowed mother, he was exempt from assuming military duty. The War, therefore, did not interrupt his creative life. With Europe involved in systematic butchery, Prokofieff found escape in his studio, in the composition of a series of strikingly revolutionary works that were soon to startle the music-world.

The first composition to engage him at this time was a ballet for Diaghilev on the subject of prehistoric nomads who roamed the steppes of Ukrania. The ballet was completed at the close of 1914, but Diaghilev—who liked the music—felt that the subject was unsuitable for the dance. Prokofieff therefore, revised his score into a purely orchestral work. In this form, the *Scythian Suite* was introduced at the Maryinsky Theatre on January 29, 1916, under the baton of the composer. This novel and eccentric music puzzled the audience. Glazunov fled from the concert hall in horror, cupping the palms of his hands over his ears to deafen them to Prokofieff's blaring dissonances. One of the violinists of the orchestra (on this or some similar occasion) was overheard by Prokofieff to say to a friend: "My wife is sick and I've got to buy some medicine. Otherwise I wouldn't play this crazy music!"

If this reception made any impression upon the composer it was certainly not one of discouragement. During the next two years, Prokofieff knew one of his most productive periods. In 1915, he composed the ballet *Chout*—which delighted Diaghilev but which was not performed at the time because the War suspended the activities of the Ballet Russe—and in 1916 an opera, *The Gambler*, after an autobiographical novel by Dostoyevsky. In 1917—in the midst of the revolution—he completed his *First Violin Concerto,* the *Classical Symphony,* two piano sonatas, and the incantation for choir and orchestra, *Sept, ils sont sept.*

In October of 1917, the second revolution—which put the communist government in power—hurled Russia into momentary confusion. The supply of food was low, the rouble was collapsing, prices soared, suffering and starvation were widespread. Prokofieff decided, therefore, to come to America. His funds were, of course, low, and a passport was not easy to procure. But both of these obstacles he surmounted in a brief period. Supplied with a generous advance from his publisher, Serge Koussevitzky— the famous conductor, who had shortly before this time established a house in Paris devoted to the publication of Russian music—Prokofieff approached government officials for permission to leave the country. "You are a revolutionary in art just as we are revolutionaries in politics," they told him. "We need you here with us. But if you really wish to go, we will not compel you to remain."

After crossing Siberia—a twenty-six day journey made perilous by the civil war—Prokofieff came to Japan where he gave three concerts to polite but not particularly understanding audiences. Then, by way of Honolulu and San Francisco, Prokofieff arrived in New York in August of 1918.

At the time of Prokofieff's arrival in America, the American music-public had not as yet acquired tolerance towards modern expression in music. In view of this fact, the cordial welcome Prokofieff received everywhere is extraordinary. It is true that his music—when he featured it at his own piano recitals, and when the Russian Symphony Orchestra gave the world première of the *Classical Symphony*—puzzled America and encouraged many acrid opinions. But Prokofieff, himself, was treated respectfully. He received many important engagements and commissions—the most important of which was from the Chicago Opera House for a new operatic work to be featured in 1921.

Early in 1921, Prokofieff completed his circuit of the globe by crossing the Atlantic Ocean in order to confer with Diaghilev in Paris about a projected performance of the ballet *Chout*. After the score had undergone slight revision, *Chout* was introduced by the Ballet Russe at the Théâtre de la Gaîeté on May 17, 1921. The whimsical story, derived from a folk-tale of the Archangel region—depicting the mad exploits of a buffoon—found marvelous expression in the whimsical and highly spiced musical score by Prokofieff. *Chout* was a partial success in Paris. When, however, it was introduced in London, it was attacked severely by the critics.

Prokofieff was back in America towards the close of 1921 to attend the first performance of two of his important works recently completed. Early in December, he was the soloist in the première of his *Third Piano Concerto*—one of his most important creations—at the concerts of the Chicago Symphony Orchestra. Later that month, the Chicago Opera House gave the world's first performance of his opera, *The Love for Three Oranges*.

The text of the opera was drawn from a "fiaba" of Carlo Gozzi, who wrote the play and produced it in Vienna in 1761 to poke fun at two other Venetian authors who at the time were monopolizing the stage—Chiari and Goldoni. For this charming piece, Prokofieff produced what is probably his wittiest score. He has rarely been more audacious in the concoction of sparkling theatrical effects in his music nor in conceiving melodies of an impudent flippancy. Unfortunately, this musical style was far too advanced for Chicago of 1921. The opera was, therefore, received with hostility both by the critics and the audience. In more recent years, several of the orchestral excerpts from this opera have achieved world prominence on symphony programs everywhere—principally the *Scherzo* and the *March*.

4.

After the première of his opera in Chicago, Prokofieff returned to Europe and later established his permanent home in Paris. From this time on, his life has been feverishly active. He has roamed the globe freely in concert-tours of his own music that have brought him to the principal music-centers of the world. At the same time, his creative pen has been indefatigably active. Writing has always come easily to him; and the production of musical works has always been, with him, abundant.

In 1924, Prokofieff composed his second symphony, subsequently producing two more works in the same form: the third, in 1928 (with thematic material drawn from an early opera), and the fourth in 1930 in honor of the fiftieth anniversary of the Boston Symphony Orchestra. In these works he has achieved his greatest terseness and effectiveness in orchestral writing. He likewise completed two new piano concertos (the last of which was given, in October of 1932, a magnificent world-première by the Berlin Philharmonic Orchestra, Wilhelm Furtwängler conducting), as well as recomposing the *Second Piano Concerto,* the score of which had been lost during the Revolution in Russia, only sketches of the piano part surviving.

His most ambitious works, however, were for the ballet. In June of 1927, Diaghilev introduced *Le Pas d'Acier (The Age of Steel)* at the performances of the Ballet Russe. In this work, Prokofieff attempted a tribute to Soviet Russia, dedicating the work to the social values of factories and to the dignity of labor. In a strident score, constructed of muscle and sinew, Prokofieff spoke of the bolt "more beautiful than the rose," and the machine more awe-inspiring than Nature. Two other significant ballets followed in the footsteps of *Le Pas d'Acier: Le Fils prodigue (The Prodigal Son)* introduced by the Diaghilev ballet in 1929, and *Sur le*

Borysthène, commissioned by the Paris Opéra and produced by it in December of 1932.

During this time—it should be recorded—appreciation of Prokofieff's works became commensurate with their fame. His startling musical style had inevitably courted the attention of the music-public. It had, therefore, never been difficult for him to procure a hearing for his works. However, it had been nothing more substantial than curiosity that drew audiences to performances of Prokofieff's music —not appreciative understanding. A decade ago, however, Prokofieff's full significance as a creative artist became universally accepted. Triumphant tours—particularly to Soviet Russia and the United States—brought him tributes that were as sincere as they were enthusiastic. Performances of his major works in the principal music-centers of the world—particularly those of his opera *The Love for Three Oranges*—were extraordinarily successful.

Recently, Prokofieff has transferred his permanent home from Paris to the Soviet Union, where he has assumed an important pedagogical post.

Serge Prokofieff is of medium height and solid in build. His face is spherical, its features markedly Slavic—particularly in the thick lips and the broad, flat nostrils. It is an extraordinarily youthful face, with considerable warmth and softness to it. His hair, which is blond, has lately begun to thin. His brow is high, and his eyes extremely sensitive.

In conversation, he talks volubly with considerable heat and enthusiasm, irrespective of his topic. Strongly opinionated, he frequently transforms arguments into a monologue. A pungent sense of humor endows sparkle to whatever he is saying; he has an instinctive bent for the ironical.

In his art, his life's mission is to attain a simplicity such as Stravinsky had in mind when, one day, he confided to Prokofieff that he hoped at one time to compose music which would consist of no more than two melodies. "I want a simpler and more melodic style for music," Prokofieff has said in interviews, "a simpler, less complicated emotional state, and dissonance again relegated to its proper place as one element of music, contingent principally upon the meeting of melodic lines."

His musical preferences are, more or less, catholic. His preference for the music of Mozart, frequently assumes sheer adoration; he has confessed that Mozart has probably had the greatest influence upon his own art. Among modern composers, Prokofieff esteems Stravinsky highest, and has no hesitation in saying that, in his own opinion, he himself occupies a place next to Stravinsky.

MANUEL DE FALLA

VII

MANUEL DE FALLA

1.

DURING the past six or more decades, the foremost composers of Spain have been motivated by one predominating ideal: to interpret their country musically for the rest of the world. The music of the modern Spanish school, therefore, is touched with the faint incense of the Orient, speaking of a land of Moorish ancestry, of magnificent cobalt skies, of sun-baked patios and moonlit terraces, of gypsy dances and songs, of baroque architecture and mosaic tiles. It mirrors the temperament of a languorous, warm-hearted people.

The nationalistic music of modern Spanish composers, however, is far different from the so-called Spanish music which the rest of Europe has for a long time exhibited as the authentic product. For years, non-Spanish composers in Europe—such as Moritz Moszkowski, Georges Bizet, Chabrier or Rimsky-Korsakoff—have taken some of the more superficial attributes of Spanish music and have constructed from them musical works which have been faithfully accepted as authentic Spanish music. This "pseudo-Spanish music" has exploited some of the more obvious Spanish rhythms, such as those of the malagueña, habañera and the bolero, simulated the tortuous melodic line of the Spanish folk-song, exaggerated its sentimentality and aped its colorful, lambent harmonizations. The externals of Spanish folk-music were caught felicitously enough; but, as true Spaniards have lamented, the heart, soul and spirit of Spain were absent. As one Spanish composer, Enrique Granados, wrote: "The musical interpretation of Spain is not to be found in tawdry boleros and habañeras, in *Carmen,* in anything accompanied by tambourines and castanets. The music of my nation is far more complex, more poetic and more subtle."

True Spanish music—such as is found in the works of the more important modern Spanish composers—is as different from the concoctions in that name of non-Spanish composers as Spain itself is from any other European nation. The melodies of Spanish folk-music rarely consist of the mawkishly sentimental whinings conceived by some imitators. The emotion of true Spanish music is much more restrained, its form is more elusive, almost Oriental in its design. Spanish music abounds in subtle modulations, supple changes from one mood to another, from one atmosphere to another. Its rhythms are often complicated, failing to fall in the neat stereotyped patterns conceived by Frenchmen or Germans writing in the Spanish idiom. Its atmospheric charm is as delicate as a faint touch of Oriental perfume, whose emotional appeal is hidden deeply within the texture of the music, whose construction is frequently so complex that it requires the searching ear of the musical analyst for dissection. It is, in short, music not half so popular in appeal as that which the rest of Europe has fashioned, but much more subtle and original.

The first composer to point the way for the Spanish musical creators of our time was Felipe Pedrell (1841-1922), who is often referred to as the "father of modern Spanish music." Pedrell's importance in the field of musical research far exceeds his significance as a composer. What I have heard of Pedrell's music has convinced me that his mediocrity would long ago have engulfed him in obscurity were it not for the fact that his pioneer work exerted such a powerful historic significance. As a composer, he is stilted, unimaginative, and self-conscious; his music is pieced together as deliberately and as uninspiredly as a carpenter might piece together blocks of wood. However, he was the first composer in Spain to realize the wealth of ideas and richness of spirit latent in the Spanish folk-song, and to understand that great Spanish music must derive its character and quality from indigenous models. Through his blundering compositions, which utilized folk material extensively, through his valuable publications of Spanish folk-songs, through his indefatigable journalistic work and through his pedagogical influence he brought the importance of Spanish folk-music to the attention of his fellow-composers. His researches into the music of Spain's past were significant enough in unearthing many gems from the bowels of obscurity; but their greatest importance must rest in the fact that they succeeded in convincing Spanish composers of the existence of a remarkable storehouse of native material from which they could draw their inspiration.

The first important composers to be influenced by Pedrell's zealous missionary work were Isaac Albéniz (1860-1909), Tomás Bretón (1850-1923) and Enrique Granados (1867-1916). Albéniz stemmed from Catalonia; he drew upon the characteristics of many parts of Spain, notably the hot-blooded songs and dances of Andalusia. His famous "Iberia" consists of twelve "Scenes" from different corners of Spain. Bréton, a Castillian composer, has given expression to the national idiom in his "Zarzuelas," or one-act operas. Enrique Granados, perhaps the most gifted of this trio of composers, produced at least one work which, though drenched with Spanish color and tradition, exerted a potent fascination to which the rest of the world responded sensitively—the opera *Goyescas*.

The foremost artistic figure in the modern Spanish school of composers is unquestionably Manuel de Falla. In him, all of the tendencies of Spanish music of the past fifty years are crystallized, unified, reach their surest artistic expression. The music of Falla sums up the aspirations of every pioneer Spanish composer that preceded him; and it brings them to their most successful artistic realization.

Manuel de Falla's music is more important artistically than that of his predecessors because, for one thing, he achieved a remarkable wedlock of form and content in all of his works. His technique he derived from the French, from whom he learned dexterity in development of musical ideas, taste in instrumentation and variety in harmonic writing. This technique, which became in his hand a supple instrument, he applied to the Spanish message, succeeding in voicing effects and qualities which were far beyond the grasp of his immediate predecessors. Moreover, Falla's music is much more imaginative than even the best works of Granados and Albéniz, because unlike these composers Falla hardly ever directly borrowed folk-songs for his music. The style, the spirit, certain technical features of Spanish folk-music he attempted to reproduce in his own works. But the invention of thematic material was predominantly his own. As a result there is a greater variety of material and much more individual personality in de Falla's music. Too frequently, the music of Granados and Albéniz is what Falla himself has called "caricature." Falla's music, on the other hand, always rings true, always seems to penetrate to the very source and heart of Spanish life.

2.

Cadiz, the famous southern port of Andalusia, two hours' distance across the Gulf from North Africa, was the city of Manuel de Falla's birth, on November 23, 1876. He was a descendant of a Spanish family that could trace its ancestry for several centuries: his father was of Valencian stock, while his mother's ancestors were Catalonian. The Falla home in Cadiz was known by the neighbors to be a setting of culture, in which music played an important rôle. The mother, an extraordinarily good musician, gave Manuel his first piano lessons even before he had learned to read or write. His progress was so rapid that professional instruc-

MANUEL DE FALLA

tors were soon engaged to give him an intensive musical education: Mlle. Elois Galluzo became his teacher in piano-playing, and Alejandra Odero and Enrique Broca his instructors in harmony and theory. While still a child, Falla made a public appearance in Cadiz, together with his mother, in a performance of a four-hand piano arrangement of Haydn's *Seven Words from the Cross.*

One of the most vivid impressions that Falla received as a child came in 1886 when his parents took him for a short visit to Seville to witness a festival. The picturesque religious pageant which he saw moved the child so strongly that he could not withhold his tears. For many years after that, this scene remained in his mind a symbol of the grandeur of Spain; it nursed and fed his national spirit.

It was not until after adolescence that Falla heard his first orchestral concert, in Cadiz, in a program that included Grieg and Beethoven. Falla frequently commented that his musical life began officially when he heard his first symphony orchestra. It was probably his first complete realization of the true vastness and scope of the musical art which, until now, he had associated only with pieces for the piano and the voice. As he listened to the ebullient lyrical spirit of Grieg and the tempestuous strength of Beethoven, Falla knew that music must remain his sphere of activity.

His parents, therefore, sent him to Madrid to enter the Conservatory of Music. There he came under the influence of two great teachers: Felipe Pedrell, the great pioneer in Spanish music, and José Tragó, the celebrated Spanish pianist. Both of these teachers recognized in Falla a native talent, fine musical sensibilities and a valuable artistic temperament. They felt strongly that if this nervous, high-strung, hypersensitive and flamingly idealistic boy directed his energy and enthusiasm through the proper channels without dissipating them he would develop into an extraordinary musican. José Tragó hoped to make of Falla a great virtuoso; he was convinced that Falla was destined for a

pianistic career particularly when the student won first prize
and then an additional special award in piano playing. But
of the two teachers Felipe Pedrell was the stronger influence. It was because of Pedrell that, even in his youth,
Falla was convinced that he would become a composer
rather than a concert artist.

When Falla was a student at the Conservatory, Felipe
Pedrell was about fifty years old, his most valuable researches in Spanish church-music and folk-music still stretch-
ing before him. However, Pedrell's entire life had already
been guided and directed by the glowing ideal to bring Spanish music a worthy place in the artistic sun, to direct the
energy and genius of Spanish composers to the production
of a music whose sources were unmistakably indigenous.
He was disgusted with the sham Spanish music which non-
Spanish composers had created throughout Europe as examples of Spanish folk-music and which all of Europe
smugly accepted as the genuine article. He, therefore,
dreamed of the time when Spanish composers by their combined efforts and coöperative endeavor would teach the rest
of the world the true nature of the Spanish musical folk-art.
As the significant cornerstone in the erection of such a Spanish musical edifice, Pedrell had already composed an opera
(*Los Pirineos*), written his trenchant pamphlet, *Por nuestra
música*, in which he firmly maintained that national music
must rest upon the foundations of the folk-song, and had
unearthed many remarkable examples of authentic Spanish
folk-songs from the distant past.

Pedrell imbued his pupil, Falla, with his own passionate
ideals for Spanish music. He poured into the boy's alert
ears those arguments which, years back, had convinced him
to consecrate his own life to one artistic mission. He introduced Falla to the fabulous wealth of Spanish folk-songs
and proved to him how different this music was, in form and
spirit, from the clichés which were masquerading throughout the rest of Europe as authentic Spanish art. He argued

that it was the duty of every Spanish composer to derive the character and personality of his art from the folk-music of so colorful a people. Again and again he told Falla that no greater ideal can inspire the Spanish composer than to interpret the glamour, mystery and charm of his own country. And Falla—reminded, perhaps, of the religious pageant he had seen in Seville several years before this—was convinced of the truth and wisdom of Pedrell's artistic mission.

The influence of Pedrell upon Falla was, as de Falla himself has confessed,[1] cataclysmic. The remarkable unity of purpose in Falla's career, the straight line of his direction, the extraordinary devotion to one artistic ideal are all the direct results of Pedrell's teachings. When Felipe Pedrell died in 1922 he knew well that his own music was destined for obscurity. But he also knew that his preachings had not been in vain. Native music of Spain had by this time acquired artistic significance and dignity in the eyes of the world, due principally to the efforts of such composers as Bréton, Albéniz, Granados and Falla who had put his theories into successful practise.

When Falla completed his course of study at the Conservatory, his eyes were directed towards that center of modern musical activity in Europe at the time—Paris. In Paris he hoped to complete his studies and reach final artistic development. To procure the necessary funds for the voyage, Falla composed several light musical scores for the Spanish theatres. Unfortunately, this temporary concession to necessity—the only such concession that Falla was ever to make—was fruitless. Spanish theatres at the time were inhospitable to unknown composers. Falla, therefore, immediately abandoned hack-work and turned to more serious artistic endeavors. He worked intensively at his piano-playing, performing in chamber groups and in concerts, and

---

[1] "It is to the lessons of Pedrell," Falla has said publicly, "and to the powerful stimulation exercised on me by his works that I owe my artistic life."

even succeeding, in 1905, in winning the Ortis y Cusso prize for piano-playing. He likewise devoted himself industriously to composition, in which he hoped to embody the principles of his master, Pedrell. He was planning a work Spanish to the core, based upon models of Spanish folk-music.

For a subject, he selected a libretto of a friend, Carlos Fernandez Shaw, entitled *La Vida Breve*—a very poor libretto, as a matter of fact, whose theme bordered dangerously upon the hackneyed (it bore a striking resemblance, for example, to the book of Mascagni's opera *Cavalleria Rusticana*). But it appealed strongly to Falla because of its strong Spanish color and because of the opportunities it offered him for the composition of authentic Spanish music.

In 1905, Falla brought *La Vida Breve* to completion. Although it was refused for performance by over-cautious managers, it brought Falla his first sensation of recognition by achieving the first prize in a competition for a national opera conducted by the Real Academia de Bellas Artes.

Falla's declining health, in 1907, compelled him to take a cure at the waters of Vichy, France. Once having crossed the border into France, Falla could not resist the temptation of paying a visit to Paris, even though his purse would be sadly taxed thereby. He bought a seven-day round trip ticket, planning his budget so that he might spend five days in the French capital. He remained, however, for seven years.

At that time, Paris was quivering with unusual musical activity. Such composers as Claude Debussy, Paul Dukas and Maurice Ravel were in the limelight. Gabriel Fauré was at the height of his creative power; the name of Erik Satie was the object for debate and dissension. It was impossible for a young and sensitive composer, arriving from a country of comparative musical aridity, not to be thrilled by what he saw, heard and experienced in this feverishly active musical metropolis. He met Debussy personally, was given a rousing welcome by Paul Dukas who always had a warm greeting and an outstretched hand of friendship for the unknown and struggling composer. Such younger composers as Florent Schmitt, Albert Roussel and Maurice Ravel generously accepted him in their circle. In such a musical environment—charged as it was with the electricity of important performances, productions of works in new idioms, discussions, arguments—Manuel de Falla felt that he was in his element.

The Paris adventure was fraught with hardship brought on by a poverty that was so intense that even the immediate necessities of life were frequently unprocurable. There were periods when Falla was on the verge of starvation, days when he feared that he would freeze to death.

An amusing episode which took place at this time almost brought Falla permanent relief from this stifling poverty. His friend, Ricardo Viñes, the pianist, pitying the young musician's plight, brought him one day the address of a prosperous French family searching for a piano teacher for the daughter. The remuneration was excessively generous, adequate to provide Falla with all his needs. Falla decided to make contact with the family without delay. Since the home of his prospective pupil was not distant from his own laundry, Falla decided to save an additional trip by taking with him a bundle of his soiled shirts which he might leave at the *blanchisseuse*. Unfortunately, the laundry was closed for the lunch hour, compelling Falla to make his visit to his prospective pupil with his soiled bundle under his arm. Timidly he rang the doorbell, stiflingly self-conscious of his large and unpleasant-looking bundle. When the servant opened the door, she mistook Falla for a tradesman and viciously upbraided him for using the front entrance instead of the rear door assigned to tradesmen. Humiliated and flushed with embarrassment, Falla sheepishly made his way to the rear entrance. There the mistress of the house awaited him, likewise with a stinging rebuke on her lips for his impudence in using the front door. Rather than make a long and ridiculous explanation, Falla stammered his apology and fled—back into the more welcome arms of poverty.

Creatively, the years that Falla spent in Paris were almost barren. His only productions were a setting of three poems by Théophile Gautier and four morsels for the piano entitled *Pièces espagnoles*. But though Falla was creatively idle, these years were by no means wasted. He was busily gathering impressions. He was absorbed in the study of the music of his French friends, acquiring their remarkable sense of form and instrumentation. Falla has frequently maintained that his personal contact and conversations with Debussy were the greatest single influence in his artistic life, with the exception of Felipe Pedrell. Above all else, he was achieving intellectual maturity.

On April 1, 1913, Falla's early opera, *La Vida Breve,* was performed for the first time at the Casino Municipal in Nice with such success that in January of the following year the Opéra Comique of Paris introduced it into its repertoire.

Nostalgia for his native country brought Falla's sojourn in Paris to a termination in 1914. He felt that such musical education as he could acquire in Paris was now his; and the feeling lingered with him that to do important creative work in a Spanish idiom it was necessary for him to return to his own country, imbibe its atmosphere and be intimately in contact with its spirit and culture.

Thus, evading the outbreak of the World War in France by several months, Falla returned to Spain in 1914. A few months later, *La Vida Breve* was performed for the first time in Spain, receiving thunderous acclaim. To Spanish audiences, not too accustomed to witnessing familiar Spanish themes in their opera-house, *La Vida Breve* struck a responsive chord. Particularly Falla's music—the corybantic dances, the sinuous monologues that resembled Andalusian folk-songs, the hot-blooded melodies. Overnight, therefore, Falla became a famous composer in his own country.

For the next few years, Falla traveled extensively throughout Andalusia, expressly to derive a closer glimpse of Spanish life, finally settling in Granada. At the same time he began an ambitious program of creation in the Spanish vein. In 1915, he completed *El Amor Brujo (Love, the Sorcerer)*, a ballet, with voice and orchestra, based upon a libretto by Gregorio Martinez Sierra which, in turn, was derived from an Andalusian gypsy folk-tale. The legend speaks of Candela, a beautiful gypsy, who—after the death of her husband—falls in love with Carmelo, a bronze-faced, broad shouldered youth. The ghost of Candela's dead husband haunts her until, shrewdly, Carmelo persuades Lucia, a seductively attractive gypsy, to flirt with the ghost. Even in death, the husband of Candela cannot resist a pair of beautiful eyes. The ghost becomes a slave to Lucia's enchantment—and Candela is given the peace to pursue her love-affair with Carmelo.

The first performance of *El Amor Brujo* took place in Madrid at the Teatro del Lara on April 15, 1915, with only moderate success. A suite for orchestra and voice, drawn from the ballet, was first featured at the concerts of the Sociedad Nacional de Música under the direction of Enrique Fernández Arbós. The suite has since become famous on symphony programs throughout the world of music.

El Amor Brujo was followed by another important Spanish work, *Nights in the Gardens of Spain,* for piano and orchestra. Completed in 1916, it was first performed in that year under Arbós' direction. While Falla attached no specific program to his orchestral work, the subtitles of the three movements suggest the Spanish pictures that Falla wished to evoke in his music. The first movement is entitled "In the Gardens of the Generalife"; the second, "A Dance Heard in the Distance"; the third, "In the Gardens of the Sierra de Cordoba."

With these two works, Falla became recognized as the foremost musical spokesman of his country. In 1919, therefore, Serge Diaghilev—contemplating the introduction into the programs of the Ballet Russe of an authentic Spanish number that would synthesize the Spanish arts—commissioned Falla to produce the musical score for a scenario fashioned by Martinez Sierra from the lustily witty novel of Don Antonio Pedro de Alarcon, *The Three Cornered Hat*. The protagonists of *The Three Cornered Hat* constitute the triangle of a miller, his beautiful wife and a lascivious governor. The governor effects the miller's arrest so that he may better be able to make advances to the beautiful wife. The wife playfully teases the governor with a dance, eluding his outstretched embrace with sinuous contortions of the body until the governor, savagely pursuing her, topples over a bridge into a stream. The governor removes his clothes and, while waiting for them to dry, slips into the miller's bed. Suddenly the miller returns and finds the governor in his bed. To avenge himself, the miller hurriedly exchanges his own clothing for that of the governor, scratches a note on the wall to the effect that the governor's wife is quite as beautiful and as desirable as his own and, jauntily whistling a roguish tune, exits from the scene.[2]

The tremendous enthusiasm that greeted *The Three Cornered Hat*—when it was first performed by the Ballet Russe, under the baton of Ernest Ansermet, at the Alhambra Theatre in London on July 23, 1919—marked probably the most formidable victory of Spanish terpsichorean art in the rest of Europe. For *The Three Cornered Hat*—much to Diaghilev's credit—was Spanish to its very roots. The book and music were, of course, native Spanish products, as were the dances, modeled closely after the native gypsy dances of Granada and Seville. And the exotic settings and

---

[2] This same subject served as the theme for Hugo Wolf's only opera, *Der Corregidor*.

costumes were the imaginative conceptions of Pablo Picasso, Spain's foremost painter.

A pathetic story is connected with Diaghilev's production of Falla's *The Three Cornered Hat*. Diaghilev—while attending a festival of gypsy dancing in Seville for the purpose of gathering impressions for his forthcoming Spanish production—was attracted to the dancing of one young boy whose subtle gyrations of the body and eloquent thrusts of the hand seemed to speak eloquently of the gypsy temperament of the Andalusian. Diaghilev contracted the boy to train the principal dancers of the Ballet Russe—Massine and Karsavina, particularly—in Spanish dance routines. The boy was something of a half-wit; thoughts and speech came to him slowly. However, he was the very incarnation of the dance. He who, at all other times, was so hopelessly inarticulate, suddenly became transfigured in dance, his body the expression of music and poetry at once. The boy, therefore, was of immeasurable importance in training members of the Ballet Russe in authentic Spanish dances. As the day of the performance of *The Three Cornered Hat* approached, the slow and stolid mind of the boy became seized with the delusion that it was he who was to be the center of all the dancing activity in the production and who was to perform the central rôle in the ballet. When Diaghilev told him firmly and explicitly that he was not to appear publicly, that he had been engaged only to train the dancers, the boy became sullen and morose. From that moment on he moved as though in a daze, oblivious to his surroundings. The night of the première of *The Three Cornered Hat* arrived, and the ballet was a stirring success. On that same night they found the boy dancing madly upon a dark altar of a deserted church in London. The following morning the boy was incarcerated in an insane asylum.

Three years after the creation of *The Three Cornered Hat*, Falla composed a charming score for a puppet-show, *El Retablo de Maese Pedro*—based upon scenes from Cervantes' *Don Quixote*—which was introduced in the Paris salon of Princesse de Polignac in June of 1923. There followed a work of far different character, perhaps the purest music that Falla created and one of his few works not written to express Spain. It was the *Concerto for Harpsichord, Flute, Oboe, Clarinet, Violin and Violoncello,* dedicated to that great performer on the harpsichord, Mme. Wanda Landowska, and introduced by her at a festival of Falla's music conducted by Pablo Casals in Barcelona in November of 1926. Mme. Landowska has explained the origin of this unusual work. "Four years ago, I spent several days with my friend Falla in Granada and at that very moment he was working at his *Retablo,* a part of which he devoted to the harpsichord. I had my harpsichord with me (being, of course, on a concert tour through Spain) and I was able to play for him a great deal and to speak about the various possibilities of the instrument. He became more and more interested, and after a few days' conversation between us he grew so enthusiastic that he resolved to write a concerto for harpsichord. He took three years to compose the work, which was finished in September of 1926. But when one becomes acquainted with the music, one understands that the master carried with him a long time such a deep work that needed to come to life little by little."

Since the *Concerto,* Falla has been laboring upon a composition which is perhaps his most ambitious canvas to date —*La Atlantída* for solo voices, chorus and orchestra, based upon a great Catalonian poem of Jacinto Verdaguer.

3.

Manuel de Falla lives the year round in Granada, atop a hill that removes him from the city itself and which is crowned by the ancient Alhambra, only a few minutes from his door. Near his home, too, are the mountainous caves of the Andalusian gypsies—reverberating with the click of castanets and dancing heels and ringing with the nasal, high-pitched singing of gypsy songs. Falla, therefore, has at his very elbow the tradition and spirit of Spain. Its beauty, too—for from his window he can see the snow-capped peaks of the Sierra Nevadas and the Vegas.

Falla is small of build; his body is so frail that he gives the impression of excessive timidity. His bullet-shaped head consists of a broad forehead, an arched nose, a weak chin and a complexion of bronze. By far the most expressive part of his face is his eyes, dreamy and melancholy which, in their suggestion of mysticism, remind one of the introspective eyes of an El Greco painting.

A recluse by temperament, Falla rarely leaves Granada where his life has become systematically routinized. He rises early each morning, takes a prolonged walk, and attends Mass at the Church San Cecilio. Falla then devotes himself to several consecutive hours of intensive composition. A siesta follows the noon-day meal, after which friends and neighbors are entertained at his home. Some more work follows later in the evening and, at an early hour, Falla retires for the night.

The Andalusians who live near him know him as a man of the utmost simplicity and humility. They refer to him as "master" and they know that he is a great man because rarely does a foreigner climb the tortuous road atop the hill without inquiring for the Alhambra and the home of Manuel de Falla. However, though they venerate him, they freely accept him as one of their own. When in their company, he is capable of speaking their vocabulary; his unpretentiousness and simplicity have made it possible for them to accept him as one of them despite his world prestige.

CHARLES MARTIN LOEFFLER

VIII

CHARLES MARTIN LOEFFLER

1.

THE death of Charles Martin Loeffler in the spring of 1935 removed from the American scene one of the most significant musical creators to have emerged there during the past fifty years. It is difficult to speak of Loeffler as an American composer, because in temperament he was far removed from the American spirit, and his musical style —in its purity and delicacy—suggests nothing that is intrinsically American. Truth to tell, Loeffler was never particularly interested in creating an American style of composition. Throughout his long and fertile career, during which he came into contact with various American influences, he rarely permitted them to touch his personal speech. He loathed fashions and fads in composition, and he succeeded in remaining aloof from all stylish tendencies. In his music, as in his life, he preferred monastic seclusion. For twenty-five years he ensconced himself in a small town in Massachusetts, where he rarely came into contact with society. In his art, he retired to an even remoter and less accessible ivory tower of escape. He never sought the limelight, nor did he ever court attention. He refused to become sensational or obviously individual. One of the most passionately sincere and artistically inviolate of contemporary American composers, he embodied the highest ideals of his art. And his entire creative life was guided by one mission alone: he sought to translate upon paper those feelings and sensations which he experienced so keenly. No one who has heard his best work will attempt to deny that he has done this with unique and matchless felicity.

2.

Charles Martin Tornov Loeffler was born in Mühlhausen in Alsace on January 30, 1861. His father—a specialist in chemistry, agriculture and horse-breeding—was fond of music; his mother's artistic preference was poetry.

While he was still a child, Charles Martin Loeffler was brought to a small country town in the province of Kiev, Smjela, whither his father had come to work for the government. Loeffler's earliest impressions in music, therefore, were received from Russian folk and church music, the plangent pathos of whose melodies and whose lusciously rich harmonic colors made so forceful an appeal to him that, as long as he lived, he never forgot them. In later life, as a composer, he revealed the strong influence these early musical experiences had exerted upon him with such works as *Veillées de l'Ukraine* and *Memories of My Childhood,* in both of which he embodied folk-music.

On his eighth birthday, Charles Loeffler received from his father the gift of a violin. He responded to the instrument with more than the mere curiosity of a child, and was soon able to draw fragments of melody from the strings. Before long, a competent instructor was sought, and found in the person of a German musician from the Imperial Orchestra in St. Petersburg who spent his summers in Smjela.

Before long, the Loeffler family once again changed its home, settling this time in Debreczin, Hungary, where father Loeffler received a pedagogical post in the Royal Agricultural Academy. In Hungary, young Loeffler was subjected to a new musical influence, as strong as that which he had encountered in Russia—namely, the folk-music of Hungarian gypsies which he literally absorbed and which, for a few years, was the only satisfaction his growing musical appetite received.

Loeffler was fifteen years old when he decided definitely that he would become a professional musician. He had by

CHARLES MARTIN LOEFFLER

this time acquired by himself a flexible technique on the violin, and he was determined to continue the study of the instrument with greater assiduity. The opportunities for intensive study offered by a small Hungarian town being impoverished, Loeffler decided to go to Berlin. There he became a violin pupil of Eduard Rappoldi—as a preparatory course for the violin class of Joseph Joachim—and a student of harmony of Friedrich Kiel. The Berlin course of study was not altogether satisfying to Loeffler and, before long, he left Berlin for Paris where he studied the violin under Massart and composition from Ernest Guiraud.

For a full year, Loeffler earned his living by playing in the violin section of Pasdeloup's orchestra in Paris, and in the private orchestra of Baron Paul von Derwies in Nice and Lugano where he was associated with César Thomson, famous French violinist. Then, in 1881—equipped with letters of introduction from Joseph Joachim to Leopold Damrosch and Theodore Thomas—Loeffler crossed the Atlantic and settled permanently in the country, of whose composers he was soon destined to become the recognized dean.

The season of 1881-1882 Loeffler spent in New York City, playing in all of Leopold Damrosch's orchestral and choral concerts. In 1882, his name came to the notice of Henry Lee Higginson—eminent Boston patron of music— who at the moment was devoting inexhaustible industry in developing the newly-founded Boston Symphony Orchestra. Higginson, who was eagerly scanning the musical horizon for important talent to import into Boston, was impressed by Loeffler's gifts and immediately engaged him for the orchestra. From 1885 to 1903 he shared the first desk with Franz Kneisel. Five years later, Loeffler's status as an American was officially established when he received his citizenship.

It was not long before Loeffler emerged as an important creative force in American music. In 1891, Loeffler's first orchestral work, *Les Veillées de l'Ukraine,* inspired by

Gogol, was introduced at the concerts of the Boston Symphony Orchestra with considerable success. *Les Veillées de l'Ukraine,* Loeffler's nostalgic reminiscences of his boyhood contact with Russian folk-music, was only faintly suggestive of Loeffler's later impressionistic style; but its sure-handed construction, its maturity of conception and its moving emotional quality brought enthusiastic response from the audience. *Les Veillées de l'Ukraine* was followed six years later by *La Mort de Tintagiles,* inspired by Maurice Maeterlinck's drama of that name composed in the summer of 1897 and first performed at the concerts of the Boston Symphony Orchestra on January 8, 1898, *La Mort* definitely increased Loeffler's artistic stature. Meanwhile, Franz Kneisel had founded his world-famous string-quartet which introduced Loeffler's *String-Sextet* at one of its concerts in 1893.

In 1901, Loeffler produced the first characteristic works of his artistic maturity: a *Poem,* for orchestra, inspired by an aubade of Paul Verlaine to his bride, entitled *La Bonne chanson* and a Symphonic Fantasy, after Rollinat, entitled *La Villanelle du Diablé.* Both works were first introduced by the Boston Symphony Orchestra in 1902. Several years later, Loeffler revised and reorchestrated the former, and in this new form it was first performed by Pierre Monteux in Boston in 1918.

Loeffler, having now found his creative pace, was not slow in creating his first accepted masterpiece. In 1901, he completed a chamber composition, *A Pagan Poem,* inspired by two love songs of Damon and Alphesiboeus in the eighth eclogue of Virgil. Four years after this, the work was remodeled by Loeffler and scored for full orchestra. In this new version, *A Pagan Poem* was introduced by the Boston Symphony Orchestra in 1907. It asserted itself immediately as a classic in modern American music; since 1907 it has enjoyed a prominent place on symphony programs everywhere as one of the rich specimens of American musical expression.

A Pagan Poem definitely established Loeffler as a composer of the first importance. In 1903, therefore, he resigned from his violin post with the Boston Symphony Orchestra to devote himself entirely to creative work. Later, he bought a farm in Medfield, Massachusetts— fifteen miles from Boston—which for the remainder of his life was to be his home. From this time on, he lived in monastic retirement—his life consecrated to musical composition as though it were a religious ritual—and guarded his seclusion so jealously that biographical material about Loeffler's later life becomes impoverished, consisting of hardly more than a record of works composed and performed. He avoided the glare of public attention so fastidiously that—though his position as the foremost living American composer was conceded without question or debate—until the end of his life little was known about him personally. For thirty years, he was as far removed from the world of frenetic activity as though he were on a different planet. The most important interruption in this life of retirement took place on December 8, 1910 when Loeffler was married to Elise Burnett Fay. Elise proved to be uniquely sympathetic and understanding of her husband's temperament, and fastidiously preserved the life of simplicity and seclusion in which the composer was happiest.

In the works which Loeffler produced during the thirty years of his retirement from activity as a violinist, he maintained a high level of beauty, poetry and artistic genuineness from which he rarely swerved. His works were not many in number because his conscience was severe and he labored slowly; but whatever emerged from his workshop was stamped with distinction and integrity of high artistry. The most significant of these works—those whose permanency seems most assured—are the *Hora Mystica,* for men's chorus and orchestra, composed in 1916, the famous *Memories of My Childhood,* created in 1924, and the *Evocation,*

the last of the Loeffler masterpieces. His most famous
work is the *Pagan Poem*.

Memories of My Childhood received the $1,000 first
prize in a competition sponsored by the Chicago North
Shore Music Festival, where it was first performed on May
29, 1924. The printed score of this celebrated work contains the following preface by Loeffler which gives us an
insight into the program of the music: "Many years ago,
the composer spent more than three years of his boyhood in
a Russian small town Smjela (government of Kiev). He
now seeks to express by the following music what still lives
in his heart and memory of those happy days. He recalls
in the various strains of his music Russian peasant songs,
the Yourod's Litany prayer, 'the happiest of days,' fairy
tales and dance songs. The closing movement of the symphonic poem commemorates the death of Vasinka, an el-
derly peasant Bayan, or story-teller, singer, maker of
willow pipes upon which he played tunes of weird intervals
and the companion and friend of the boy who now, later in
life, notes down what he hopes these pages will tell."

In 1931, United States celebrated the seventieth birthday
of Charles Martin Loeffler with adulatory articles in the
press and festival concerts in Boston, Cleveland and New
York. To commemorate the event—and to inaugurate at
the same time the official opening of its new concert-hall—
the Cleveland Symphony Orchestra commissioned Loeffler
to prepare a special work for that organization. The work,
Evocation—for chorus and orchestra—was Loeffler's eloquent reply. It is one of the most moving pieces of music
that Loeffler produced, has all that rich blend of poetry,
mysticism and elegiac calm of his best compositions. Old
age, obviously, never could set into Loeffler's creative life.

Loeffler's chief diversion, during the last years of his life,
was to train a boys' church choir, in his home town, in the
singing of Gregorain chants. Carl Engel, that eminent
musicologist, met Loeffler one year before the composer's

death, and has given us a vivid paragraph describing the great musician in his old age.[1] "He bore the marks of physical suffering. But his razor-blade mind still showed occasionally its flashing edge. His mood was genial, reminiscent. The good things of the table still appealed to him. His wonderful eyes would still twinkle as he unraveled some favorite story, not less amusing for being not altogether new. His precarious cardiac condition did not prevent him from asking the waiter to bring me particularly rich cigars. He acknowledged eagerly how charmed he had been with the person of Arnold Schönberg. His thoughts roamed the length of contemporary music. On hearing the hotel musicians play a certain composition, he made a face and confessed that for him the appeal of Karl Maria von Weber had long ago ceased. From one thing to another the talk swayed along its circuitous course, not as fast as formerly, but just as absorbing."

Charles Martin Loeffler died as he had lived, gently and peacefully, at his farm in Medfield, Massachusetts, on May 19, 1935. His death was mourned by an entire world of music, for it had lost one of its more precious spirits.

3.

Charles Martin Loeffler frequently referred to himself, not as a composer or as a musician, but as "the farmer of Medfield." This self-designation gives an eloquent insight into the man's utter simplicity and lack of affectation. There was nothing about him to suggest his artistic calling; few composers of any age have been so devoid of postures, self-advertisement or little idiosyncrasies and peculiar mannerisms as Loeffler. He loved the country intensely, everything about it. He enjoyed watching the crops grow, and he was a great fancier of horses.

In appearance, he suggested the scholar. He was tall,

[1] *Musical Quarterly,* October, 1935.

well-built and erect, even in old age. He exuded an air of
professorial dignity. His head was almost like an inverted
triangle extending from his broad bald scalp and converging
into a short pointed beard. His nose was aquiline, descend-
ing from a high brow; his face was long and lean.

His musical preferences were orthodox. He worshipped
the music of Bach, and seemed to derive greatest artistic
satisfaction from the contrapuntal works of the sixteenth
and seventeenth centuries. He had also the greatest
admiration for Beethoven. Among moderns Fauré and
Debussy were perhaps his favorites.

He was equally interested in many branches of art, deriv-
ing pleasure from painting and sculpture and being
particularly intimately acquainted with literature. The
American scene, in all of its facets, was an endless source
of interest to him. He admired the poetry of Edgar Allan
Poe, the novels of Mark Twain and the humor of Will
Rogers. He even confessed deriving pleasure from good
jazz, which he believed to be a true musical expression of
American temperament—and held the highest respect for
George Gershwin and Duke Ellington.

4.

The artistic creation of true genius is not a spasmodic
change from one style to another. It is, rather, an inevitable and logical growth which develops from the most
elementary roots and blooms, finally, into full flower. In the
lifework of true genius one can perceive his individual style
and his identifying fingerprints, however embryonic, even
in his earliest works. The Beethoven of the first period is
most assuredly not the Beethoven of the *Missa Solemnis*—
and yet we already hear, in embryo, the distinctive speech of
Beethoven in the pain and despair of the slow movement of
the Opus 10, no. 3 Piano Sonata and in the *Adagio* preceding the fourth movement of the String Quartet Opus 18,

no. 6. The sparkling *C-major Symphony* that Mozart wrote at the age of eight, and the ebullient *Adelaide Concerto* created at the age of ten are, emphatically, not of the stature of the *Jupiter;* yet who can deny their unmistakable Mozartean traits? The Wagner of *Rienzi* already disclosed the traces of a style which he was to develop with such passion and force of genius in the *Ring*. True genius, I feel strongly, is not chameleon; it does not discard styles and mannerisms as though they were pieces of garment. The later work of every great composer must be an unmistakable outgrowth of all his earlier fumblings.

This is eloquently true of Charles Martin Loeffler. Even in the earlier pages of his compositions—the *Poem,* for orchestra, and the more mature *A Pagan Poem*—there is that placidity of style, that fine ability to etch tone colors of the greatest delicacy and the most elusive suggestiveness, that other-worldliness of beauty which is half sensual and half ethereal, which bring the great works of his later period to such high levels of artistic greatness. In these early works—as we listen to them today—the hand that shaped this music is plainly the hand of Loeffler, even though we may realize that it has not as yet learned the cunning and subtlety which come only with long experience.

Loeffler was essentially the disciple of Impressionism—one of the few distinguished devotees in America of the Debussy period. The expression of beauty in a fluid outflow was the high ideal to which he clung tenaciously throughout his entire life; and he sought to express this beauty with a sensitive delicacy of sounds and colors and sensations. But it would be a fatal mistake to consider Loeffler merely as an imitator of the composer of *Pelléas*. As a matter of fact, Loeffler continued where Debussy left off, and brought the art of musical Impressionism to its inevitable—perhaps final—destination. Loeffler's music, fragile though it is, is not merely perfume in sound; it is not merely a sensuous experience of a very emotional poet.

Exquisitely refined and rarefied though it is, this music has a very definite muscle and sinew, a perceptible spine, a solidity and depth. The beauty of the *Hora Mystica,* the unforgettable poignancy of the *Evocation,* the nebulous mystery and serenity of *Canticum Fratris Solis,* for example, can never become cloying in the same fashion that so much of Debussy's music does after frequent hearings. It is never over-sensualized. Always is a perfect balance maintained, always a fine play of contrast and shadow. Thus, though the music might never have existed had Claude Debussy never composed his series of immortal tone-pictures, it very definitely possesses a quality uniquely its own, in which the personality of the composer is clearly recognizable.

A born instinct for orchestration, a feeling for form and design which seem to have been intuitive with him from his earliest years as a composer, and a technical grasp which is consummate have always made it possible for Loeffler to achieve the most felicitous mould in which to couch his feelings. Each of his later works has a perfection of style and form that make them a perpetual joy to listen to and study. His music is very much like a precious gem that has found a setting of equal perfection. In Loeffler's music content and form borrow qualities from each other in an inextricable wedlock of beauty.

Mr. Lawrence Gilman once wrote of Loeffler's *Evocation* that this "music, radiant, serene, Hellenic, spoke with irresistible effect the thought of a mind which has never forgotten that the ultimate ritual of the spirit is the worship of that loveliness which is outside of time." I know of no more fitting epitaph to carve upon the tombstone of America's foremost composer.

BÉLA BARTÓK

IX

BÉLA BARTÓK

1.

WHEN Béla Bartók was twenty-four years old (his formal music study had by this time come to a close) he spent a few days at the country home of a friend in the interior of Hungary. While there, he accidentally overheard one of the servants singing to himself a tune so exotic in character and content that he questioned its source. The servant explained that he had acquired the melody from his mother who, in turn, had heard it as a child-in-arms from her parents. Upon further questioning, the servant disclosed the fact that there existed a prolific number of similar melodies—all Magyar in origin—which were sung in the smaller towns of Hungary, bequeathed as a heritage from one generation to the next.

This was Bartók's first realization that there existed a storehouse of Hungarian folk-music far different from the weeping sentimentality and meretricious decorations of those melodies publicized by Brahms and Liszt as authentic Hungarian folk-music—and a folk-music which was a much truer expression of the Hungarian people. Those sentimental songs that had been recorded by Brahms in his dances and Liszt in his rhapsodies—and which were identified by the rest of the world as indigenously Hungarian —were not Hungarian in origin, as Bartók knew well. They had been imported into Hungary by itinerant gypsy caravans who, in turn, had created this music from an indiscriminate *mélange* of influences acquired from the many countries they visited. As Bartók studied the songs hummed to him by the servant, he realized that it was here—and not in mawkish gypsy airs—that rested the musical tradition of his country.

His curiosity aroused in this little-known music of his own country, Bartók decided to travel extensively throughout the land to collect folk-song data. He visited the more remote corners of Hungary, small hill towns and secluded villages nestling in the valley. There he lived with the peasants, sometimes worked with them in the fields, frequently drank liquor with them—and, at all times, made copious notes about the songs he heard them sing.

During this trip, he stumbled across a fellow-musician, Zoltan Kodály. Kodály, who was later to occupy a position next to Bartók as an outstanding Hungarian composer,[1] was a member of the faculty of the Royal Hungarian Academy where Bartók was soon to teach the piano. They were not a little surprised to meet each other in so far-flung a district of Hungary. Their surprise, however, expanded to amazement when they learned that they were on a similar mission: for Kodály, too, had learned of the existence of a native Hungarian folk-music and was in search of it.

Bartók and Kodály decided to join forces. Thus, together, they roamed over prairies, hills and in villages, copying on paper the songs they heard peasants sing.

For the next ten years, Bartók—frequently aided by his friend, Zoltan Kodály—consecrated himself to the herculean task of unearthing Hungarian folk-music from its neglect and obscurity and bringing it to the notice of the music-world. During the next decade, Bartók wandered from the Carpathian mountains to the Adriatic, from western Slovakia to the Black Sea—always equipped with notebook and a recording apparatus—making profuse notes. In that time, he collected more than 5,000 folk-melodies which had been the property of the Hungarian peasant for generations but which, strange to say, were almost completely unknown

[1] Some of Kodály's music has become world-famous, particularly *Háry János, Psalmus Hungaricus* and *Dances of Marosszek*.

in the large cities of Hungary, not to mention the rest of the world. Several thousand of these folk-melodies were published, under the editorship of both Bartók and Kodály.

These excavations had an effect analogous to Pedrell's explorations in Spanish folk-music; they revealed to the world that Hungarian folk-music possessed an individuality which the gypsy song, known to the rest of the world, could not even faintly suggest. Hungarians are not, by temperament, a mawkishly sentimental race. They are made of sterner stuff—made hard and callous by suffering and labor. To a great extent they are a reticent folk.

True Hungarian folk-music is not so tinklingly melodious, so emotionally uninhibited, so pleasingly seductive to the ear as gypsy airs. It is much severer in structure, with hard surfaces of sound. Authentic Hungarian folk-songs are constructed from modal scales (and, like all modal music, have a subtle and elusive charm which is not always perceptible on first hearing), and highly intricate rhythmic patterns. They are frequently drenched with sombre grays, far different from the vivid purples of gypsy music.

As with Manuel de Falla of Spain, and Ralph Vaughan-Williams of England, Béla Bartók's devoted researches in folk-music influenced his musical writing. But this influence has been much more elusive and less strongly accentuated in Bartók's works than in those of the other two composers. At first hearing, Bartók's principal works do not flaunt their national influence. His music is strongly modern, sometimes atonal in harmony, avoiding the more obvious patterns of melody and employing a highly individual harmonic language. With the exception of his children's pieces— *Pro Deň,* for example, or *A Gyermekeknek*—Bartók never uses folk-songs directly. Even the more recognizable technical qualities of the Hungarian folk-song are not discernible in his music at first glance.

It is only after an intimate familiarity with Bartók's music that its affinity with Hungarian folk-music becomes appar-

ent.   Like the folk-song, his melodies are often derived
from the modal scales. Like the folk-song, Bartók's rhythms
are complex, with edges as pointed as the blade of a saw.
Like the folk-song, there is often a shadow of sombre
despair hovering over his music. Bartók is too much the
individualist ever to be an imitator. But he has permitted
the spirit of the Hungarian folk-song to touch his own music
ever so lightly and to spread over it a spell, as though it
were a faint perfume.

2.

Béla Bartók was born in Nagyszentmiklos, Hungary
(now Jugoslavia), on March 25, 1881. His father, the
director of an agricultural school, died when Béla was eight
years old. The burden of supporting the family fell upon
the shoulders of the mother who, assuming the profession
of school-teaching, was forced to travel frequently 'from one
section of Hungary to another, teaching in its various
schools. Thus, as a mere child, Bartók was given an
intimate glimpse at different corners of Hungary, and permitted to acquire a knowledge of the many-patterned
customs of his country people.

Despite this nomadic life, the education of young Béla
was not neglected. Revealing unusual musical aptitude, he
was launched in the study of the piano at the age of six. At
nine he was already creative, producing a group of small
pieces for the piano. One year later, he made his first
public appearance as pianist.

When Béla reached his twelfth year, his mother acquired
a post in Pressburg, at the time the most advanced musical
city in Hungary. There, she placed the boy under competent musical teachers: László Erkel was engaged to teach
him the piano, and Ernst von Dohnanyi [2]—four years Bar-

---

[2] Later world-famous as concert-pianist, conductor and composer.

tók's senior—became his friend and adviser. Under their guidance, Bartók's musical progress was fleet.

In 1899, upon the advice of Dohnanyi, Bartók entered the Royal Hungarian Academy of Music where he was enrolled as a piano student of Stephan Thoman and as a pupil of composition of Koessler. He remained in the academy for four years, earning recognition as one of the most brilliant pupils both in piano and composition that the Conservatory produced.

Following his graduation from the Academy, Bartók knew desperate poverty. He did some concert work as pianist, made some musical arrangements and engaged in some teaching. But his earnings from all three endeavors were so meagre that they were hardly sufficient to supply him with threadbare necessities. Poverty and suffering did not smother his contagious enthusiasm and his enormous zest. Even though hunger and cold were frequent companions, he absorbed himself with intensive music study and composition. A scholarship, won in 1905, helped him for a time. But not until 1907, when Bartók was engaged as teacher of the piano at the Royal Academy was he guaranteed comfort and recess from physical duress.

During these student days, Bartók was subjected to several important musical influences. The first of these was Brahms, whose romanticism Bartók frequently attempted to ape in his first works. Then he heard a performance of Richard Strauss' *Thus Spake Zarathustra,* which profoundly affected him. He felt now that in Strauss' pungent and dramatic writing, musical expression had achieved its apotheosis. For several years, Strauss was his idol; many of Strauss' most personal mannerisms—principally his predilection for chromatic writing—asserted themselves in Bartók's music. Finally, Bartók found Liszt: Liszt who at first had repelled him because of his pseudo-Hungarian effects but whose great significance he now realized.

Bartók's earliest works—such as the rhapsody for piano and orchestra, and the first suite for orchestra, both composed during his student days—were, therefore, obviously derivative. In fumbling for his own vocabulary, Bartók freely borrowed that of those composers who had impressed him most. But—for all its imitative strains—there was already perceptible the shadow of Bartók's later personality, particularly in his disposition for riotous rhythms, and in his almost barbaric savagery of speech which, every once in a while, forced an emergence from the prison bars of his classical form.

3.

It was in 1905 that Bartók was first attracted to Hungarian folk-music. Between 1905 and 1914 he divided his time among his intensive travels throughout Hungary in search of native musical material, his teaching assignments at the Royal Academy (after 1907) and, most important of all, his creative work.

Bartók's struggle for recognition as a composer has been a bitter one; and not even today can we say that he has achieved full victory. His purely personal style has brought him life-long antagonism and misunderstanding. His music, compounded of asperity and desiccated emotions, was bitterly condemned. Such an early work as *Kossuth,* a symphonic-poem, composed in 1903, found an enthusiastic audience because, strongly imitative of Richard Strauss and drenched with nationalistic ardor, it was easily comprehensible to the musical intelligence of early twentieth century Hungary. But as Bartók's personality evolved and became integrated, and as he achieved his own individual speech, the music-public turned sharply from him and was not diffident in openly showing its hostility. In the *Two Portraits* for orchestra and the *Bagatelles* for piano, Bartók emerged with his peculiar counterpoint, with a melody that was

BÉLA BARTÓK

severely outlined, and with emancipated rhythms. With the
First String Quartet he definitely blazed his own trail. After
that, each performance of a new work by Bartók was
received in Hungary with antagonism and intolerance which
frequently crushed its composer's spirit and broke his heart.

During the War, Bartók—who had resigned from his
pedagogical position in 1912—lived in complete seclusion,
occupying himself with his creative activity. His industry
remained unaffected by the trying conditions brought on by
the War and the physical suffering to which his country was
subjected. It was at this time that he received one of the
few successful ovations that had been accorded to him
during his career. In 1917, a ballet, *The Woodcut Prince,*
was performed in Budapest to what was probably the first
welcome sound of applause and cheering that Bartók had
heard as a composer in more than a decade.

Subsequently, Bartók's fame grew slowly but inevitably.
An opera, *Bluebeard's Castle,* was found in 1918 to be a
remarkable fusion of drama in music; its composer, therefore, received a handsome measure of praise from the
critics. So has the pantomime, *The Wonderful Mandarin,*
because of the dramatically conceived musical score, in spite
of the hostility of certain audiences. Finally, three additional string-quartets—in which Bartók has achieved his
most compressed and incisive writing—a *Dance Suite,* for
orchestra, composed in 1923 in honor of the fiftieth anniversary of the union of Buda and Pesth, a *Rhapsody,* for
violin and orchestra, dedicated to Joseph Szigeti (which has
likewise been arranged by the composer for violoncello and
orchestra, in honor of Pablo Casals) and a concerto for
piano and orchestra (one of the most pulsating and dynamic
pieces of music of our time) earned for Bartók the designation of Hungary's greatest living composer.

Yet, even though his imperial position over Hungarian
composers is generally conceded, it would be absurdly
extravagant to say that Bartók has ever achieved that

world-wide fame that he deserves. The reception his music has received since the War is impressive only in contrast to the hostility that preceded it. For one of the most uniquely endowed and imaginative composers of today, and one of the most alive and vital forces in twentieth century music, Bartók has never been accorded a fame commensurate to his genius and significance.

Critics and musicians have, it is true, recognized Bartók as one of the undisputed glories of contemporary music. But the public remains surprisingly indifferent to his art. In his concert-tours (in 1922, Bartók visited England, and in 1927-1928 he traveled extensively throughout America) he has been received respectfully enough. But composers who are undoubtedly his inferiors have been accorded by audiences an enthusiasm more feverish and a welcome more spontaneously boisterous than those which greeted Bartók. Moreover—and what is much more important—performances of Bartók's works are startlingly few and far between not only in America but in European countries outside of Hungary as well.

Béla Bartók lives in a residential section of Budapest. Under his window is the incessant turmoil of the city; the sound of moving tramways, heavy automobile traffic and hurrying crowds frequently inject a jarring note to the atmosphere of serenity with which his home is permeated. His apartment reflects his own great national pride. It is so cluttered with objects of Hungarian interest—strips of peasant embroidery, bodices, national costumes, native pottery and furniture—that it might very aptly serve as something of a national museum.

Despite the fact that he has made his home in a central part of the city, Béla Bartók is almost a recluse in his love of solitude. His many years of life in Hungarian villages and plains have probably made him unsuited for the social salon. Public receptions or social functions he avoids like the plague; in a company of admirers, he moves uneasily.

Essentially, he is a man of great humility and unostentation, of a simplicity that is devoid of any pretense or affectation, of a softness and gentleness that are almost kittenish. After speaking to him, it becomes impossible to conceive of his using a vitriolic phrase or a harsh sentence; equally, it is impossible to conceive of him harboring either envy or malice. Thus, cynicism or irony play no part in his speech; rather a warmth of feeling and excessive generosity.

He is small and slight, built lithely, his movements supple and graceful. At first glance he appears to be a man who has grown prematurely old. Some of his features are extraordinarily youthful. On the other hand, his hair is gray, and his face is deeply lined. His life has not been easy, and the futility, despair, disillusionment and hardship which he confronted seem to speak eloquently from his ineffably sad eyes. Likewise, his spirits are touched with a bitterness of which he cannot rid himself successfully.

ERNEST BLOCH

ERNEST BLOCH

X

ERNEST BLOCH

1.

SOMETHING of the ecstasy of the Hebraic prophet has moulded the artistic career of Ernest Bloch. No Biblical Jeremiah consecrated himself to the pronouncement of prophetic truths with more passionate idealism and self-abnegation than Ernest Bloch to the composition of music. To Bloch, the creation of music in general—and Hebrew music in particular—has been a sacrosanct mission. It has been recorded that as a child Bloch wrote upon a slip of paper a vow that he would devote his life to music. This slip of paper he placed under a mound of rocks over which he burned a ritual fire. Bloch's career, thus launched, assumed in his eyes the aspect of religious consecration. And a consecration it has remained to the present day.

Few composers of any day have been so unswervingly true to themselves and to the artistic principles they adopted in early manhood than Bloch. Like the ancient Hebraic prophet, he has always been sublimely sure of himself, always intoxicated with the self-assurance that the truth rested with him, fully convinced of the significance of his artistic mission. To Bloch, as to the Biblical prophet, love for and faith in humanity were essential parts of his *Weltanschauung*. Bloch's music, therefore, has been a conscious attempt to uplift man, to reveal to him new conceptions of beauty and truth.

The Hebrew prophet comes to mind in any personal contact with Bloch. Even now that he has removed that Messianic black beard that for several years had given him a patriarchal appearance, he seems to have stepped out of

173

the pages of the Old Testament. His face, in its strength and serenity (strength in the broad cheek bones and prominent chin; serenity in the spiritual quality of his intensely expressive eyes) might well have been that of a prophet of old. There is in Bloch a savage sincerity, an integrity that cannot recognize concessions, an immaculate honesty, and an idealism that reach the stars, qualities which might have been found in an Isaiah or Jeremiah. This savage sincerity has always made him speak his mind openly on every question, and has consequently made him many enemies. Bloch recognizes neither tact nor expediency; only honesty and frankness. Therefore, he is almost brutally critical of shams and postures in music. He has again and again denounced composers who, as a pose, ruthlessly break laws and shatter tradition. Bloch has a piquant sense of humor, but the humor is essentially Hebraic in its satiric acidity. When, therefore, he is denunciatory in his criticism, his tongue can annihilate an opponent with one devastating remark.

Another quality of the Biblical prophet is a dominant trait of Bloch's character—his deep-rooted mysticism. Bloch is not a religious man in the formal and accepted sense of the term; nor is he so racially chauvinistic as his Hebraic music might suggest. His religion is, rather, a world religion, and his God a spiritual Being for all men. It is the spiritual and poetical qualities of religion that appeal so sensitively to him.

It is these personal qualities of the Biblical prophet in Bloch that have compelled him, in several decades of artistic self-expression, to cling tenaciously to those ideals and standards he adopted in his youth. And it is these qualities that bring to all of his music a nobility of conception, a profundity of expression, almost an other-worldliness which are Bloch's most distinguishing traits as a composer.

2.

Ernest Bloch, the son of a Swiss clock merchant, was born in Geneva on July 24, 1880. From his parents he inherited neither his religious consciousness nor his musical talent. His father and mother were bourgeois shopkeepers in whose lives both religion and music played a negligible part.

His parents aspired to make of their son a self-respecting business man. The resolve to become a musician, however, was so strongly entrenched in Ernest Bloch even in childhood that he was soon able to override successfully the opposition of his parents. In his fourteenth year, therefore, Bloch began the study of composition under Jacques Dalcroze and the violin under L. Rey in Geneva. The first taste of music so intoxicated him that he turned instinctively to musical creation, producing within two years an *Oriental Symphony* and an *Andante* for string-quartet.

In his seventeenth year, Bloch left Geneva for Brussels for a more intensive musical training. He studied the violin with Eugene Ysaye and composition with F. Rasse. After a few years of such study, Bloch went to Germany where, as he himself has recorded, "my master was Ivan Knorr, at Frankfort-on-the-Main. He was a profoundly great pedagogue. He taught me to teach myself. For it is only what you unturn through your own efforts, what you discover after grim and long pondering that really benefits you. I had studied harmony and mastered it to the satisfaction of my teachers before going to Frankfort. However, I insisted on Knorr's going over the ground with me, and within a few months I conquered it for myself. . . . After that I went to Munich and studied with Thuille. I composed my first symphony in Munich and then went to Paris."

The *First Symphony*—it was in the key of C-sharp minor —was completed in 1902. Bloch's inability to gain a hearing for the work either in Paris or Germany—coupled with

the news of the growing financial duress of his family—
brought him back to Geneva in 1904 where he became book-
keeper, salesman and traveling merchant for his father's
shop. "I will write music as I feel I must," he said at
the time, "and if it is good it will be heard; otherwise it
will not. Meanwhile I will be a merchant." But business
—though it required prodigious energy and time—did not
absorb all of Bloch's interests. Several hours each week he
lectured at the University of Geneva on metaphysics. In
1909, he became a conductor of subscription concerts in
Lausanne and Neuchâtel. And, during the night (Bloch
never required more than a few hours of sleep) he belonged
to his first and greatest love—composition.

During these hours of night, Bloch composed a series of
works which brought his musical idiom to high development: *Poèmes d'automne,* for voice and orchestra, *Hiver-
Printemps,* two symphonic sketches, and made elaborate
plans and outlines for an opera, *Macbeth,* on a libretto by
Edmond Fleg. In these early works, the style which is
today recognizable as Bloch's is already manifest in embryo.
That barbaric ferocity and passion, savage in their intensity,
fill this early music with an enormous energy and vitality;
the fully developed melodic lines and the free use of the
rhythmic elements are already clearly apparent. Moreover, certain Hebraic qualities—use of Oriental intervals
and vivid harmonic colors—rear their heads. And already
one can discern in this music the high idealism and nobility
of a great heart which speak so unmistakably in Bloch's
later works.

In 1909, Bloch completed his opera *Macbeth* which, with
many misgivings—almost on a gamble—he despatched to the
management of the Paris Opéra Comique. To his bewilderment the opera was accepted for performance. On November 30, 1910, it was given its première, arousing considerable discussion and conflicting opinions. Certain critics, like
Arthur Pougin, denounced it vigorously. Others, however,

found in it a new and important voice. Pierre Lalo spoke
of the opera as "one of the most profoundly interesting
works which has been given on the operatic stage in these
last years; a work in which the singularly powerful nature
of a dramatic composer reveals itself—a work to which
the extraordinarily direct expression of feelings and of
moods, the vibrant and quivering musical speech, the
mysterious intensity of color, the atmosphere of darkness
and terror, in which the characters are enveloped, give a
gripping force."

One of the critics in Paris who believed in Bloch was
Romain Rolland, celebrated author of *Jean Christophe*.
This was the result of perusing the manuscript score of the
C-sharp minor Symphony. To express his great faith in
Bloch's genius in no uncertain vocabulary, Rolland made the
trip from Paris to Geneva to meet and talk to the young
composer. Rolland has described the astonishment at finding Bloch sitting behind a high desk, in the store of his
father, working patiently over the business accounts. Bitterly, Rolland expressed his indignation to Bloch that a
composer of such promise should devote his time to business. It may have been that Rolland's words fell upon
receptive ears, or else that the praise which *Macbeth* encouraged from certain quarters gave Bloch the assurance he
needed. At any rate Bloch was now convinced that he was
through with business. Henceforth, he was to devote himself completely to music.

Long after this—in 1915—there took place a complete
performance of Bloch's *Symphony in C-sharp minor*—in
Geneva under the baton of the composer, with Romain
Rolland—now watching keenly the work of his discovery—
in the audience. The letter that Rolland wrote to Bloch
after the performance must have caused the heart of the
neglected composer to throb with ecstasy. "Your symphony is one of the most important works of the modern
school. I don't know any work in which a richer, more

vigorous, more passionate temperament makes itself felt. It is wonderful to think that it is an early work! If I had known of you at the time, I should have said to you: Do not trouble about criticism or praise, or opinions from others. Don't let yourself be turned aside or led astray from yourself by anything whatsoever, either influence, advice, doubts or anything else. Continue expressing yourself in the same way, freely and fully; I will answer for your becoming one of the masters of our time. From the very first bars to the end of the music one feels at home in it. *It has a life of its own;* it is not a composition coming from the brain before it was felt!"

In 1911, Bloch's position as a conductor came to an end when, after a series of cabals, one of his pupils succeeded in superseding him. Much to Bloch's credit, he expressed neither bitterness nor rage in relinquishing the baton. Instead, he applied himself more conscientiously to his creative work. In 1915, he coupled his creative work with a series of lectures on composition and æsthetics at the Geneva Conservatory of Music.

It was at this time that Bloch's style underwent a definite evolution, that he became imbued with the ideal to create a Hebrew music that would give expression to his race. Truth to tell, the development of Bloch's music from the first period of the *Symphony in C-sharp minor* to the Hebraic period was not quite so sudden as so many critics have been tempted to suspect. The careful ear can discern many qualities in Bloch's early works that are Hebraic. One need but note the elegiac sadness in portions of this symphony and the almost Chassidic mysticism of the fugue of the last movement, the religious fervor of the *Poèmes d'automne,* the Oriental flavor of Bloch's harmonizations and the Semitic intervals in his melodic line to realize that Bloch evidently felt the Hebrew spirit keenly from the very first and attempted to transfer it into his music. However, it was not until a little more than ten years after the *Sym-*

phony in C-sharp minor that Bloch openly acknowledged himself to be a Jewish composer. "Racial consciousness is absolutely necessary in music even though nationalism is not," he announced as his æsthetic creed. "I am a Jew. I aspire to write Jewish music not for the sake of self-advertisement, but because it is the only way in which I can produce music of vitality—if I can do such a thing at all." At another time, in explaining his Jewish music, Bloch wrote: "It is not my purpose or my desire to attempt a 'reconstruction' of Jewish music, or to base my work on melodies more or less authentic. I am not an archæologist. I hold that it is of first importance to write good, genuine music—*my own music*. It is the Jewish soul that interests me, the complex, glowing, agitated soul that I feel vibrating throughout the Bible . . . the freshness and the naïvete of the Patriarchs, the violence of the prophetic Books; the Jew's savage love of justice; the despair of the Ecclesiastes; the sorrow and the immensity of the Book of Job; the sensuality of the Song of Songs. All this is in us, all this is in me, and it is the better part of me. It is all this that I endeavor to hear in myself, and to translate in my music; the sacred emotion of the race that slumbers far down in our soul."

With such works as the *Two Psalms* (137 and 114), for soprano and orchestra, *Trois Poèmes Juifs,* for orchestra (composed in the memory of his father) and *Psalm 22,* for baritone and orchestra, Bloch definitely rediscovered his race and associated himself with it. By the close of the year of 1916, Bloch was to travel even deeper into the Hebraic world he had recently begun to explore with the completion of such works as *Schelomo,* for violoncello and orchestra, a portrait in tone of a great Biblical Jew, and *Israel Symphony,* a proud and exultant affirmation of his race.

It is this Hebrew period that has produced many of Bloch's most famous works. While I, personally, do not

accept all of these works with the unqualified enthusiasm
that some other critics do, there can be no denying that, at
its best, this music speaks with a sublime vocabulary. Bloch's
music, at its best, has a profound depth, an enormous vision,
an inspiring eloquence and a contagious enthusiasm. Its
tremendous vitality is irresistible; and we seem, in this music,
to catch a new glimpse at the soul of beauty. However, it
is my personal feeling that both the *Israel Symphony* and
Schelomo (always with the exception of sporadic superb
passages) are too self-conscious. Certain elements of
Hebrew music—the Oriental color, the ritual trumpets, the
augmented-second intervals in the melody—have been
superimposed on the music and are not integral and inevitable parts of it. Both of these works fail to convince
as Hebrew documents. They are at their best when the
Hebrew message is less strongly emphasized. It is almost
as though, freed from the constraining necessity of composing music essentially Hebrew in technique, Bloch could
give his inspiration free reign, and it was able to soar and
expand.

3.

Early in 1916, Ernest Bloch came to America as conductor of the Maud Allan troupe that had been booked for
an extensive tour of the country. The sudden bankruptcy
of this venture left Bloch stranded in a foreign country
without friends or resources. For a few months, Bloch
experienced starvation. Then, a few prominent musicians,
discovering his plight, combined their efforts to snatch him
from his undeserved obscurity. There followed a series of
important performances of Bloch's music that definitely
established his reputation and placed him among the most
significant creative figures in America. In December of
1916, the Flonzaley Quartet performed the *String Quartet
in B-minor* with great success. Several months later, Dr.
Karl Muck invited Bloch as a guest conductor of the Boston

Symphony Orchestra to direct his *Trois Poèmes Juifs*. Artur Bodanzky, in New York, devoted an entire program of the Society of Friends of Music to Bloch's works, and one year later Bloch personally directed another program of his music with the Philadelphia Symphony Orchestra. In 1919, the award of the Elizabeth Sprague Coolidge prize of $1,000 for the *Suite for Viola and Orchestra* brought several performances to this work. These performances finally succeeded in bringing Bloch that international fame as a composer that Rolland had prophesied a few years before this.

In 1920, Bloch was appointed director of the Cleveland Institute of Music. Though he was never happy either as an administrator or as a teacher—principally because too frequently his high ideals were in direct conflict with expediency and practicality—he held this post for five years. In this position, he composed several extraordinary works, including the *Baal-Shem Suite,* for violin and piano (1923), the *Quartet Pieces* (1924), the *Concerto Grosso,* for string orchestra and piano (1924-1925) and, what is probably the greatest music of Bloch's career, the *Quintet,* for piano and strings (1924). It is interesting to mention that the *Concerto Grosso* was composed by Bloch partly with an eye to some of his pupils whose compositions were needlessly elaborate, to show what could be done with simpler means.

In 1925, Bloch resigned his directorial post with the Cleveland Institute, having been antagonized by its more political aspects. A pedagogical position brought him at this time to San Francisco. There, in 1927, he composed his symphony *America,* which won the $3,000 award offered by the magazine *Musical America* for an outstanding American musical work for large orchestra. The symphony *America* (submitted, as prescribed by the rules, under a pen-name) was the unanimous selection of the judges, and it was performed simultaneously by the leading symphony orchestras in America, including the New York Philharmonic, and the Boston, Philadelphia and Chicago symphony orchestras. Following *America,* Bloch produced a work as a tribute to his native country, *Helvetia.*

In the works ranging from the *Concerto Grosso* to *Helvetia* Block seemed to have digressed from his Hebraic path. The discerning critic will realize, however, that the digression is not quite so marked as might first be suspected. The *Piano Quintet,* the *Concerto Grosso,* the *America Symphony* and *Helvetia* may not be, in body, Hebrew compositions; but who can doubt that they are the creations of a Jew? It has been well pointed out by Dr. Isaac Goldberg that the Indians of the *America Symphony* dance with Chassidic feet. Bloch may have permanently deserted Hebrew music, but Hebrew music has refused to part with him. As a matter of fact, the *Piano Quintet* is, in my opinion, the most successful of his attempts to give expression to his race. It is a profoundly religious document. Its religion does not consist in artificial exteriors, but rather in the religion of philosophers. Through its pungent harmonies Spinoza trumpets his intellectual love of God; the meditative mysticism of Chassidic folk-lore seems to speak in the cool counterpoint. The religion of the *Quintet* purifies and exalts; it shows us more clearly than any other of Bloch's music the true soul of the Hebrew religion.

In *America* and in *Helvetia,* Bloch pays tribute to his two countries. If both these works are disappointing, it is only because the composer does not seem to feel his country's spirit so intimately as he does that of his race. There are unquestionably moments of power and majesty in *America,* pages of heroic grandeur and strongly felt emotions. But *America* and *Helvetia* lack conviction. In *America* the anthem that Bloch fashioned for the close is not a culminating pæan of praise that one had the right to expect; it is a trite and effete melody such as might have been penned by a schoolboy.

However, with his more recent works—the *Sacred Service*

and *A Voice in the Wilderness,* for violoncello and orchestra
—Bloch has returned to his original path. He has rightly
realized that the Jew in him is too strong to be discarded,
and that, if he is to compose music of ability and strength,
he must write in the Hebrew idiom.

4.

A generous endowment by one of San Francisco's art
patrons enabled Bloch to give up the teaching of music, in
1931, and to devote himself completely to creative work.
He left America, for a far-flung corner of Switzerland—
Ticino, Roveredo, near Italy—to compose a work which he
had been planning for several years. It was to be a work
which, he felt, might very well become his crowning achievement—a musical *Sacred Service* for the Sabbath morning
prayers of the Jewish synagogue. However, in constructing the work, Bloch intended it to become something
infinitely more than a ritual service for his race; he hoped
to create a monumental song of Faith for all humanity.
"Though intensely Jewish in roots"—I am quoting Bloch
himself—"the message seems to me above all a gift of
Israel to the whole mankind. It symbolizes for me, far
more than a Jewish service, but, in its great simplicity and
variety, it embodies a philosophy acceptable to all men."
A singularly descriptive letter from the hand of Bloch's
daughter, Suzanne, describes the conditions under which
Bloch produced his ritual work. "In this beautiful spot of
Switzerland, he found the quiet and peace needed for the
creation of such a work. The village of Roveredo is as
primitive a place as could be imagined. A few stone houses
grouped together, a cobblestone path passing under dim
arches, form the main street. The only other 'musician'
living nearby is the village half-wit who, as twilight falls,
sits in his loggia playing an accordion, making the most
fantastic sounds. . . . On some beautiful evenings in

Roveredo, Bloch liked to walk slowly up the hill to the next town, Bidognio. About eight o'clock it is very still in front of the old church. All the peasants are inside; one hears the priest's voice—then suddenly a Gregorian chant breaks forth in rough, drawling, almost goat-like voices, dragging over each syllable. In this semi-religious and profane atmosphere, with the lake of Lugano at his feet, the mountains rolling to Italy, lying before him, Bloch wrote his latest work."

The *Sacred Service* was composed at a time of great moral crisis, from which it possibly derives its especial vision and significance.

When the *Sacred Service* was completed, Bloch returned to America, after an absence of three years, to direct the first performance of the work at a concert of the Schola Cantorum in New York on April 11, 1934.

The *Sacred Service* is one of Bloch's most deeply felt works, in which "the sacred emotion of the race that slumbers far down in our soul" has been given eloquent expression. It is a work which has tenderness and passion, power and humility. It has visions of unearthly beauty which imposes upon the spirit of the listener an angelic serenity that uplifts and ennobles him.

There are passages in this work which an honest critic cannot accept: passages such as the closing orchestral passage to Part One, and the *Yimloch* chorus which closes the second part—empty bombast and hollow pomp. But acknowledging these defects and lamenting them, the *Sacred Service* is a work of importance. Listen to the awe and grandeur of the *Shema,* followed immediately by the heartbreaking poignancy of the *Veohavto;* listen to the superb majesty of the *Tzur Yisroel;* listen to the terrifying mystery of the *Kodosh*—listen to these passages and you will hear a music springing from inspiration, a music born out of pain and stress and ascending towards a new world.

FREDERICK DELIUS

XI

FREDERICK DELIUS

1.

IN THE winter of 1929, Frederick Delius—then in his sixty-seventh year, totally paralyzed and blind—was brought in his invalid's chair from his home in France to London to witness the outstanding triumph of his artistic career. After more than thirty years of production of fragile masterpieces which are almost without equal in the musical expression of our time, he received for the first time that recognition of his own country that he had so eminently deserved—and that should have been his twenty years before.

From his chair, placed prominently in front of the mezzanine, Delius heard a monumental festival, spanning no less than six concerts, devoted to his principal works. He received, too, the adulatory attention of a music-public whose tribute was intensified by the realization that its gesture of recognition—so long belated—had not come too late. Crowds swarmed the doorway of the concert-hall to await the composer after each performance, and fought for an opportunity to catch a glimpse of him; and, as Delius was carried from the Queen's Hall, with almost regal dignity, he was cheered as though he were some political dignitary.

His friends reported to him his victory on every possible front. Phonograph records of his music outsold in London those of any other modern composer. Over the radio, an evening of his music was broadcast to the four corners of England. The newspapers prominently displayed his photograph and life-story as they might that of a new cinema

star; the critics were effusive in their panegyrics. From the
University of Oxford he received an honorary degree. In
short, a musical prophet was, at last, being appreciated in
his own country.

Thus, magnificently, was the last chapter written to the
life-story of a neglected composer who had never received
the attention that his music warranted. It was written none
too soon. Five years later, Delius was dead; but he died
knowing that his music had finally won its place in the world
of modern art.

2.

Frederick Delius was born in Bradford, England, on
January 29, 1862,[1] into a large family that included ten
girls and two boys. His father, a prosperous wool merchant, raised his children with an autocratic hand. From
earliest childhood Frederick was in terror of him.

Delius was, as his sister recently disclosed in a remarkably informative biography,[2] a healthy, normal, athletic boy,
his intellectual development sufficiently normal to permit
him to devour greedily the English equivalent of "dime
novels." Adventure stories fed his imagination until he
began to identify himself with the picaresque characters of
the novels. At one time he ran away from home "to seek
his fortune," and was discovered, fifteen miles away, tired,
dusty and hungry. Upon another occasion, he was inspired
with the ideal of becoming a circus performer; he rehearsed
equestrian feats upon his horse until he was thrown from
the saddle and so seriously hurt that for an extended period
he was confined to bed.

In one respect, he was far different from his young
friends—in his unusual love and adaptability for music. As

---

[1] Delius himself believed that he was born in 1863, which is the year that
is given in all existing reference books. Shortly after Delius' death it was
discovered that not 1863 but 1862 was the date of his birth.

[2] *Delius: Memoires of My Brother,* by Clare Delius.

a mere child, he played the piano by ear, frequently delight-
ing his family circle with his imaginative improvisations.
He was taught the violin on which his progress aroused the
speechless admiration of his teachers. Delius, however,
was not permitted to take the study of music too seriously.
His father had every expectation of making him a business
man, perhaps a junior partner in his rapidly expanding wool
establishment.

After completing some elementary schooling, Delius was
sent to Germany in his nineteenth year to study the wool
business more intensively as a preparation for entering the
paternal firm. There he heard performances of Wagner's
Die Meistersinger and Karl Goldmark's *Queen of Sheba*
which stirred him so tempestuously that he was for the first
time fired with the ambition of becoming a composer. Business he hated with an instinctive detestation, so that before
long he began, as an escape from wool, to harbor dreams of
a musical career more and more persistently. Soon—somewhat timidly—he wrote to his father asking permission to
give up business for music. Then, in a stormy session, he
was reminded that he was not to question the career that
had been chosen for him. Always terrified by the thunder
of his father's anger, Delius docilely acquiesced to his
father's wish. In 1882, he was sent to Manchester where
his uncle had a large business.

Two years of the wool business convinced Delius emphatically that this was not the career for him. Moreover,
his early passion for adventure—which had by no means
deserted him—was making him squirm with restlessness.
He was eager to try unfamiliar paths in brave, new worlds,
not to remain a prisoner in a Manchester office. One day,
therefore, he definitely announced to his somewhat bewildered father that, if he must become a business man, he
wished to abandon wool and to turn his hand to planting
oranges in Florida. Why Florida, and why the planting of
oranges? Delius had always been attracted to the glamour

of America since his boyhood days; the instinctive need to escape from people and to find himself through solitude convinced him that he would be happiest in the warm and languorous climate of a small and distant Florida town. He had also read that Florida was a state devoted to orange plantations. He decided, therefore, that he would work at the soil.

In March of 1884, Delius left for Florida to superintend the orange plantation, Solano, which his father had purchased for him. Solano was a distant point on the St. John's River, a three days' trip from the nearest large city—Jacksonville. In its primitive desolation it seemed an eternity away. Delius was the only white person there. He was as far removed from the European civilization of the late nineteenth century as though he had penetrated the heart of Africa. He was surrounded by bronze skins, Negro spirituals, the plangent whine of the banjo, and the almost sensual languor of Negro life. And he succumbed to their spell. The orange plantation, as a business, soon wearied him, and he left its management to an overseer. Instead he spent his days in reading, and in quiet contemplation. He would spend his time in a canoe on the St. John's River, accompanied by Negro friends who played and sang their folk-music. In the evenings—the mellowness of which was as soothing as ointment—he would walk in the woods, permitting the peace and serenity of his world, and the benediction of a star sprinkled sky, to cast their magic over him. Eventually, this life, to be fully complete, required an avenue of artistic expression. Fortunately, he had brought with him his violin, and upon this he worked assiduously.

Progress in the study of the violin aroused Delius' dormant musical appetite. He decided, soon, to make the three days' journey to Jacksonville for the purpose of buying a piano and arranging for its shipment to Solano. While he was trying out various instruments in the music-house, a stranger approached him—attracted to the imaginative

chords and the unusual melodic passages that Delius evoked
from the various pianos in his aimless improvisations. This
stranger was Thomas F. Ward, organist in Jacksonville.
That moment marked the beginning of a devoted friendship, the influence of which upon Delius' musical development was profound. Each became attracted to the other's
musical sensitivity. Delius prevailed upon Ward to return
to Solano with him. The idea of a vacation appealed
strongly to Ward; so did Solano. For six months Ward
remained Delius' guest, paying for his board by teaching
the avid young musician lessons in harmony and counterpoint. These lessons brought Delius straight into the arms
of creation. At this time he conceived his first ambitious
work, his musical impressions of America entitled *Appala-
chia,* for chorus and orchestra.

After six months, Delius became convinced that his future
rested with music, and with music alone. He deluged his
father with letters pleading for permission to pursue music
study intensively, but the old man turned a deaf ear.
Finally, Delius decided to abandon his plantation and to
make his own way with music. He came to Jacksonville
where he sang in the choir of a Jewish synagogue. Then,
equipped with glowing letters of introduction from the
Chief Rabbi of Jacksonville, he went to Danville, Virginia
—only one dollar left in his pocket—and eventually became
a music teacher at the Old Roanoke Female School. Eight
months later, he was a professional organist in New York.
About this time his father suddenly relented; within a few
months he was completing his musical studies in Leipzig, on
an allowance. This had for some time been a cherished
dream. He was enrolled in the Conservatory as a pupil of
Sitt, Jadassohn and Reinecke.

In the summer of 1887, Delius took a walking trip
through Norway, where he made friendships leading eventually to a meeting with the famous Scandinavian composer,
Edvard Grieg, when the latter came for a visit to Leipzig

the following winter. Grieg was convinced of Delius' gifts
—particularly after an impromptu performance in Leipzig
of an early Delius composition, *Florida*. When, therefore,
Grieg came to England that same year, he contacted Delius'
father and urged him not to hinder any longer an artistic
career that was so rich with promise. Grieg's reputation
won the day. Although Father Delius provided only a
scanty allowance for his son, he promised faithfully that he
would henceforth raise no further obstacles in his son's
artistic path.

From Leipzig, Delius went to Paris where a kindly uncle,
sympathetic to his aspirations, relieved him of all monetary
problems by giving him a generous income. The years that
followed were devoted not only to the study of music but
more especially to the gathering of artistic impressions and
to assimilating them. He was introduced to such important
artistic figures as Gaugin, the painter, and Strindberg, the
dramatist, in whose circle he moved freely. He also devoted himself to some composition. In 1892, his first published work—a *Légende,* for violin and orchestra—was
released in Paris. This was followed by a Fantasy Overture, *Over the Hills and Far Away,* and a *Concerto for
Piano and Orchestra.*

During this period in Paris, Delius first met Jelka Rosen,
a girl of enormous talent and cultural background who was
equally adept in poetry, music and painting. Jelka Rosen
recognized Delius' creative gifts and was magnetically attracted to the appeal of his strong personality. She, therefore, invited him one day to lunch at the home of her
mother, who lived in a suburb of Paris, Grez-sur-Loing.
Before long, Delius became a frequent household guest of
the Rosens.

Delius, at first, was not strongly drawn to Jelka; as a
matter of fact, though he delighted in speaking with her
about art, he did not seem to take much notice of her
feminine charm or personal appeal. And there was good

reason. For, during his American stay, twelve years before this, Delius had formed an extraordinary attachment for a young Negress, whom he was unable to remove from his thoughts. She obsessed his thoughts so completely that he was unable to create a strong bond with any other woman. Finally—with sudden impetuousness—Delius decided that he would sweep discretion to the winds; he arranged for a return voyage to America so that he might claim his beloved Negress as his bride. For this purpose—and for this purpose alone—he crossed the Atlantic a second time, in the summer of 1897. He remained only a brief period. His search completely fruitless, Delius returned to France.[3]

Upon his return to France, Delius went straight to the home of Jelka Rosen in Grez-sur-Loing, and settled himself and his baggage there permanently. Soon afterwards, Jelka and Delius were married. This marriage, which seems to have had so haphazard an origin, proved to be preeminently successful. Jelka was an extraordinary wife, patient, solicitous, encouraging, understanding and unselfishly devoted until the very last day of her husband's life. For his part, Delius worshipped her—and could never speak of her to his friends without revealing his profound love for her and his prodigious admiration for her talents.

Shortly after the marriage, Delius left with his wife for Norway, brought there by a commission to prepare incidental music for a political play by Gunnar Heiberg, *Folkeraadet*. This commission was almost accompanied by a fatal tragedy. In his score, Delius utilized the Norwegian national anthem in a satirical vein, a fact which so infuriated the Norwegians that they denounced Delius' music vituperatively. At one performance, a patriotic spectator

[3] This extraordinary incident in Delius' life—which has been discreetly omitted from all existing biographies and biographical sketches on the composer—was disclosed by a life-long friend of Delius, the eminent American musician Percy Grainger, in a singularly informative series of articles on the composer.

became so enraged that he fired several revolver shots at the composer, which, fortunately, missed their target.

In 1899, Delius' mother-in-law bought him a gift of a secluded country home in Grez-sur-Loing, Delius' retreat for the remainder of his life. Situated as it was in a small French town, a few steps from the village church, and surrounded by spacious and well cultivated grounds which protected him from the outside world, this villa provided Delius with that feeling of solitude and peace which he always sought and needed, and with that spirit of tranquillity in which he could work most fruitfully.

3.

During the next decade and a half, Delius created his series of masterpieces upon which must rest most firmly his significance as a composer. Following the completion of such pioneer attempts as the opera *Koanga*—a work with Florida as its background and Negroes as its principal characters—and the orchestral pieces, *Paris* and *A Life's Dance*, Delius achieved his personal idiom in its purest and most crystallized form. In 1901, he completed the opera *A Village Romeo and Juliet*, based upon a tale of Gottfried Keller. Within the next two years, two significant choral works were added to his productions, *Sea Drift*, inspired by the poem of Walt Whitman, and *A Mass for Life*. There followed a string of immortal poems for orchestra, *Brigg Fair* (1907)—based upon a famous English melody—and *In a Summer Garden* (1908), *Summer Night on the River* (1911-1912), and *On Hearing the First Cuckoo in Spring* (1911-1912), all three musical translations of country scenes at or near Grez-sur-Loing.

This music, at its best, is pictorial painting in tone produced by a poetical temperament—music highly sensitivized, suffused with a tranquillity and repose which seem far removed from our time. Refinement of speech and delicacy

of tone, restraint of emotion and fragility of construction
are their outstanding qualities. It is a baffling task to place
a label on Delius' music. It is too eclectic, moulded by as
many influences as have touched Delius in his wanderings.
His style is sometimes touched with Negro blues, and sometimes affected by Scandinavian austerity. Often German
romanticism and French impressionism moulded his idiom
at one and the same time. These many influences, Delius
has blended into a speech that is so completely his own that
his personality—that of a dreamer, poet and philosopher—
escapes from every page he has written.

There is an elusive quality to Delius' music, an almost
amorphous quality which makes it difficult to grasp on first
hearing. Delius' music appears, at first, like a perfume—a
fleeting sensory experience without body, shape or substance,
leaving behind it a blurred but pleasing memory. It is only
upon intimate acquaintance that the subtle outlines of
Delius' form become clearly perceptible, and that the remarkable construction of his works is disclosed in the fluid
flow of the music. And it is only upon frequent hearing that
the individual beauty of his message begins to exert a necro-
mantic spell over the listener.

It is for this reason that Delius' recognition as a composer came slowly—much more slowly than it has come to
any other outstanding modern composer. When on May
30, 1899, Delius personally arranged an entire concert of his
own works at the St. James' Hall in London, his music had
only a partial success. During the years that followed, performances of Delius' works were sporadic in England, and
were received with hardly more than casual politeness.

Germany was more appreciative of Delius' work, and it
was in Germany—and not in England—that the first performances of Delius' outstanding works took place. *Ap-
palachia* was featured at the Lower Rhine Music Festival in
1905, followed one year later by a performance of *Sea
Drift* at the Tonküntslerfest in Essen. In 1904, Fritz Cas-

sirer conducted the opera *Koanga* at the City Theatre in Elberfeld, with Clarence Whitehill singing the principal rôle. *A Village Romeo and Juliet* was introduced in Berlin in 1907. These performances were greeted courteously enough by the German music public; in some cases with enthusiasm. "I never dreamt that anybody except myself was writing such good music," commented Richard Strauss on first hearing a work by Delius.

A handful of disciples in England—principally among them Sir Thomas Beecham, the conductor, whose herculean efforts on behalf of Delius during more than two decades was most responsible for the composer's eventual recognition—patiently worked for him, spread propaganda on his behalf, performed his music upon every possible occasion and tried to impress its beauty upon the consciousness of an indifferent public. The battle was a long one, but—as his disciples knew—victory was inevitable. With the beginning of 1920—when Delius' opera *A Village Romeo and Juliet* was successfully revived at Covent Garden under Sir Thomas Beecham's guidance—the English music public began to react favorably to Delius' music. During the years that followed, Delius' works were given more and more frequent performances until 1929 when a magnificent six day festival devoted to Delius' outstanding works proclaimed the fact that England had, at last, accepted Frederick Delius as one of its greatest composers of all time.

4.

When the thunder of German cannon shattered the peace and tranquillity of Grez-sur-Loing, Delius—burying his most valuable belongings in his cellar—escaped with his wife from France, taking with them only one possession, a painting of Gaugin. They came to London where, during the years of the War, they were the household guests of influential musicians. During these tempestuous years—

years that crushed Delius' spirit—he wrote, among other works, a *Requiem,* dedicated to all the young artists who had fallen in battle.

When the War ended, Delius returned to his home in Grez-sur-Loing. He was beginning to disclose alarming symptoms, in the form of a stifling weariness of flesh and spirit. That these were harbingers of physical disintegration soon became appallingly evident. In 1922, paralysis set in; by 1925, Delius was blind as well.

What this tragedy meant to Delius only those who knew him well can guess. He who loved travel and freedom of movement was now enslaved to an invalid's chair. He who adored Nature with an almost religious adoration was now blind to its beauty. And he who could live so fully and completely—who could derive such an intense delight from every phase of life, sensual as well as spiritual, physical as well as mental—was now robbed of all the major pleasures of living.

However, it cannot be said that Delius was incapable of heroism. He bore his cross—crushing though it was at times—with a sweetness of spirit that amazed those with whom he came into contact. He could never reconcile himself to his tragic fate. Yet he was rarely heard to complain, and his suffering was always done in silence. At times, he was even capable of a witticism or an ironic thrust. His spirit, at least to the outside world, seemed unruffled and serene. When he was brought downstairs each day at noon, there would be that ineffably poignant smile on his thin lips as he whispered: "Well, here we are."

During the afternoons, he would sit in the garden which he loved so intensely, sometimes in the company of intimate friends. Illness and proximity to death did not succeed in making him any more the Christian than he had been in his younger years. He had frequently felt that culture, art and the mind had been routed by Christianty, and he frequently repeated this belief in his last years. Yet, though his philosophy did not tread in the formal route of religion, there was something indescribably spiritual about him, which moved and inspired those who met him. His fine face—with its majestic Roman profile—was touched with an other-worldliness, accentuated by the pallid, hollow cheeks and the stark, unseeing eyes, denying the life of indulgence that he had led.

In discussions on æsthetics, religion, art or philosophy, he always expressed himself fearlessly and individually. Particularly in music were his opinions unorthodox and courageous. He detested Brahms, disliked Haydn and Beethoven, and was bored by Debussy and Richard Strauss. Mozart, he thought, was one of the most naïve composers of all times. At one time, he told a friend that no one who liked Mozart could possibly be a good musician! He admired Bach, Chopin, Wagner and Grieg—spasmodically. But truth to tell—and Delius sometimes confessed it—he really enjoyed nobody's music but his own. One of the greatest pleasures he acquired during the last years of his life was to listen endlessly to phonograph recordings of his own works.

During these years of sickness, Delius did not abandon composition, even though creative work demanded on his part such gargantuan effort that, after an hour, he became limp with fatigue. Fortunately, in his composition he had the coöperation of a young musician, Eric Fenby, who wished to be of some service to a composer whom he venerated so highly. Guided by his blind master, Fenby brought many of Delius' early works into final shape. And with Fenby, as amanuensis, Delius dictated his last works, note by note. It was thus that Delius' last work, an *Idyll* for soprano, baritone and orchestra, was brought to completion in 1933.

Frederick Delius died at his home in Grez-sur-Loing, June 10, 1934. One of his last requests was that he be buried near a church, somewhere "where the winds are warm and the sun friendly." One year after his death, his wish was fulfilled. His body was transported from France to the warm sun of southern England—Limpsfield. A concert of his works took place at the church under the direction of Sir Thomas Beecham. To the elegiac strains of the *Summer Night on the River* and *On Hearing the First Cuckoo in Spring,* Delius was buried in the church graveyard, under a tree a thousand years old. His grave was lighted by two hurricane lamps, and was lined with laurel leaves.

PAUL HINDEMITH

PAUL HINDEMITH

XII

PAUL HINDEMITH

1.

SHORTLY after the Nazis assumed control of Germany, they promulgated their musical creed to the world as a part of their nationalistic program. "Only that music," it was announced officially, "which expresses the highest ideals of the German people and which is untainted by foreign influences, will be encouraged." Under the flying banner of this æsthetic creed there followed a wholesale *Sauberung*—"cleansing"—of German music. All musicians who—either because they were Jews or else because they were not in full sympathy with the new government—were not full-blooded Germans in the eyes of the Nazis were peremptorily expelled from the country. There followed a veritable hegira of great German musicians out of their fatherland—conductors, composers, virtuosi, musicologists, teachers—perhaps the greatest exile of genius that civilization has seen. Then, having purged Germany of "non-German" musicians, this *Sauberung* next took place with the music itself which was then being performed in Germany. Performances of works by composers of Jewish origin were strictly *verboten*. Finally, it was made clear that music of an experimental nature was not to be encouraged; for radicalism in music—according to Dr. Richard Eichenauer, in one of the unofficial publications of the Nazi party [1]—is essentially the offspring of distorted Jewish minds.

It was during this purification of German music that Paul Hindemith was decreed an unwholesome and undesirable influence in German music. Paul Hindemith was not a Jew,

---

[1] *Musik und Rasse,* by Richard Eichenauer.

and his music—in its essence and spirit—was German. Yet, to the Nazi officials—who by this time had converted their æsthetic precept into a religious dogma—Hindemith was a pernicious influence in German music, an influence of which it was essential to be completely purged.

The "Hindemith-affair"—reverberations of which were heard around the world—was precipitated by the première of an orchestral suite (entitled *Symphony*) drawn from the opera *Mathis der Maler,* performed in Berlin in the spring of 1934 under the direction of Wilhelm Furtwängler. Shortly after this performance, which had been widely publicized in the German press, the Kulturkammer issued the opinion that Hindemith did not measure up to the fastidious requirements of a true Aryan composer and that, therefore, it could not look with favor upon performances of his music.

The case against Paul Hindemith, clearly outlined by the Kulturkammer, was as follows: (1) Though an Aryan himself, Hindemith was tainted because his wife was Jewish; (2) Hindemith was the violist of the Amar Quartet which included two Jewish representatives; (3) Hindemith had at one time made phonograph recordings with such Jewish artists as Emanuel Feuermann, violoncellist, and Simon Goldberg, violinist; (4) the subject of many of Hindemith's works, particularly his operas, was objectionable to Nazi philosophy, examples of pernicious *Kultur Bolshevismus.*

Following closely in the heels of this official verdict, came vicious attacks on Hindemith's music from many quarters in Germany. *Die Musik*—a musical journal which, in previous years—had lauded Hindemith's music with extravagant adjectives—now devastatingly denounced Hindemith's work as "unbearable to the Third Reich." Richard Strauss insisted that a ban be placed on all of Hindemith's music. Many prominent musical organizations in Germany openly boycotted Hindemith. There were, however, some dissenting voices. Professor Gustav Hartmann, head of the Third

Reich Music Association, protected Hindemith's Aryanism and upheld Hindemith as an artist. And Wilhelm Furtwängler, in his now famous defense of Hindemith, answered point by point the damning accusations of the Kulturkammer.[2] Hindemith, ran his argument, could not justifiably be blamed for associations, marital and artistic, which took place long before the Nazi government came into power. As for Hindemith's music, Furtwängler pointed out that it was quite true that the choice of some of his operatic librettos had been unfortunate and that some of his early chamber works were antagonistic to Nazi principles. But these, after all, were the indiscretions of youth, the growing pains of an artist, so to speak. Since his maturity, Hindemith had produced music as high-mindedly German as the classics of Bach, Beethoven and Schubert. "It is a crime," concluded Furtwängler in his passionate plea, "to attempt to defame and drive him from Germany, since none of the younger generation has done more than he for the recognition of German music throughout the world. In an age that offers so few productive musicians, Germany cannot afford to abandon Hindemith."

Furtwängler's arguments fell on deaf ears. For his stubborn stand on this issue, Furtwängler was severely taken to task by the Kulturkammer and, for a time, resigned all his conducting posts. At the same time, the Kulturkammer officially banned all the works of Hindemith from the concert programs throughout Germany.

Even to a world well hardened to the follies of the Nazi régime, the banishment of Hindemith's music came as an electric shock. For years, the name of Paul Hindemith has dominated modern music. His works had been performed in every musical center in the world, and there were few

[2] It is not necessary, here, to explain the motives that impelled Furtwängler to protect Hindemith—motives more selfish than idealistic. These have been clearly and forcefully revealed by Mr. Herbert F. Peyser, foreign musical correspondent of the *New York Times*.

who did not agree that this composer was one of the most genuinely significant forces in modern musical expression. In Germany, only Richard Strauss enjoyed a greater fame and artistic significance than Hindemith. Moreover, it was obvious that Hindemith was a growing figure. With each work he was showing a greater enrichment of style and a fuller development of his personality. He was promising much more for the future than he had already fulfilled in the past. It was, therefore, difficult to believe that the Kulturkammer could be so myopic as deliberately to set its face against a creative spirit that was so vital and dynamic.

2.

Paul Hindemith was born on November 16, 1895, in Hanau, Germany. His love for music became apparent at such a tender age that he began the study of the violin and the viola even before he could read or write. He was, therefore, literally born with "music in his bones," as one critic pointed out; "he sucked it with his mother's milk."

Hindemith's parents objected violently to his musical preoccupations. Rather than renounce music, Paul Hindemith ran away from home. For an extended period, beginning with his eleventh year, he earned his livelihood—which, at best, was threadbare—by playing in cafés, dance bands and movie-houses. However, he did not neglect his own musical development. In the Hoch Conservatory of Frankfurt, where Hindemith was a pupil of Arnold Mendelssohn and Bernhard Sekles, he received a comprehensive training not only on the viola and the violin but also in harmony, counterpoint and composition. He was a brilliant pupil and captured many school prizes. It was while he was still a pupil at the Hoch Conservatory that Hindemith began composition seriously.

In 1915, Hindemith joined the orchestra of the Frankfurt Opera House as concertmaster. He remained there until 1923, rising to the post of conductor. Meanwhile, his importance as a musician had branched out generously into several significant directions. He founded and became the violist of the Amar String Quartet—a powerful force for the dissemination of propaganda for modern chamber music throughout Germany. He had likewise attracted note as a composer. In 1921, 1922 and 1923 his early chamber music was featured prominently at the Donauschingen Festival in Baden-Baden—so prominently that his music was soon the feature attraction of the festival. In 1922, his *Second String Quartet* (Opus 16) was successfully performed in Salzburg, followed one year later by a triumphant performance of the *Clarinet Quintet* (Opus 30).

Hindemith's musical style was not completely personalized until 1925, with a *Kammermusik*—a concerto for piano and twelve solo instruments—introduced at the Festival of Modern Music in Venice. In this work, Hindemith revealed forcefully a tendency which had been asserting itself spasmodically in his previous works—a tendency which extended as far back as Bach. In his previous works—particularly in the sonatas for violoncello and piano, and viola and piano (Opus 26) and in his magnificent song-cycle *Das Marienleben*, based on poems of Rainer Maria Rilke— Hindemith disclosed a strong predilection for polyphonic writing; in the *Marienleben*, frequently, the melodic line of the solo voice moves completely independent of the piano accompaniment. However, counterpoint became fully integrated into Hindemith's style with the *Kammermusik* of 1925. From this time on, Hindemith's music was to be a combination of Bach's polyphonic principles with the harmonic, rhythmic and melodic innovations of twentieth century music. He was, with rare felicitousness, to infuse the modern spirit into old forms. His music, for all its leanings on seventeenth century counterpoint, is crisp in idiom, often stingingly acid, strong-fibered in architecture, muscle and sinew rather than heart and nerves. Yet it derives from Bach its sense of perpetual movement, the lucid clarity of its construction, and the inextricable unity which binds it into a coherent whole. It was this strange marriage of modern musical devices with Bach polyphony that tempted more than one critic to refer to these works of Hindemith as "Brandenburg concertos upside down."

In 1926, Hindemith's name assumed especial significance in the world of modern music when his *meisterwerk,* the opera *Cardillac,* was introduced at the Dresden Opera under the baton of Fritz Busch. This was not Hindemith's first adventure into operatic form. In 1921-2, he had produced a series of three one-act operas whose rawness and immaturity have relegated them to an obscurity they probably deserve. The year after that, a play with incidental music, *Tuttifäntchen,* was given a first-performance in Darmstadt—an opera which proved to be so inept a union of drama and music that, shortly after the first performance, a quip was circulated throughout Germany which quoted the composer as saying: "Never again, as long as I live, will I compose an opera of which I haven't read the text!"

Cardillac was, however, Hindemith's first mature and full-grown composition in operatic form. The opera was based upon E. T. A. Hoffmann's novel, *Das Fraulein von Scuderi.* The scene of *Cardillac* is seventeenth century Paris where Cardillac, a goldsmith of singular ingenuity in fashioning things of a delicate beauty, plies his trade. It is soon discovered that a curse pursues all those who buy Cardillac's works of art. An officer, who is in love with Cardillac's daughter, determines to solve the mystery of the curse and learns that Cardillac is a diabolical murderer who injects into his moulds a lethal poison.

In *Cardillac,* Hindemith did not blaze new trails for the music-drama as Alban Berg did, for example, in *Wozzeck.* *Cardillac* is an opera in traditional form, a combination of arias, duets, recitatives, etc. Its great strength lies in its architectonic construction, the design of which is as taut as a violin string. One critic astutely remarked that in *Cardillac* Hindemith applied the form of some of his concertos: the first act resembles an exposition, the second act a development, and the third act something of a recapitulation. In style, the opera has the compactness of writing, the terseness of expression, the lucidity of structure and the moving beauty of polyphony which mark the best pages of Hindemith's chamber works. There are few moments in modern opera so deeply stirring as the final scene of the opera.

Cardillac definitely placed Hindemith at the head of the younger German composers, "the most full blooded talent," as Hugo Riemann referred to him. His creative significance brought him, in 1927, a professorship in composition at the Berlin Normal School as well as a membership to the German Academy—an amazing distinction for a composer who had only recently seen his thirty-second birthday.

Cardillac was followed by a still more sensational opera which, for a time, enjoyed an overwhelming vogue among German music-lovers. It was *Neues vom Tage,* produced in Berlin in June, 1929, when it received an electric response from the audiences. Built about a libretto which was a swiftly moving and acid comment on modern life, written with the raciness and gusto of a tabloid news-column, *Neues vom Tage* delighted a jazz-mad era. The opera, for all the sparkle and vitality of its score is, however, the most transitory of Hindemith's works; its greatest appeal lay in its timeliness. The story is a complicated one in which an unhappily mated couple—who suddenly find that their domestic quarrels and pursuit of a divorce have brought them into the public eye through the glaring publicity of the tabloids—are the central characters. In the face of such fame and glory, they desire to be reconciled, but their public won't let them. They are finally offered a magnificent theatrical contract. This trite libretto, too absurd and complicated to be effective either as satire or as humor, received a musical treatment that too often lacked dramatic genuineness. Tabloid realism is certainly unsuitable for the composition of inspired music. Hindemith's earnest attempt to treat the plot flippantly in his music was, for the most part, futile. His hand was too heavy for such absurdities; his music too severe.

It was the inartistic theme of *Neues vom Tage,* as well as such works as the *Kammermusik no. 5,* a concerto for viola and orchestra (whose last movement appeared to be a satire on a German military march), and such *Gebrauchsmusik* as his manufactured pieces for pianola, radio, talking screen and even ether-wave instrument, that aroused the displeasure of the Kulturkammer of the Nazi government.

At about this time Hindemith visited Paris and London. On January 22, 1936, he was scheduled to introduce his latest work, *Der Schwanendreher,* a concerto for viola and small orchestra, at a concert at Queen's Hall under the auspices of B.B.C. The death of King George V cancelled the prospective concert. It was decided to substitute on that date a special studio concert in memory of the King, with Hindemith playing some appropriate music on his viola. For three days, Hindemith searched musical literature for some appropriate work for viola and orchestra, but could find nothing. He decided, therefore, (since the concert was only two days off) to compose an original work for the occasion. That morning he set to work upon *Funeral Music,* a composition for viola and string orchestra. Late that afternoon the work was completed. The following day it was rehearsed. And the evening after that it was given its first performance on a nationwide broadcast.

"Such a feat," remarked the English critic, Walter Leigh, "can rarely have been accomplished since Handel's day in the sphere of serious music. Only a composer with a complete mastery of technique and an exceptionally fertile invention could perform it successfully. It is the more remarkable because the work bears no trace of speed, other than its simplicity; and this very simplicity is one of its great merits."

In the spring of 1937, at an invitation of the Elizabeth Sprague Coolidge Foundation, Paul Hindemith came to the United States for the first time. He was forty-one years old now, but—in the almost boyish expression of his round face and the ingenuous quality of his eyes—he appeared much younger, so much younger that it seemed difficult to believe that for more than a decade already he has been a dominant figure in the world of modern music. The regal reception that Hindemith was accorded not only by the outstanding musical organizations of this country but by the music public as well was an eloquent tribute to a great musical figure—and an eloquent answer to the country, across the ocean, that had ejected him because he was an "unwholesome influence."

ARNOLD SCHÖNBERG

XIII

ARNOLD SCHÖNBERG

1.

FOR the past thirty years, Arnold Schönberg has been one of the most original and dynamic forces of modern music. There may be arguments about the inherent greatness of Schönberg's music, but there can never be a doubt about his far-reaching significance, as a personality, for the music of our generation. As a teacher, he has inspired a group of disciples whose work is leaving a definite impress upon contemporary musical expression; a musician who has guided and directly influenced a composer like Alban Berg, creator of *Wozzeck*, cannot be hastily dismissed. As a theorist, Schönberg has produced what is probably the most coherent and penetrating analysis of modern musical technique, the *Harmonielehre*. As a composer, he has created music which may or may not have the deathlessness of great art, but whose individuality and strength, sureness of purpose and fearlessness have unmistakably affected the character and style of modern music.

It was Arnold Schönberg—and not Igor Stravinsky— who was the first in the advance-guard of modern composers. *L'Oiseau de feu* was composed in 1910, *Petrushka* in 1911 and *Le Sacre du Printemps* in 1913. But as early as 1903, Schönberg had sketched and composed the greater part of the *Gurre-Lieder* which contained in embryo some of the revolutionary qualities of his later style. Even in 1913 (when the *Gurre-Lieder* made its belated appearance) this was considered music of an unparalleled nature. "It is more advanced than any contemporary German music," wrote the astute Ernest Newman in that year, "and yet it was written three years before the *Symphonia Domestica* and six years before *Salomé*. It is quite evident that Schönberg's style is quite native to him. It could not have developed out of Strauss, say, for there is simply nothing in Strauss out of which Schönberg's rich harmonic language could have evolved."

Schönberg's original style has inspired many vicious attacks during two decades, and for a generous variety of reasons. But none is more ridiculous than that which accuses Schönberg of insincerity in the creation of his music. There are those who believe that Schönberg expressly adopted a distorted speech for the purpose of attracting comment, publicity and the limelight. In view of the fact that Schönberg has known a lifetime of devastating antagonism that would have smothered a spirit less strong than his (and in view of the fact that to compose music in an orthodox, romantic vein would have been for him the path of least resistance—the shortest route to fame and recognition had he desired them) it is absurd to question Schönberg's integrity. As a matter of fact, only an artist sublimely convinced of the truth of the message and immaculately honest could have followed his undeviating direction in the face of the laughter and ridicule of virtually an entire music-world during a period that spanned more than twenty years.

Schönberg's musical style, consisting of the most startling harmonic combinations (drawn from a unique system which he himself evolved—the "twelve-tone system"), the most unexpected progressions and the most bewildering combination of tonalities, is based upon the almost religious belief, more instinctive than intellectual, that music must consist not only of beautiful sounds but of ugliness as well. Schönberg's world, therefore, is frequently a fantastic one, full of "horrid shapes and shrieks and sights unholy."

Schönberg's music, however, is not the product of theories and rationalizations. It is music which he feels with intensity, and to which he must give expression whether he wishes to or not. As he once said to me with the utmost sincerity and simplicity: "Theories are no good to a composer. If a composer doesn't write from the heart, he simply can't produce good music. I have never had theory in my life in composing my works. I get a musical idea for a composition, I try to develop it into a certain logical and beautiful conception, and I try to clothe it into a type of music that exudes from me naturally and inevitably. I don't consciously create a tonal or polytonal or polyplanal music. I write what I feel in my heart—and what finally comes on paper is what first coursed through every fibre of my body. It is for this reason that I cannot tell anyone what the style of my next composition will be. For its style will be whatever I feel when I develop and elaborate my plans."

Revolution for revolution's sake does not interest Schönberg. More than once has he sharply reprimanded his students for bringing in exercises which he knew were written atonally only to cater to him. Schönberg has frequently urged his pupils to create romantic music in the traditional style, if that is the music that is the natural expression of the student. Good music, Schönberg repeats endlessly to his pupils, comes naturally and spontaneously from the composer. Schönberg has written in an unusual style because that is the music he has felt. When he thinks differently—and there are signs that he is beginning to do so—he will not hesitate to change the character and personality of his music completely.

2.

Arnold Schönberg was born in Vienna on September 13, 1874. His father, a Jewish merchant, died when Arnold was sixteen years old, leaving the boy in a precarious financial condition. By this time, Schönberg had already acquired a good musical training and a strong taste for the art. He had begun the study of the violin in the Real-schule in his eighth year. A few years later, he began to teach himself the elements of violoncello playing. Before long, he attempted composition—creating several trios and a string quartet for a group of schoolmates with whom he was, at the time, playing chamber music regularly.

Shortly after his father's death, Arnold Schönberg showed one of his chamber works to an American who was so impressed by this music that he arranged a meeting be-tween the young composer and a well-known theorist and composer in Vienna, Alexander von Zemlinsky. To Zem-linsky, Schönberg brought an entire bundle of original works. There was latent such an original force in this im-mature outpouring of sound that Zemlinsky decided to take Schönberg under his wing. From that time on, Zemlinsky was not only Schönberg's teacher, but his friend and coun-sellor as well. To assist him financially, Zemlinsky engaged Schönberg as violoncellist in the Polyhymnia orchestra, of which he was at the time the conductor.

From then on, Schönberg moved in a strictly musical environment, discussing music, breathing music and think-ing music. He frequently visited the Café Landtmann, opposite the Burgtheatre, where he discussed with his musical friends the latest æsthetic theories. Wagnerism was the topic-of-the-day in advanced musical circles in Vienna, and from his friends Schönberg acquired a profound veneration for Wagner in general and *Tristan* in particular. Under such Wagnerian influence, Schönberg composed a string-quartet in 1897. This was Schönberg's first com-position to receive public performance, introduced the same year by the Wiener Tonküntsler Verein. The following year, the string-quartet was given performance once again, this time by the Pfitzner Quartet. Upon both occasions it was well received because—cast in traditional mould—it was warmly romantic and buoyantly youthful, full of emotional appeal.

Following the string-quartet, Schönberg produced a series of songs which were featured at a concert by Professor Gärtner, with Zemlinsky serving as the accompanist. Slightly more original in treatment—particularly in the polyphonic accompaniments—these songs created a mild disturbance among the puzzled audience. Thus, for the first time, Schönberg experienced the resentment of the music-public. "From that time on," Schönberg himself has said, "the scandal has never ceased."

The most important work of Schönberg's formative period came in 1899—the *Verklärte Nacht,* originally a sextet, but later scored by Schönberg for string-orchestra, the form in which it is best known. *Verklärte Nacht,* inspired by a poem of Richard Dehmel—speaks of the transfiguration of the world.in the eyes of a lover, brought about by his self-abnegation in forgiving his sweetheart for her sin. In this work, strongly influenced by the Wagnerian idiom, there is lucid, fluent contrapuntal writing in which the exquisite mood of a sensuous night is caught in gossamer, delicate tone-colors. The mood of suspense and drama, with which the very night seems pregnant, is painted with suppleness. Its background is a scintillating scenic painting. *Verklärte Nacht* remains Schönberg's most beautiful work.

During this period, Schönberg earned his living by conducting several groups of men's choruses in the suburbs of Vienna. One spring evening, Schönberg was celebrating with one of his choral groups in a wine tavern. A whim of the moment, inspired the group to make a nocturnal excursion to a nearby mountain. The walk through the woods, on a night of unusual beauty and tranquillity—culminating before the scene of the dawn rising from the trees—inspired Schönberg with a portion of a new musical work, the *Gurre-Lieder.* The *Gurre-Lieder,* however, conceived along monumental lines of design, was a task requiring several years for completion.

In 1901, Arnold Schönberg was married to the sister of his teacher, inspirer and friend, Zemlinsky. Shortly after the marriage, Schönberg came to Berlin to assume the position of conductor of the Wolzogen Buntes Theatre, a smart cabaret for the sophisticated. At this time, he composed a short poem for orchestra, *Pelleas and Melisande,* which was later to be performed in Germany and Holland under his own baton.

The *Gurre-Lieder,* however, was Schönberg's major creative problem of the time. By 1901, he had sketched the entire work and written down a great part of it. A portion of the manuscript, Schönberg showed to Richard Strauss, who was so strongly moved by the original character of the music that he procured for Schönberg the Liszt stipend, and a position as a teacher of composition at the Stern Conservatory.

In July of 1903, Schönberg was back in Vienna, living in the same house with Zemlinsky, and devoting himself to the teaching of harmony and counterpoint. At this time, Schönberg gathered about him a clique of students who were to become his disciples and band into a school of modern composition which glorified Schönberg's style of creation and accepted as its truth his æsthetic principles. To these pupils—including Alban Berg, Erwin Stein, Anton Webern, Heinrich Jalowetz and Egon Wellesz—Schönberg was more than a mere instructor in harmony. He influenced their thinking, their philosophy of life, their cosmic viewpoint. As one of his students, Anton Webern, once remarked: "Schönberg instructs his pupils in every branch of humanity. He is their master, in the highest sense of the word. He develops their personality to the point of self-expression."

At this time, too, Schönberg met and became a friend of Gustav Mahler, the great conductor and composer. Mahler, in his contacts with Schönberg, electrified and inspired the younger musician. What Mahler meant to Schönberg—not only as a composer, but as an example of idealism, integrity and moral fortitude—might be guessed by the dedication of the *Harmonielehre,* which appeared eight years later. "This book is dedicated to Gustav Mahler. It was hoped that the dedication might give him a small measure of pleasure while he was still living. . . . Gustav Mahler has had to forego far greater joys than that which this dedication might have given him. This martyr, this saint had to leave the earth before he had brought his work to such a point of perfection that he could bequeath it to his friends in all tranquillity. I should have contented myself with offering him this satisfaction. But now that he is dead, it is my wish that my book may bring me this esteem, that none may gainsay me when I say: 'Truly, he was a great man!' "

The influence that Gustav Mahler exerted on behalf of Schönberg resulted in the performance of several of Schönberg's works. The Rosé String Quartet featured the *Verklärte Nacht,* the *Quartet in D-minor* and, the latest of Schönberg's music up to the time, the *Kammersymphonie.* These works were too startling in idiom to be accepted complacently by the audiences. Whistling, hissing, banging of seats marked these performances. Catcalls mingled with laughter of derision until, at certain moments, it was impossible to hear the music. At a later performance of a Schönberg work (the *Quartet in F-sharp minor,* also featured by the Rosé String Quartet) there was pandemonium.

This heartbreaking reception did not discourage Schönberg, nor tempt him to question his direction. On the contrary, he went forward with greater boldness and self-assurance. The *Kammersymphonie*—which Lawrence Gilman has picturesquely described as a "two-faced mirror" which, in facing backwards, reflected Schönberg's one-time romanticism, but, in facing forwards, reflected Schönberg's experimentalism—was the first definite warning of the direction in which Schönberg's style was heading. In it he permanently discarded his former pellucid contrapuntal writing, substituting for it a melodic line as sharp and as decisive as a lash of a whip, and a harmonic language, pungent and electric. There followed a series of works, produced between 1909 and 1912, in which Schönberg's revolutionary style reached final development: the *Five Pieces for Orchestra,* the *Six Pieces for the Piano,* the song-cycle, *Pierrot Lunaire,* and two works for the stage, *Erwartung* and *Die Glückliche Hand.*

Vienna being too hostile to his art, Schönberg decided upon a change of scene. He came to Berlin in 1911, accepting the posts of instructor of composition at the Akademie für Kunst and lecturer on æsthetics at the Stern Conservatory. It was in Berlin that Schönberg finally brought the *Gurre-Lieder* to completion—after thirteen years. The plan of the *Gurre-Lieder* was so gargantuan, requiring such an oversized orchestra that—in scoring it— Schönberg was forced to order special printed music-paper utilizing twice the usual number of staves.

The *Gurre-Lieder* was first performed in Vienna on February 23, 1913, by the Philharmonic Choir conducted by Franz Schreker. The performance was—mirabile dictu!—an enormous success. The cordial and sympathetic reception that this work received was not difficult to explain. True, even in 1913, the *Gurre-Lieder* was in many respects ahead of its time. There are harmonic combinations in the *Gurre-Lieder* which are the definite expressions of a fully liberated composer; there are tonal arrangements which—created as they were in 1903—heralded the approach of the later Schönberg. However, in comparison with the fully emancipated style of the *Five Pieces for Orchestra* and the *Pierrot Lunaire,* the *Gurre-Lieder* seemed more Wagner than Schönberg—intensely melodic, richly harmonic and frequently emotional, despite

ARNOLD SCHÖNBERG

its occasional lapse into experimentation. After the
parched expression of Schönberg's later works, the *Gurre-
Lieder* appeared to the Viennese music-public uniquely
pleasing and refreshing.

3.

That Schönberg's victory as a composer was by no means
established with the success of the *Gurre-Lieder* was con-
vincingly proved only one month later. On March 31,
1913, Schönberg arranged a concert of modern Austrian
music, under the sponsorship of the Academic Society for
Literature and Music in Vienna—a program including his
own *Kammersymphonie,* a chamber work by Anton
Webern, orchestral songs by Zemlinsky and Alban Berg, and
the *Kindertotenlieder* by Gustav Mahler. Once again,
noise, hissing, pronounced jeers disturbed the performance.
At length, Schönberg made a request, through the Super-
intendent of the Academic Society, that at least the songs of
Mahler be received in the "fitting quiet and respect due to
the composer." This was the spark necessary to ignite
dynamite. Fist fights ensued in the audience; finally a riot.
The reverberations of this concert were later felt in the
law-courts of Berlin, where one of the audience had brought
suit against another for assault. At that time, a witness
explained that he had laughed himself sick during the concert because the music was funny, and he always laughed at
funny things. Another witness—a prominent physician—
testified that the music performed had been so nerve-rack-
ing that many who had been present at the concert were
already disclosing signs of neurosis attacks!

The War brought Schönberg's creative production to an
end. From December, 1915, to September, 1916, and from
July to October of 1917 he was engaged in military service. During these tragic years, musical composition was,
of course, impossible.

When the War ended, Schönberg returned to his native city, Vienna, establishing his home in Mödling. He reestablished contact with his most important pupils, and once again was their personal guide and inspirer. One of Schönberg's most important achievements was the creation of the Verein für Musikalische Privataufführungen, which for many years was responsible for first performances of the outstanding new music of young composers. One of the interesting features of these concerts of new music was the performance of works without the program revealing who their composers were, so that audience and critics might not be prejudiced for or against the work before hearing it.

The "scandals" attending performances of Schönberg's music had by no means relented—even though Schönberg had, by this time, achieved a world-wide reputation, and even though post-War Europe had accustomed its ears to musical audacities. In 1922, a performance of the *Five Pieces for Orchestra* in Paris was smothered by the stamping of feet. Six years later, Wilhelm Furtwängler introduced a new Schönberg work with the Berlin Philharmonic—the *Variations,* for orchestra—to the accompaniment of audible denunciations of the audience. And when this very same work was performed for the first time in America shortly afterwards, by Leopold Stokowski and the Philadelphia Orchestra, the usually placid and docile American music-public expressed its heated indignation in no uncertain response.

In the face of this life-long antagonism for Schönberg's music, the question of its artistic importance rises inevitably.

In his music, Schönberg has been fascinated by ugly sounds, barbaric cries and yawps. Brutal vigor is here made boldly manifest. Here, as James Gibbons Huneker wrote many years ago, we have the "very ecstasy of the hideous—for pain can be, at once, exquisite and horrible." In this music, Schönberg is often the cerebral mathematician of music. Overdressed orchestrations have begun to repel him; sentimentality and emotion have grown cloying. He strove to denude music of all superficiality, of all extraneous material, of all unnecessary appendages of sound, and present his message succinctly and lucidly. And into this task Schönberg hurled himself with the devotion of a prophet. The music that followed the *Gurre-Lieder* is, for the most part, barren, parched, withered of all emotion. Brevity is the soul of its wit. Furthermore, his orchestration is threadbare; it consists only of those instruments which are absolutely essential to the message. Schönberg felt that he must pierce to the very heart of his music; he must write strictly to the point, without any circumlocutions; he felt that he must reveal his message in its baldest guise. And that is precisely what he accomplished in all of his later works.

Unmistakably, Schönberg's revolution has opened a limitless field for music. Music has acquired more plasticity, its boundaries have been extended indefinitely. New poignant effects, new qualities of tone, new meanings seem to have been added. These are some of the fruits of the revolt; the weeds are just as numerous. With Schönberg, music has become naked and ugly. It has become as intellectual as a syllogism or a mathematical formula. Schönberg's music, therefore, may be important in that it has opened new vistas for musical expression; it is never, however, great music in itself. It lacks emotion, depth, and, above everything else, human experience. We derive a certain kinæsthetic pleasure from the sting and bite of his harmonies and atonality. We are at times intoxicated by his masculine vigor, his healthy vitality, and his unique originality. But his music never inspires us nor carries us into other spheres, as all immortal music does. And it is only momentarily impressive; its influence deserts us as soon as we stop listening to it. It never haunts us or becomes a part of us.

I am, therefore, confident that Schönberg's music will eventually go the way of all flesh. But his importance as a musical personality should make musical history. His name will live longer than his music.

4.

In 1934, Austria celebrated the sixtieth birthday of Arnold Schönberg. A volume of adulatory essays was the gesture of honor extended by his many disciples to their beloved master.[1] Moreover, several of Schönberg's works were performed, and—in respect to his world prestige— were received with courteous appreciation.

This reception came at a time when Schönberg's career had reached a completely new phase. For one thing, he had permanently changed his home. The rise of Fascism in Europe generally, and in Germany in particular, was a severe blow to him. As an escape, he expatriated himself, crossed the Atlantic in the winter of 1933, and settled in America. For six months, he was on the faculty of the Malkin School of Music in Boston and New York. One year later, an appointment as professor of music to the University of Southern California, brought him to the western coast where he established his home.

During the first few years in America, Schönberg has brought to completion several new works—a *Concerto for String Quartet and Orchestra,* based upon a Handel concerto grosso, a concerto for violoncello and orchestra, a suite for string orchestra, a chamber symphony and an opera on a Biblical subject, *Moses and Aaron*—which suggest that Schönberg's musical style has undergone a radical departure. Grating atonality is no longer his natural expression. Instead, he is producing music more in the style of the neo-classicism of Stravinsky's latest period—refine-

---

[1] *Arnold Schönberg zum 60 Geburtstag* (essays by Anton Webern, Jalowetz, Broch, etc.).

ment instead of babarity, classical forms replacing complete emancipation. For this change, Schönberg has offered only one explanation: "I always write music the way I feel it. My ideas recently required a different idiom, that is all. I did not consciously change my style. Some time in the future, other musical ideas of mine will be best expressed in the idiom of *Pierrot Lunaire*. If so, I will write it that way." [2]

It is difficult to bear in mind, in meeting Schönberg, that he has been one of the most advanced rebels of present-day music. Short of stature, and slight of build, he gives the impression of excessive timidity. And excessive gentleness. His face possesses an expression that combines ingenuousness and sensitiveness. It is a face full of warmth and kindness; the lines are refined; the eyes are affectionate; the lips, soft. Everything about him is suggestive of softness. His voice has almost the quality of a flute. His hand, when you shake it, is limp. His temper is generally equable. Rarely has a man's personality and his art been so strikingly at polar points!

During the first few moments with Schönberg, one finds little about him impressive. He is a small man, highly strung and nervous, with little dignity or solemnity. It is only after a prolonged conversation with him that his true stature becomes apparent. His sincerity, idealism and faith in his art are reflected in everything he says; his enormous intellectual range as well. His mind is clear and analytical. His ideas are expressed succinctly and clearly; he soon discloses the fact that he detests confused thinking and is impatient with aimless verbiage. Moreover, he has a cultural background that extends far beyond the realm of music. He is not only a great musician and a profound theorist, but he is also a poet, metaphysician and mathematician. He even paints—well enough to have given several exhibitions of his canvases in Berlin and

2 In an interview with the author.

Vienna which have encouraged the enthusiastic comments of the critics.

His conversation reveals knowledge of many things, and a profound knowledge of some. However, it should not be assumed that he is either pompously pedantic or affected. He is too much a man of utter simplicity to make a meretricious display of his learning. He is just as likely to talk to you about a recent game of tennis or ping-pong (in both of which he indulges enthusiastically) or to tell you about his favorite hobby, bookbinding, as he is to discuss æsthetic theories or indulge in abstruse subjects.

He has one pronounced musical preference—Johann Sebastian Bach, a few of whose organ works he has arranged for the modern symphony orchestra. He has never—tactfully enough!—expressed publicly his opinions on modern composers, although it is known that some of them are devastatingly iconoclastic. Where his own music is concerned, there is very little attempt on his part at false modesty. He believes implicitly in his importance as a creator. However, he rarely attends a performance of his own works—conditioned, no doubt, by the hostile reception his works received over a period of many years. As a result, there are still many of his works which he has never heard at a public concert.

FRANCESCO MALIPIERO

XIV

FRANCESCO MALIPIERO

1.

IN THE little Italian hill-town of Asolo, two hours' distance by automobile from Venice, Francesco Malipiero has his permanent home. Asolo is a curiously appropriate setting for a composer like Malipiero whose artistic roots reach back several centuries. It is several centuries old, revealing its age in every corner and cobblestone. The center of the town is almost of thumbnail size. Here are an old hunching inn, seeming to stoop under the weight of its own age, and a church whose face is marred and scratched by the winds and rains of four centuries. In the distance looms a historic ruin. The various homes of the Asolo inhabitants—probably no more than a handful in number—are sprinkled at formidable distances from each other along tortuous roads that twist and wind like veins from out the public square.

My first impression upon arriving in Asolo was that any composer selecting so secluded a niche for his home must by temperament be a recluse. Yet this is far from the truth. Malipiero is not a misanthrope who must seek solitary confinement. As a matter of fact, he is uniquely warmhearted and gregarious, and the society of pupils and friends means much to him. One of his greatest delights comes on Sundays when his home becomes alive with visitors; pleasant social palaver over teacups finds him an enthusiastic participant in the musical discussions that take place in his study. The solitude of Asolo, however, is indispensable to an artist who wishes to work as industriously as Malipiero does. Once each week he goes to Venice to

enjoy the society of friends, crowds and metropolitan life;
occasionally, he interrupts the routine of his work days to
make special trips to European capitals. But except for
these intermissions, he works continuously and richly—and
because distractions in Asolo are few and far between.

The Malipiero villa is surrounded by an impregnable
wall—very much as a monastery might be—and it stands in
bleak isolation from the rest of the town. It is in many
respects a home of incomparable tone, whose spirit and
atmosphere bespeak the warm, genial and witty personality
of its owner.

Over the doorway of the villa is inscribed the following
quotation from the Latin: "To the obscene all things are
obscene." I learned from Malipiero that some time back
he had composed an opera to a text by D'Annunzio which
was removed from the stage because of its immoral theme.
This made Malipiero an object for suspicion and disdain
among his townspeople. Attack is always the best defense,
as Malipiero realized. Before his townspeople could express their indignation in so many consecutive thoughts,
Malipiero placed the quotation above his doorway. "After
that," Malipiero said with a broad grin on his face, "my
townspeople were a little ashamed to condemn me."

I had not been more than a few minutes in Asolo when
I was given further examples of Malipiero's unorthodoxy.
Upon ringing his doorbell, the bell rang sharply and pro-
longedly as though the button of the bell had slipped and
established a permanent contact. Nor did the bell stop
ringing until the maid opened the door for me. Malipiero
chuckled warmly when he saw my embarrassment in the
face of this prolonged and obstreperous ringing. "I assure
you that the fault is not yours," he explained hurriedly.
"I had the bell constructed that way purposely so that if
anyone rings it continues to sound until the maid opens the
door. I'll tell you why. Frequently, a timid admirer comes
to visit me—making the unpleasant trip from Venice ex-

pressly for that purpose. If the maid delays in answering him, he becomes so terrified while waiting that he runs away. The loud ringing of the doorbell, on the other hand, so startles him that he remains rooted to the ground until the maid opens the door for him."

Inside the villa, the first disconcerting thing to strike the eye is a prominent sign on the wall: "Do not trust your host. You can never be quite sure who he really is." And then, before you have had the opportunity to recover from the shock of this warning, you stumble grotesquely on a false step which has been painted on the foot of the stairway with such skill that it is truly deceptive. Asked for the reason for this false step, Malipiero answered (and it was impossible not to detect the malicious sparkle in his eyes): "Sometimes people come to visit me who are half-sleepy and arrive at my studio with deadened intellects. If so, by stumbling over that false step they suddenly become fully awakened and can come into my studio clear-headed and alert."

The above remarks and incidents gave me a clue to Malipiero's innocently malicious sense of humor. I was soon to learn that combined with this love of wit was a generosity, an affectionate nature, a tender heart and a softness that is almost effeminate—qualities which make Malipiero one of the most lovable men I have ever met.

His qualities as a human-being are suggested, to a great degree, by his appearance. He is not a handsome man, but he has a regal bearing, and an expressive and sensitive face. The slopes of his cheeks are soft, and his eyes are the gentlest I have ever seen. His voice is, as one might expect, thin and pleasant; his gestures, which are frequent, invariably express affection. He exudes a charm that spreads an atmosphere of warm pleasantness about him, making those near him feel close to him even after a cursory acquaintance. He is a born host, gracious, well-poised and solicitous.

When he took me by the arm and conducted me about his garden, he stopped at a favorite flower to stroke it affectionately as though it were human. He stepped for a moment into the barn to introduce me to his goat, patting it with infinite tenderness and speaking to it as though it could understand him. When he accidentally stumbled across his dog in the garden, he tipped his hat (in all seriousness!) and apologized.

An anecdote about Malipiero is particularly illuminating in illustrating his love for living things. It occurred to him that it might be wise to raise chickens and have them fresh from his own garden for his Sunday dinner. Malipiero bought a dozen or more chickens, built a coop and began to raise them himself. In a few days, however, he became so warmly attached to the chickens that not only did he firmly refuse to slaughter any one of them for his Sunday dinner but when one of them fell seriously ill he frantically called a physician from Venice to care for it. It has been said that, ever since Malipiero acquired his coop of chickens, fowl on his Sunday dinner-table has been noticeably infrequent!

In everything he says or does are his nobility of character and generosity of heart apparent. We were, for example, discussing the younger Italian composers. Where he could praise, his enthusiasm was lavish. Where, however, honesty demanded blame, he discreetly refused to voice his opinion. Harsh words were a definite effort for him. Likewise he is altogether incapable of envy. Time and again, in our talks, he figuratively bared his head in respect to some imposing achievement of a modern composer. He admires Stravinsky profoundly; Ravel and Prokofieff, too. His enthusiasm for his fellow-musicians is always genuine and sincere. There is the case of his relationship with Toscanini, for example. Since 1918—the result of a petty and a disagreeable quarrel between Toscanini and Malipiero—the maestro has stubbornly refused to conduct a work by

the composer. Many another composer would, with justification, feel considerable resentment towards Toscanini.
But Malipiero worships Toscanini's art, considers him the
greatest interpretative artist of our age and has no hesitation in expressing this opinion. As a matter of fact, whenever Malipiero is in the north of Italy he always pays a
cordial visit to Toscanini's villa in Lake Maggiore to in-
quire after the health of the conductor and to exchange
conversation.

The relationship between Malipiero and his pupils is
likewise characteristic of a teacher who is also a great
human-being. Malipiero is not only their teacher but
father and friend as well. He nurses them with the fastidious watch of a hen guarding her brood. Shortly after my
visit to Asolo, I had an appointment with Malipiero at the
Liceo Benedetto Marcello in Venice (where he has a special
class in composition once each week). Leaving the Liceo,
Malipiero was surrounded by his pupils, one of whom he
held by the arm, while affectionately embracing another.
Between teacher and pupil there was warmth of feeling
and affection which was very apparent as they strolled
down the streets of Venice, talking at the top of their voices,
laughing unrestrainedly at frequent intervals. Passing a
café, Malipiero herded his pupils into it and urged them
to drink milk with him.

At another time, I met Malipiero in Venice when he
begged me to wait for him a half-hour because, at that
moment, he was terribly occupied. "You see," he explained, "one of my pupils is leaving for Brussels to study
conducting. I am buying his train ticket for him, getting
his traveler checks and arranging everything so that his
trip might be made easier." Incidentally, at that very moment, Malipiero was even holding packages belonging to
his pupil!

The most important musical influence upon Malipiero
has, of course, been early Italian music. He has made ex-

tensive and valuable research into old Italian music, and
has edited the works of such Italian masters as Monteverdi,
Cavalli, Cavaliere, Scarlatti, Galuppi, Jomelli, Marcello
and Tartini. These Italian masters, who are Malipiero's
favorite composers, have nurtured his spirit and have most
strongly affected his artistic direction and musical style.
Malipiero likewise possesses an enormous knowledge of
painting and a fabulous acquaintanceship with Italian
poetry. Frequently, the cadences and strophes of old
Italian lyrics definitely give shape to the contours of his
melodic line.

2.

The music of Malipiero can best be understood when his
great preoccupation with old Italian music, poetry and
painting is recalled. He is not an Italian composer if by
the term we bear in mind only the singableness of Puccini,
Verdi and Rossini. He is more dramatic than lyrical. He
is also, frequently, more contrapuntal than homophonic—
his contrapuntal writing deriving its personality from the
Gregorian chant.

Essentially, Malipiero's Italianism is much subtler and
truer than that of Puccini or Rossini. It is the pure classical spirit of the Renaissance, drenched with the colors,
movement and spiritual intensity of Renaissance art. His
music is, like all Italian music, permeated with lyricism; but
it is a lyricism that has its own quality and flavor. Malipiero prefers a crisp melodic line of a swiftly moving pace
which derives its dramatic character from the recitatives of
Cavalli and Cavaliere. On the other hand, he prefers a
recitative made more flexible by the freer use of melody.
Thus there is frequently very slight difference between his
recitatives and his melodies.

Malipiero's music is essentially a dramatic expression—
even when he abandons the opera for symphonic and cham-

ber music. Frequently, it has the gleam of a mischievous wit and irony strongly reminiscent of the Italian opera-bouffe of a previous century. Occasionally, it assumes a philosophic pensiveness, a contemplative and introspective serenity. I am inclined to think that Malipiero's music is at its best and most imaginative when it avoids nervousness and agitation, wit and malice, and assumes the spiritual tranquillity of the Renaissance paintings. This classical Renaissance tranquillity and spirituality, which Malipiero has couched in forms of musical writing that are essentially modern in technique is, I believe, his most personal speech, and the one by which he can most clearly be identified.

3.

Gian Francesco Malipiero is descended from an old Venetian family which, in an earlier age, included many important dignitaries of state and later numbered some prominent musicians. His grandfather was a well-known composer of popular operas, a rival of Giuseppe Verdi. His father was a distinguished pianist who subjected his children to a rigorous musical training. As a result, not only Francesco, but two other sons as well, became professional musicians.

Francesco Malipiero was born in Venice on March 18, 1882. He was born to a profoundly musical environment, and began the study of the violin in his sixth year. It is said that as a child he revealed greater enthusiasm for painting, even expressing the wish at one time that he aspired to become an artist rather than a musician. His father, however, was insistent upon a musical career. Young Francesco devoted himself to his music-study with an assiduity that brought with it rapid progress.

When Malipiero was eleven years old, a family catastrophe—which Malipiero has always been reluctant to disclose—compelled the father to exile himself, his mother and his oldest son, Francesco. For seven years, theirs was a nomadic life, during which time the boy acquired a unique attachment for his grandmother. During this time, both father and son earned their living by playing in various small orchestras. After a period in Germany, the Malipieros came to Vienna where, in 1896, an affluent Polish nobleman became so convinced of Francesco's musical gifts that he offered to finance his musical education. In this way, Malipiero began his first systematic study in musical theory at the Vienna Conservatory, principally under Professor Stocker.

After a year in Vienna—a year fraught with discontent and unhappiness brought on partially by poverty and partially by the death of his beloved grandmother—Francesco Malipiero returned to Venice, where he became a pupil of Marco Enrico Bossi. A bond of friendship developed between teacher and pupil. When, therefore, Bossi was appointed director of the Liceo Musicale in Bologna, Malipiero accompanied him. It was there that Malipiero's first orchestral work, *Dai Sepolcri,* was performed with considerable success.

In 1902, two important influences changed the course of Malipiero's artistic life. In that year, he heard Wagner's *Die Meistersinger,* and for the first time realized that there existed an operatic world far different from that of the Italian composers. Of even greater importance, however, was Malipiero's discovery in a library of a series of manuscripts of musical works by old Italian composers. In this music he found such a spiritual affinity that he plunged deeper and deeper into its study. Eventually, he became one of the foremost authorities on old Italian music. Eventually, too, his own musical creation was subtly but unmistakably shaped and formed by the style of the old Italian masters.

In 1910, Malipiero married the daughter of a famous Venetian painter. For the next three years, he lived in

FRANCESCO MALIPIERO

comparative retirement, absorbed with the study of old Italian music and poetry. There was some composition too —principally such orchestral works as *Sinfonia degli Eroi* and *Sinfonia del mare;* but with all of these early works Malipiero was stiflingly dissatisfied. Instinctively, he knew that he was failing to achieve that happy fusion of the old style and the new which he intuitively sought. He was irritated by the stiltedness of his thoughts, by the lack of fluidity of his musical expression. He arrived at the conclusion that his technique was at fault—which, to be remedied, required an intimate contact with the style of the modern composers. The only modern music that Malipiero knew at the time consisted of Debussy's *L'Après midi d'un faune* (which he admired profoundly) and some of Strauss' tone-poems. Sensing that there existed an important world of music of which he was completely unfamiliar, and realizing that familiarity with this music was indispensable if he was to achieve full artistic development, Malipiero left Venice for Paris in 1913.

In Paris, his fellow countryman, Alfredo Casella, opened for him all musical doors. Malipiero mingled with such composers as Debussy, Fauré, Ravel and Stravinsky; he heard their music and analytically studied their forms and technique. He was in the celebrated audience that heard the first performance of Stravinsky's *Le Sacre du Printemps* —a shattering experience for him because it disclosed how expansive the world of modern musical expression could be. This intimacy with modern music gave Malipiero a new mastery of form, a greater plasticity of style, and more technical adroitness—and it inspired him to indulge in a new burst of creation.

One day, in Paris, Malipiero read an announcement in the newspapers that a national competition was being conducted in Italy for original musical works. Without thinking of possible consequences, Malipiero submitted five works under five different names. To his confusion and embarrassment, he learned from the papers that four out of the five awards were conferred upon his works. The discovery in Italy that one and the same composer had, by utilizing different names, confiscated the first four prizes aroused such bitter resentment that the newspapers combined to attack Malipiero. It was a difficult situation which required much tactful explanation. Malipiero rushed to Rome to explain that he had not attempted anything fradulent in submitting five works. But his explanation hardly failed to placate his opponents. When, therefore, one of his prize-winning compositions, *Arione,* was performed at the Augusteum on December 21, 1913, it was received with a carefully planned hostility; hissing, stamping of feet, raucous shouts disturbed the progress of the music. An even more bitter reception awaited the performance of his opera *Canossa* at the Costanzi Theatre in Rome on January 24, 1914—a reception so bitter that Malipiero begged the authorities to remove the opera from the repertoire after the first performance.

These unpleasant contacts with audiences hardened Malipiero to public opinion. He returned to Venice where—in the town of Asolo—he once again secluded himself from people, composing fecundly, but making very little effort to have his works performed. During this time Malipiero composed what is frequently considered the first of his masterpieces, the second series of the *Impressioni dal Vero,* for orchestra, a set of sensitive tone impressions of Nature.

Then the first cannon of the World War disrupted Malipiero's peaceful creative life.

These cannon completely shattered Malipiero's peace of mind and spirit. How strongly the War affected him can best be judged by the fact that, for more than two years, he—who could be so prolific—could not write a line of music. The creation of art seemed to him a pusillanimous gesture in a time when madness and wholesale butchery prevailed. The only escape from this horrible reality of bloodshed, Malipiero found by burying himself in the scores of old Italian music, whose tranquillity and repose were like soothing balm to his blistering spirits. It was at this time that he edited many works of Monteverdi, Galuppi, Tartini and others, and resuscitated such significant examples of early Italian dramatic music as Luigi Rossi's *Orfeo* and Cavaliere's *La Rappresentazione di anima e di corpo*.

Finally, even such labors became impossible when the War came to Malipiero's very door. In October of 1917, Asolo was invaded by the Second Army which was in flight before the approaching enemy. With the threat of War under his window, Malipiero and his wife decided to flee. Taking with them only a few precious manuscripts, they made what was at that time an arduous trip to Venice. It took them two days, most of the journey being done on foot. Everywhere, Malipiero saw the dead and the dying, pools of blood, destruction and devastation. The sights turned his stomach and wrenched his heart. When, finally, he made the trip from Venice to Rome, his friends—terrified by his ghastly appearance and by the incoherence of his raving—seriously feared that he was losing his mind.

Returning to composition, at last, Malipiero inevitably expressed his sentiments about War. He put to paper one of the most neurotic conceptions in music, a ballet *Pantea,* "the struggle of a soul hurling itself into the strife for liberty only to find, after a thousand sufferings, Death and Oblivion." A year previously he had composed one of his most moving pieces of orchestral music, the *Pause del Silenzio*.

A personal rift between Toscanini and Malipiero has kept Toscanini, despite his partiality for modern Italian music, from conducting anything by Malipiero. There are two or three versions for this quarrel, which need not be detailed here. Eventually, friendship between the two was renewed. But, though Malipiero was a frequent guest at the home of the Toscaninis and even though Toscanini from time to time has expressed enthusiasm for Malipiero's works, the maestro—with his characteristically sublime stubbornness—has refused to perform any of Malipiero's music.

Following the War, Malipiero returned to his retreat in Asolo. For the next decade and a half, his life was not particularly eventful in dramatic incidents. But it was rich in production of musical works and in their performances throughout Europe. A series of important works placed him at the head of living Italian composers and among the most fruitful musical voices of our time. These works included the operas *L'Orfeide, Torneo Notturno* and *Tre Commedie Goldoniane;* the *Sette Canzoni* (a series of exquisitely beautiful lyrics from the fourteenth, fifteenth and sixteenth century which Malipiero set to music and gave a scenic adaptation); the cantata, *San Francesco d'Assisi,* for solo baritone, chorus and orchestra—one of Malipiero's most tender conceptions; the charming orchestral suite of Cimarosa melodies, *La Cimarosiana,* and the *Concerto for Violin and Orchestra* and *Concerto for Piano and Orchestra.* In 1920, Malipiero achieved fame in the United States when his best known chamber work, the *Rispetti e Strambotti,* for string-quartet, won the Elizabeth Sprague Coolidge prize of $1,000 for the best chamber work submitted in the annual competition.

In the midst of this prolific creation, Malipiero's life was one of serenity and seclusion, which not even the political upheaval could disturb. Malipiero, who has never been politically minded, became even less so with the rise of Fascism in Italy. The Fascist government—as part of its cultural program—accepted him as one of the great living composers, giving him full freedom to pursue his creative career without disturbance and giving frequent performances to his works. The *Sette Canzoni* was magnificently performed in Turin in 1926; the oratorio, *La Cena,* was one of the outstanding musical events in Italy in 1933. And in April of 1934, Malipiero's Symphony, *Like the Four Seasons* was featured prominently at the festival of modern music in Florence.

Thus—removed from the political maelstrom by his secluded life in Asolo—Malipiero's life was one of intense creative activity. Occasional interruptions from his work came when, from time to time during these years, he traveled to England, France, and Germany to attend important performances of his works. But most of the time in Asolo, composing, editing, writing and studying. During this period, Malipiero married a second time—an English woman of considerable cultural background, charm and sweetness of personality.

Once—in March of 1934—Malipiero came into direct conflict with the Fascist officials. At that time, his new opera, *La Favola del Figlio Cambiato*—which had had a successful first performance in Brunswick, Germany, the previous January—was introduced in Italy. The opera, based upon a play of Pirandello, received a stormy reception. There were some to denounce it on moral grounds: some of the characters in the play were prostitutes. The Vatican and Fascist officials, however, made a more grievous charge: they found in the theme a subtle satire against royalty and Authority. At the first performance, there was so much hostility on the part of the audience that Malipiero was compelled to flee from the theatre to escape physical maltreatment. The following day, it was publicly announced that Mussolini banned the opera from all future performances on "moral and political grounds."

Malipiero's reinstatement in the favor of the Fascist officials, however, was not slow in coming. His ensuing works—probably consciously planned to placate the infuriated authorities—were an oratorio, *La Passione,* a sequel to the successful *La Cena,* setting a sixteenth century mystery play to music, and an opera, *Julius Cæsar.* Both works succeeded in restoring their composer to the high esteem of the government. Particularly *Julius Cæsar*, which in its attempt to speak the grandeur and magnificence that was Rome and in its favorable delineation of Cæsar as a Latin hero, struck a responsive chord with Mussolini. *Julius Cæsar*, with the blessing of the government on its brow, was introduced in Italy in 1936 with great success—a success which it failed to duplicate when it was introduced in America by the Schola Cantorum of New York, Hugh Ross conducting, on January 13, 1937.

ROY HARRIS

ROY HARRIS

XV

ROY HARRIS

1.

OVER the horizon of modern American music the name of Roy Harris has soared like a meteor. In 1931, he was virtually unknown even to many of those who keep close watch of the musical skies. Yet within a few years his became—without being guilty of overemphasis—the most important name in contemporary American music. His works have been performed by such outstanding American symphony orchestras as the New York Philharmonic, the Boston, Chicago, Philadelphia, Portland, Washington, Minneapolis and Los Angeles orchestras. On February 28, 1936, for example, almost within the same hour, both the Boston Symphony and the Philadelphia Symphony orchestras featured the premières of Roy Harris' works—the former with the *Second Symphony,* and the latter with the *Farewell to Pioneers.* Most of his major works are recorded by the Columbia and Victor phonograph companies (an amazing fact when one realizes that there are talented composers not only in America but in Europe as well who do not even boast of a single major work on phonograph records!). Commissions from leading musical organizations, as well as from the recording companies, to compose new works to be featured by them, descend upon his head like blessed manna. Finally, when in 1935 the New York Philharmonic Symphony Society conducted a nation-wide poll among its radio listeners for an all-request program, the name of Roy Harris appeared first among the American composers—just a few votes less than César Franck.

The wonder of it is that Roy Harris' music has none of

that contagious appeal which ignites the enthusiasm of a wide music public with seductive melodic phrases or impressionable rhythms as, for example, Ravel's *Bolero* or Gershwin's *Rhapsody in Blue*. It is highly intellectual music, elaborately complicated, which requires a long intimacy to be appreciated. Roy Harris' melodies are not such as to tempt you to whistle them after a first hearing; they are intricately carved, and grow and expand through many bars before they stop to catch breath. The subtlety of his design is not visible immediately, and becomes apparent only after careful analysis. Harris' music consists of elaborately concocted harmonic schemes and often complex polytonal counterpoint. His music is far more the product of an analytical brain than a sensitive emotional heart. It is, therefore, strange to find him the composer of the hour.

But the composer of the hour he has undoubtedly become. He is not only the most frequently performed among American composers, and the recipient of the most commissions, but he is also esteemed the major creative talent to have emerged in our country in many years. More than one eminent critic has spoken of him as the most authentically American voice, the most thoroughly American expression among modern composers. To quote Alfredo Casella, for example: "In producing a composer such as this young master, America has placed herself in the front rank amongst those nations who are concerned with building a music for the future." He is, therefore, in the eyes of many, the "white hope" of American music.

2.

His background is rich with American tradition. He was born—appropriately enough!—on Lincoln's birthday of 1898, in a log-cabin in Oklahoma, the son of stout-fibered American pioneers. His parents, of Scotch-Irish descent, had provided themselves, before Roy's birth, with gun, ammunition, an ox-cart, some flour and sugar, and struck for the open West in the last frontier land-rush. They staked a claim in Oklahoma, built there a log-cabin and fructified the soil.

Malaria drove these pioneers from Oklahoma to the San Gabriel Valley in California where the Harrises built their own farm. Here Roy spent his boyhood, adolescence and early manhood. He saw the grainfields of Lucky Baldwin sliced into farms which were soon to become the famous orange groves of the San Gabriel Valley. He went through grammar and high school, an apt pupil who revealed an enormous interest in books and learning. He played the piano, clarinet and organ but until his twenty-sixth year had not studied composition.

In his eighteenth year, he started a farm of his own. Farming alone could never completely satisfy so restless an intellect as that of Roy Harris, and he coupled it with the study of Greek philosophy. One year later, America entered the World War. For a year, Harris served as a private in the United States Army. That year of absence from his farm lands seemed to have given him musical perspective. He returned to Southern California determined to devote himself to study. He transferred his home to Hollywood Hills, entered the Southern Branch of the University of California where he began the study of harmony, and found diversion in Hindu theology. During the day he drove a truck, distributing three hundred pounds of butter and three hundred dozen eggs each day. The evenings belonged to school and his books.

What it was that definitely decided him to turn completely to music he cannot explain today, except that he had always been interested in the art. At any rate, after he had acquired a passing acquaintance with harmony and theory, he came to Arthur Farwell, well-known theorist and composer, and begged to become his pupil. Farwell was not the teacher to take under his wing pupils who knew hardly more than the musical alphabet and the elements of its grammar. But something about Harris appealed to him strongly and he accepted him. "I was convinced," Arthur Farwell later wrote,[1] "that he would one day challenge the world. Aside from his manifest talent, my grounds for this belief lay in his mental vitality and breadth, in his insistence upon the subjecting of every accepted musical dictum and tradition, technical and spiritual, to a searching scrutiny, and a determination to work out a new, vital, and creative way in every musical sphere and relation."

For two years, Harris studied energetically under Farwell, and in that time a young man who formerly would not have known how to put upon paper anything more complex than an inverted major triad found himself the composer of a suite for string-quartet and an *Andante* for orchestra. The *Andante*, for all its artistic gropings, disclosed a fine musical instinct for the *mot juste*. This work was singled out from a mass of manuscripts submitted to the New York Philharmonic, and was performed by that orchestra under the direction of Willem van Hoogstraten at the Lewisohn Stadium during the summer of 1926.

Through the generosity of private patronage, Harris was enabled to leave for Paris soon after the performance of his *Andante*, and to continue his studies in Paris under Nadia Boulanger, that singularly inspiring teacher without whose guidance, it seems, the education of younger modern composers seems incomplete.

During Harris' initial year in Paris, he composed his first major work, a work of amazing maturity and roundness of personality when one compares it with the *Andante* that preceded it. It was the *Concerto for Piano, Clarinet and String-Quartet*, introduced in Paris by the Roth String Quartet, supplemented by Nadia Boulanger and M. Cahuzac. French critics immediately singled out the work from the entire program as the one with the most obvious

talent. "One work dominated the program," wrote Bander-
lot. "It has warmth, life, a rhythm, an accent which denotes
a nature of the first order." The artistic success of the
Concerto brought Harris the award of the Guggenheim
Fellowship.

In Paris, a misfortune struck Harris which, eventually,
proved to be a blessing in disguise. In 1929, he fractured
his spine and was confined to a hospital. When he had
partially recovered, he was forced to return to America
to undergo a major operation. For more than six months
he was confined to a hospital bed, and for diversion he composed a string-quartet. In composing this work, circumstances compelled him for the first time in his life to
dispense with the help of a piano keyboard. Thus, he
finally succeeded in freeing himself from what he terms the
"tyranny of the piano." It is his honest conviction that this
lesson, learned in an American hospital, put him at least ten
years ahead artistically. Liberated, at last, from the habit
of composing at a piano, Harris was enabled not only to
compose quicker and with greater lucidity, but even to
change the character of his music: formerly his music had
been for the most part harmonic, because his fingers
instinctively groped for chords at the piano; now it had
become more contrapuntal.

Whether Harris overemphasizes the importance of this
liberation from the piano is debatable; certainly there are
any number of excellent composers who work successfully
at the piano. At any rate, the unalterable fact remains that
although before 1929 Harris had produced only one work
of significance—the *Concerto*—he succeeded, after 1929, in
producing a consecutive series of outstanding musical works,
each clearly marked with the fingerprints of originality and
importance.

On February 12, 1928, the Lenox String Quartet—with
Harry Cumpson and Aaron Gorodner—introduced the
Concerto for Piano, Clarinet and String-Quartet in New

York. There were some kind words of praise, but its genuine distinction was not as yet fully appreciated. On June 14, 1933, the *Concerto* was broadcast over a national hookup of the Columbia network. At that time, a deluge of congratulatory letters poured into the studio, much to the amazement of both composer and performers who feared that the music might be too intricate for appreciation by the masses. Encouraged by this response, Harry Cumpson—the pianist who assisted at the performance—made, on his own initiative, a scrapbook of the flattering letters. With this, he forcefully convinced a director of the Columbia Phonograph Company that a work receiving such a spontaneous outburst of praise was well deserving of recording. The work was recorded, and to the bewilderment of all the officers of the Columbia Phonograph Company, the first recording of a serious modern American work had a very large and profitable sale.

From that moment on, Roy Harris' star soared. On February 2, 1934, Serge Koussevitzky introduced Roy Harris' new symphony, the *Symphony: 1933*. Describing the context of the symphony, Roy Harris wrote: "In the first movement I have tried to capture the mood of adventure and physical exuberance; in the second, of the pathos which seems to underly all human existence; in the third, the mood of a positive will to power and action."

The Boston Symphony performance of Harris' symphony proved to be important for Harris not only because of the glowing praise it received from the critics, but more especially because it tempted the Columbia Phonograph Company to record this work as well, thereby bringing forcefully to the attention of the competitive Victor Phonograph Company that here was a composer well worth cultivating. Without delay, Victor not only recorded many of the succeeding works of Harris—including the *Variations on a Theme*, for string-quartet, and the *Poem*, for violin and piano—but it decided to go one step ahead of its competitor by commissioning Harris to compose a special symphonic work for recording purposes. The work—an American overture, *Johnny Comes Marching Home*, based upon a famous Civil War tune which Harris, as a boy, frequently heard his father whistle while working on the farmlands—proved to have phenomenal appeal on records, in symphony-hall, and over the radio; and it was principally this work (after its performance by Otto Klemperer and the New York Philharmonic) that made Harris the first most popular American composer in the 1935 Philharmonic radio poll.

By this time, Harris was a vogue. Commissions poured in from many directions, Koussevitzky wanted another symphony as soon as possible—and before long, the *Second Symphony* was featured at the concerts of the Boston Symphony Orchestra. Mrs. Elizabeth Sprague Coolidge and Mrs. W. W. Norton commissioned Harris to compose chamber works—the results being the *Trio* and the *Piano Quintet (Passacaglia, Cadenza and Fugue)*. The League of Composers asked for a choral work—the *Song for Occupations*, which has likewise been recorded. The Westminster Choir ordered still another choral work to include on its concert programs—*The Symphony for Voices*. Jascha Heifetz requested a violin concerto. The Columbia Broadcasting System ordered a special orchestral work specifically for radio purposes.

Harris is, therefore, perhaps the only composer in America who has the enviable consolation of knowing, even before he puts pen on paper, that the new work he is contemplating will find eager hands among American conductors, musical groups, and phonograph companies, long before the ink becomes dry on the paper.

3.

How well has Roy Harris deserved this striking success? Among modern American composers, he is most thoroughly American in his idiom. His music is natively American not because he has borrowed some indigenous American vocabulary for his speech. His works do not employ the Indian idiom of Henry F. Gilbert, Charles T. Griffes or Frederick Jacobi, the Negro idiom of Rubin Goldmark, or the jazz idiom of George Gershwin. Roy Harris' music grows naturally out of European traditions, influenced by Beethoven, by such contrapuntists as Josquin des Prés and Palestrina. Yet Harris' music could not have been produced by a European; its accents have been sounded by a distinctly American voice.

One American critic, whose name eludes me at the moment, has written that Harris is as native an American product as, for example, Carl Sandburg. His melodies are obviously the speech of a Western temperament in its angular line. Its vitality is an expression of American health and youth. That admirable critic, H. T. Parker, summed up the native qualities of Harris' music when he wrote that Harris is an American, "first in a pervading directness, in a recurring and unaffected roughness of musical speech. . . . He is also American in broad design, full voice, a certain abruptness. . . . The rhythms are uneven, unconventional, changeable, irregular. There is no mistaking their propulsive force. They seem to derive besides from the West that bred Mr. Harris, in which he works most eagerly—from its air, its life, its impulses, even its gaits. His melody, in turn, partakes of this irregularity, this unevenness. . . . Suffice it for the rest to say that in this melody we hear an instinctive American quality to which we respond as instinctively." [2]

Harris does not generally employ unusual harmonies or

[2] *Boston Evening Transcript.* January 27, 1934.

tonalities. The most salient feature of his style is the long
and elaborate melodic line which becomes, in turn, the germ
of a rich and fruitful development. In a conversation,
Harris once pointed out to me that Sibelius' symphonies
were unsatisfactory to him as works of art because their
ideas were too episodic and were not given the opportunity
to expand and develop. This criticism—which I consider
neither important nor penetrating—gives us a valuable insight into Harris' principles of composition. He believes
implicitly that a musical work should, as it did with Beethoven, be permitted to evolve and grow and ripen as
naturally as a plant. In Harris' music, particularly in his
two symphonies, the developments are enormously complex,
and it requires a very intimate association with this music to
be able to distinguish subtle strands that are woven into the
fabric.

Roy Harris' music is genuine, authentic, individual, possessing no pretences or postures. Its enormous vitality and
freshness are unmistakable. It possesses none of the nervousness and restlessness of the modern age; it is the healthy
offshoot of the mid-Western plains. American to the core,
this music is the high-minded utterance of a fine and independent spirit.

5.

And as the music, so the man.

Everything about Roy Harris speaks strongly his West-
ern-American origin. His appearance suggests the open
spaces rather than the crowded city. His sparing build is
angular and supple, his face—revealing strength in high
cheek-bones, and assertive chin—knows repose, his gray
eyes and his elastic skin are fresh. He has the simplicity
and unpretentiousness of one who has lived the greater part
of his life in a secluded farm-house with books. Essentially
reticent, he feels himself to be out-of-place in the New York

music salon. His gestures are almost awkward, and he speaks with a perceptible drawl.

He is not the man to assume poses of dignity and grandeur because his music has made him a famous man. He has been known to meet journalists or distinguished musicians in his study and, while talking to them, to take off his jacket and vest and sprawl lazily across the couch. Nor can he assume poses of modesty and humility either, merely because it is demanded of a successful composer. He is convinced of his direction, sublimely sure of himself, and does not hesitate to tell this to the first person who asks him.

His pastimes include tennis and chess, in both of which he is more than passingly proficient. His intelligence being alert and restless, he likewise finds enormous fascination in reading—particularly in philosophy and the social sciences. Politics—he inclines towards the left—interest him greatly. Where music is concerned, he finds greatest satisfaction in the works of the fifteenth and sixteenth centuries—those of Dufay, des Prés, Palestrina and Orlando di Lasso. Among other famous composers, his greatest respect is for Bach and Beethoven. After Beethoven, he feels, the art of music degenerated. And this degeneracy, he believes, is most apparent in the works of such composers as Berlioz, Liszt, Wagner, Richard Strauss and Rimsky-Korsakoff.

RALPH VAUGHAN WILLIAMS

XVI

RALPH VAUGHAN WILLIAMS

1.

WITH the death of Sir Edward Elgar, the first position among living English composers passed, without question or debate, to Ralph Vaughan Williams. Truth to tell, Vaughan Williams fills the rôle of dean of English music more gracefully than Sir Edward Elgar ever did. Elgar was an English composer more by accident of birth than by the quality of his musical speech. Vaughan Williams' music, on the other hand, is more essentially English, more an expression of English character and temperament and more firmly rooted in English tradition than the works of Elgar. It shows less noticeably any foreign influence. Much of it is, in content, Anglo-Saxon both in its expression of a serene beauty and in its often tight-lipped restraint.

During the early years of his career, Vaughan Williams borrowed his musical subjects directly from English folk-music, a field in which he made monumental research. Subsequently, he abandoned the folk-song, utilizing for the most part only material of his own invention. But the influence of folk-music upon his art never completely deserted him. Its structure and spirit became the bone and tissue of his musical thinking. His melodic construction acquired folk-song physiognomy. Thus, even his most original line of music has the unmistakable flavor of the English folk-tune. More than any other composer of recent memory, therefore, Vaughan Williams has succeeded in producing an authentic English musical art.

Vaughan Williams has never achieved the regal fame that was Elgar's for more than three decades. Yet I am inclined to believe that as a composer Vaughan Williams has been much more original and personal, and as an influence upon his contemporaries much more potent. Like Elgar, Vaughan Williams proved that the academic and formal style of Parry and Stanford need not be the essential qualities of an English composer. But he went one step further than Elgar in demonstrating that English music need not derive its materials from the Germans or the French to acquire sensitivity of design and emotional beauty of message. It is, therefore, not beyond the realm of possibility that when a future historian evaluates English music of the twentieth century he will point out that its renaissance began not with Elgar but with Vaughan Williams.

He was born in Down Ampney, Gloucestershire, on October 12, 1872. His father, a well-to-do clergyman with independent means, aspired to give his son a comprehensive education that would be unhampered by the necessity of preparing for earning a livelihood. Therefore when Vaughan Williams completed his schooldays at Charterhouse and a two years' course at the Royal College of Music, he entered Trinity College, Cambridge. He afterwards returned to the Royal College of Music, where his instructors were C. Hubert Parry and Charles Villiers Stanford.

In 1896, Vaughan Williams extended his studies by a visit to Germany. His travel included periods of study at the Berlin Akademie under Max Bruch. Finally, he came to Bayreuth where he heard Wagner's music for the first time. Returning to England, he continued his studies as a preparation for a creative career—taking advanced courses in music at Cambridge until he received his doctorate in 1901. At the same time he held a few minor posts (important only in that they constituted his official apprenticeship) as organist of the South Lambeth Church and as University Extension lecturer on music in Oxford and London.

It was at this time—while still immersed in music-study

—that Vaughan Williams first interested himself in English folk-music. A few examples of folk-songs from the Tudor period came to his attention, in which he found such poignancy of artistic expression and such irresistible charm that he decided to plunge deeply into the study of folk-music of his country. He joined the Folk-Song Society (of which he was soon to become one of the most active members) helping it to unearth from obscurity an entire library of unfamiliar gems. Many of these he himself reconstructed melodically, adding to them a piquantly modern harmonization or new lines of contrapuntal voices. In this rejuvenated form, many of these songs, long neglected, took a new lease upon life: principally such present-day favorites as *The Turtle Dove, Down in Yon Forest, We've Been Awhile A-Wandering, A Farmer's Son, Ca' the Yowes, The Dark Eyed Sailor* and *It's Of A Lawyer.* During the past decade or so, many of Vaughan Williams' arrangements of English folk-songs have been popularized throughout the world of music by that incomparable group of *a cappela* voices—the English Singers.

Inevitably, when he first turned to original composition in larger forms, Vaughan Williams' explorations in the folk-music of his country left their indelible traces upon his intellect. In 1905, he composed the *First Norfolk Rhapsody,* following it one year later by two additional Norfolk rhapsodies. These three compositions in rhapsody form were intended by their composer as a Norfolk Folk Symphony: the first of these was to be the Introduction and First Movement; the second, the slow movement culminating in a Scherzo; the third, the Finale. Borrowing liberally from folk material native to King's Lynn, Norfolk (including such well-known airs as *The Captain's Apprentice* and *A Bold Young Sailor Courted Me*), Vaughan Williams, in these rhapsodies, dressed folk-tunes in an elaborate but skilful orchestral garb. The latter two rhapsodies displeased the composer who, feeling strongly that they failed to achieve a satisfactory symphonic treatment of folk-music, discouraged their performance. It is, therefore, only the *First Norfolk Rhapsody* that has been performed by orchestras in Europe and America.

The first work by Vaughan Williams to receive public performance was *Towards an Unknown Region,* for chorus and orchestra, enthusiastically received at the Leeds Festival of 1907. This work, too, dissatisfied the fastidious composer. Sensing that his failures and self-disapproval might be largely the result of a deficient technique, Vaughan Williams momentarily deserted creative work, came to Paris in 1908 and became a private pupil of Maurice Ravel. It cannot be said that the relation between teacher and pupil was altogether an idyllic one. Ravel and Vaughan Williams were opposing spirits: the one was refined and sensitive; the other strong, muscular, almost savage. They could, therefore, never see eye to eye on a musical subject or its treatment. After eight months, Vaughan Williams left Ravel, but these months of study had by no means been wasted. He acquired from Ravel a finer and surer sense of form, even though—fortunately!—his own personal mannerisms in composition had remained untouched by Ravel's entirely opposite style.

The Paris excursion—or was it only the temporary recess from composition?—radically altered Vaughan Williams' self-assumed principles of compositions. He realized that he had been too much the slave to the folk-song, thereby stifling his imagination and creativeness. He decided, therefore, to utilize folk material only sparingly in the future—and only to inject a touch of flavor just as a cook might sprinkle some condiments in a broth. This decision reached, Vaughan Williams began composition anew. From this time on, he produced works which spread his name and reputation to two continents.

The first work in which his own personal idiom revealed itself strongly was *In the Fen Country,* in which he freed

RALPH VAUGHAN WILLIAMS

himself permanently from a slavish use of folk-music but derived the quality and character of his own melodies from folk-song formulas. In 1910, Vaughan Williams produced a still more significant work in the famous *Fantasia on a Theme of Thomas Tallis*,[1] for double string-orchestra, featured with considerable success at the Gloucester Cathedral during the Three Choirs Festival of 1910, and since that time performed so frequently in England and America that it has become one of Vaughan Williams' best-known works.

Following the *Fantasia*, Vaughan Williams rapidly revealed his growing independence and individuality as a composer. The *Sea Symphony*, a choral setting of Walt Whitman, and *On Wenlock Edge*, after A. E. Housman, showed a greater freedom in the use of harmonic combinations and more plasticity. In the opera, *Hugh the Drover*, his aptitude for depicting background in tone, as well as his flair for dramatic musical writing, asserted themselves. Finally, now in full stride as a composer, Vaughan Williams completed in 1914 a work which was not only his most distinguished creation up to that time but which was also to place him definitely among the leading composers of England—namely, *A London Symphony*.

Commenting upon *A London Symphony*, Vaughan Williams has said: "The title . . . may suggest to some hearers a descriptive piece, but this is not the intention of the composer. A better title would perhaps be *Symphony by a Londoner*. That is to say, the life of London (including possibly its sights and sounds) has suggested to the composer an attempt at musical expression; but it would be no help to the hearer to describe these in words. The music is intended to be self-impressive, but must stand or fall as 'absolute music.' Therefore, if listeners recognize suggestions of such things as the *Westminster Chimes* or the

[1] Thomas Tallis (c. 1510-1585) was one of the most famous English church composers during the Reformation.

Lavender's Cry they are asked to consider these as accidents, not essentials of the music."

A London Symphony is not only a characteristic example of Vaughan Williams' musical style up to the time, but reveals it at its surest and best. That remarkable feeling for form—an almost intuitive sense for structure which will not permit the inclusion of any line or curve not integral to the design of the whole—is here apparent; this symphony is knit closely, developed with a hand that never falters in its aim, and derives a great part of its effectiveness from the compactness of its construction.

Here, too, is an ability to put to music the subtlest suggestions of atmosphere and background: the Thames at dawn as it passes by a city touched with the peace and mystery of sleep, or—in the second movement—a district of London saturated with fog at dusk. Finally, in this work —as in so many of Vaughan Williams' other compositions —there is a supremely deft use of popular music. To Vaughan Williams, popular music is a supple and useful means of injecting a faint touch of "local color" so to speak —or the slightest suggestion of flavor—into a work. Used with the utmost of discretion and with the most sparing economy, it never debases the composition in which it appears but rather, in turn, is raised by the composition to a high artistic level. As Vaughan Williams himself once said, in justification of the use of popular music in serious artistic forms: "Have we not all about us forms of musical expression which we can take and purify and raise to the level of great art? For instance, the lilt of the chorus at a music-hall joining in a popular song, the children dancing to a barrel organ, the rousing fervor of a Salvation Army hymn, St. Paul's and a great choir singing in one of its festivals, the Welshmen striking up one of their own hymns whenever they win a goal at an international football match, the cries of street peddlers, the factory girls singing their sentimental songs. Have all these nothing to say to us?" Certainly the appearance of that music-hall ditty *We'll All Go Down to the Strand,* in *A London Symphony,* does not vulgarize the work but, on the other hand, is immeasurably useful in instilling atmospheric color.

A London Symphony was performed for the first time in the spring of 1914 under the baton of Geoffry Toye, and was well received by an audience appreciative of its originality of treatment and imaginativeness of conception. In 1920, the British Music Society selected *A London Symphony* as the most significant native musical work produced by an Englishman.

2.

Patriotism called Vaughan Williams from his studio to the field of battle in 1914.

Despite the fact that he was already forty-two years old, he enlisted in the Territorial Royal Army Military Corps, serving as a stretcher-bearer and as a scrubber of floors first in France and then in Macedonia. Keeping floors clean or even carrying stretchers from the battlefield to the hospital did not seem to Vaughan Williams a sufficiently active participation in the War. In 1917 he passed an examination for an artillery commission. Throughout 1918, he served as a lieutenant in France in the very midst of the fighting.

When he returned from the battle-front, Vaughan Williams reverted to a musical life by joining the faculty of the Royal College of Music and becoming conductor of the Bach Choir. At the same time, he solidified his position as the foremost English composer of his time—excepting, of course, Sir Edward Elgar. In 1921, Vaughan Williams composed the *Pastoral Symphony* which, shortly after its first performance by Adrian Boult and the Royal Philharmonic Society on January 26, 1922, became one of Vaughan Williams' most famous works. The *Pastoral Symphony* once again proved the composer's extraordinary gift in reproducing tonally the most elusively haunting moods. In 1922, Vaughan Williams composed one of his most intimate and personal works, a one-act opera-oratorio entitled *Shepherds of the Delectable Mountain;* in 1926, he conceived his most ambitious work, the oratorio *Sancta Civitas.*

To those Londoners living near the Embankment, Vaughan Williams was a familiar figure during these years. With the most meticulous punctuality he passed the Embankment each day in the week and at precisely the same time. He was easily recognizable. His huge frame of a body moved with a certain angular stiffness, his magnificent head lowered in contemplation. In his sublime indifference to dress, his appearance strongly suggested the story-book composer. His coat was frequently too large for him, and more than once was it thrown completely out of shape by the fact that one of the buttons was adjusted to the wrong buttonhole. His trousers were baggy, hanging loosely at the ankles. He wore an old bowler hat which should have been discarded long before; in his hand he held a frayed carpet bag containing his books and papers. As he walked—his pace, slow and studied—he seemed completely self-immersed.

His sturdy independence of spirit—which his friends have identified as his most striking trait as a man—has often brought him to pursue new courses in his composition. Just as in 1909, he abandoned the folk-song as the basis for his musical creation, so—in more recent works—he has frequently adopted a style radically different from the tranquillity, poetry and tonal painting of *A London Symphony* and the *Pastoral Symphony.* When a new work by Vaughan Williams is announced, it is impossible to prophesy what the quality of its musical content will be. Vaughan Williams' more recent works, therefore, have caused more than one uplifted eyebrow of amazement, and no little antagonism.

The *Symphony in F-minor,* composed a few years ago, is so unlike its preceding three works in the same form that it might very easily have come from a different pen. Utilizing polytonality, Vaughan Williams has here produced astringent music with such hard surfaces that it is impossible to identify in it any of the fingerprints of the composer who fashioned the earlier romantic symphonies. On the other hand, in his opera *The Poisoned Kiss,* on a libretto by Evelyn Sharp, introduced in the spring of 1936, Vaughan Williams wrote a musical score replete with lilting dance tunes, patter-songs and formalistic set-pieces—a score at an opposite polar point from the severely intellectual *Symphony in F-minor.* And, again different in treatment, is still another recent work, the *Pavane of the Sons of the Morning,* inspired by one of the numbers from "Job"—Blake's illustrations—which is one of the few reminders, among Vaughan Williams' present-day works of the style of the *Pastoral Symphony.*

Does this spasmodic change of style denote confusion? Does this fluctuation from one idiom to another point a finger to Vaughan Williams' lack of definite direction in his recent creation? Perhaps. Perhaps, too, it denotes merely a transition from one period in Vaughan Williams' creative life to another—which, when finally achieved, may attain expression as fully personal and imaginative as the first three symphonies.

GEORGE GERSHWIN

GEORGE GERSHWIN

XVII

GEORGE GERSHWIN

1.

WALTER DAMROSCH once felicitously remarked that George Gershwin made a lady of jazz.

Truth to tell, Gershwin found jazz in the gutter and transported her into a Park Avenue drawing room. Whatever his musical shortcomings as a composer may be—and they are many—Gershwin's importance as a musical influence cannot be overestimated. Before the *Rhapsody in Blue,* jazz belonged in the musical slums. Largely through Gershwin's taste and ingenuity, his foresight in applying jazz to larger symphonic forms and his ability to make it speak a more poignant message, he has made it an important musical idiom—important enough for composers like Maurice Ravel, Ernst Krenek, Kurt Weill, Igor Stravinsky, and others to adopt.

Early in 1923, George Gershwin, a composer of ingenious jazz-songs, met Paul Whiteman, the celebrated jazz-band leader, and a friendship between the two was struck at once. Paul Whiteman, a graduate from the orchestral ranks of the San Francisco Symphony Orchestra where he had been a violoncellist, had some vague ideals about the future of jazz—ideals with which George Gershwin, himself a lover of serious music, could sympathize. More than one evening did they spend discussing the future and the possibilities of jazz. Gershwin sincerely felt that he could compose a jazz music that would be symphonic in scope, and Paul Whiteman felt that he and his band could perform such a work with sympathetic understanding.

One day in 1924, Paul Whiteman decided to bring his

cherished dream into realization. He called his band together for a series of long rehearsals; he commissioned his
friend Gershwin to create a long symphonic-jazz composition. He engaged the Æolian Hall in New York, now
demolished, but at that time the home for serious concert
performances, and sent notices to the press that he was contemplating a concert devoted to all-American music.

The skeptics greeted this plan with laughter of derision,
many musicians found the venture a subject for ironic ridicule, friends of Paul Whiteman begged him to abandon a
futile and impossible adventure. But Paul Whiteman continued rehearsing his band at the night-club, Palais Royale,
long after the dancing had stopped—until early hours of
morning. And George Gershwin continued working on a
long symphonic-jazz composition to be featured on the program.

Rehearsals continued in full swing every night in the
week. After four strenuous weeks, the entire program was
ready—with the exception of Gershwin's composition.
Patiently, Whiteman waited for Gershwin to send in the
manuscript, but as the days flew by his patience dwindled
and he was rapidly yielding to a frenzy. Would that in-
fernal work never be finished? Somewhere in the corner
of Whiteman's heart there lurked the fear that, perhaps,
the work was beyond Gershwin's capabilities, that, in short,
there would be no new symphonic-jazz work to feature at
his concert. Frantically, Whiteman kept Gershwin's telephone ringing perpetually, kept Western Union messengers
blazing an indefatigable path to Gershwin's home. But
always did he receive the same complacent answer. The
composition required more time and more revision.

A week before the concert . . . and still no sign of
Gershwin's work. In despair, Whiteman himself invaded
Gershwin's study and swore that he would not leave without
the composition in his hand. Regretfully, and with the
lingering feeling that it was not so good as it should be,

Kodály, Zoltan. "Béla Bartók." *La Revue musicale.* vol. 2, p. 205. Paris, 1921.

Leichentritt, Hugo. "On the Art of Béla Bartók." *Modern Music.* vol. 6, p. 3. New York, 1928.

Nuell, Edwin von der. *Béla Bartók: Ein Beitrag zur Morphologie der neuen Musik.* Halle. Mitteldeutsche Verlags. 1930.

Westphal, Kurt. "Béla Bartók und die moderne ungarische Musik." *Musik.* vol. 20, p. 188. Stuttgart, 1927.

Whitaker, Frank. "A Visit to Béla Bartók." *Musical Times.* vol. 67, p. 220. London, 1926.

X. ERNEST BLOCH

Downes, Olin. "Ernest Bloch: The Swiss Composer." *Musical Observer.* vol. 15, p. 11. New York, 1917.

Ewen, David. "Ernest Bloch." *Musical Record.* vol. 1, p. 422. Philadelphia, 1934.

———"Ernest Bloch." *Monthly Musical Record.* vol. 64, p. 25. London, 1934.

Gatti, Guido. "Ernest Bloch." *Musical Quarterly.* vol. 7, p. 20. New York, 1921.

Hartt, Julius. "Ernest Bloch." *La Revue musicale.* vol. 4, p. 218. Paris, 1923.

Klein, Herbert. "Ernest Bloch: Mensch und Musiker." *Zeitschrift für Musik.* vol. 8, p. 298. Berlin, 1932.

Morgan, Edward William. "Ernest Bloch." *Scottish Musical Magazine.* vol. 11, p. 79. Edinburgh, 1930.

Pannain, Guido. *Modern Composers.* New York. E. P. Dutton & Co. 1933.

Rosenfeld, Paul. "The Music of Ernest Bloch." *Seven Arts.* vol. 1, p. 413. New York, 1916-1917.

Sessions, Roger. "Ernest Bloch." *Modern Music.* vol. 5, p. 3. New York, 1917.

Tibaldi, Chiesa Mary. *Ernest Bloch.* Turin. G. B. Paravia & Co. 1933.

XI. FREDERICK DELIUS

Abraham, Gerald. "Delius and his Literary Sources." *Music and Letters.* vol. 10, p. 182. London, 1929.

Berry, Leland J. "Frederick Delius." *Musical Standard.* vol. 32, p. 40. London, 1928.

Chislett, W. A. "A Neglected Composer: Delius." *Gramaphone.* vol. 4, p. 450. London, 1927.

Chop, Max. "Frederick Delius: Sein Leben und Schaffen." *Neue Musik Zeitung.* vol. 31, p. 310. Stuttgart, 1910.

Delius, Clare. *Memories of My Brother.* London. I. Nicholson & Watson, Ltd. 1935.

Douglas, Keith. "Frederick Delius." *Heaton Review.* vol. 3, p. 53. Bradford, 1929.

Evans, Edwin. "Delius: A Personal Reaction." *Sackbut.* vol. 10, p. 118. London, 1929.

Foss, Hubert J. "Afterthoughts on Delius." *Musical Times.* vol. 70, p. 1073. London, 1929.

Grainger, Percy. "The Genius of Frederick Delius." *Musical Courier.* vol. 71, p. 39. New York, 1915.

Gray, Cecil. *A Survey of Contemporary Music.* London. Oxford University Press. 1924.

Heseltine, Philip. "Frederick Delius." *Musical Times.* vol. 56, p. 137. London, 1915.

———*Frederick Delius.* London. John Lane. 1923.

Hogarth, Basil. "Frederick Delius: A Critical Estimate." *English Review.* vol. 59, p. 154. London, 1934.

Hull, A. Eaglefield. "Delius and Norway." *Monthly Musical Record.* vol. 51, p. 196. London, 1921.

———*Delius.* London. L. and V. Woolf. 1928.

Marx, Joseph. "Frederick Delius." *Musik blätter des Anbruch.* vol. 1, p. 49. Vienna, 1919.

Pike, D. E. "The Future of Delius." *Chesterian.* vol. 49, p. 37. London, 1925.

XII. PAUL HINDEMITH

Bekker, Paul. *Briefe an zeitgenössiche Musiker.* Berlin. Max Hesses. 1932.

Benninghoven, Erich. "Der Geist im Werke Hindemiths." *Musik.* vol. 21, p. 718. Stuttgart, 1929.

Coeuroy, André. *Panorama de la musique contemporaine.* Paris. Kra. 1928.

Einstein, Alfred. "Paul Hindemith." *Modern Music.* vol. 3, p. 21. New York, 1926.

Fraser, Andrew Alstair. *Essays in Music.* London. Oxford University Press. 1930.

———"Paul Hindemith." *Music and Letters.* vol. 10, p. 167. London, 1929.

Machabey, A. "Esquisse de Paul Hindemith." *Menestral.* vol. 193, p. 65. Paris, 1931.

———"Paul Hindemith: Musicien allemand." *La Revue musicale.* vol. 11, p. 193. Paris, 1930.

Pannain, Guido. *Modern Composers.* London. J. M. Dent & Sons. 1932.

Reich, Willi. "Paul Hindemith." *Chesterian.* vol. 11, p. 33. London, 1929.

Seidl, Arthur. *Neuzeitliche Tondichter und zeitgenössiche Tonkünstler.* Regensburg. G. Bosse. 1926.

Strobel, Heinrich. *Paul Hindemith.* Mayence. B. Schött. 1928.

XIII. ARNOLD SCHÖNBERG

Armitage, Merle (editor). "Arnold Schönberg." New York. G. Schirmer. 1937.

Arnold Schönberg. (Chapters by Alban Berg, Anton Webern, Egon Wellesz, etc.) München. R. Piper. 1912.

Arnold Schönberg zum 60 Geburtstag. (Essays by Jalowetz, Webern, Broch, etc.) Vienna. Universal Edition. 1934.

Bekker, Paul. *Briefe an zeitgenössiche Musiker.* Berlin. Max Hesses. 1932.

Calvorcoressi, M. D. "Arnold Schönberg." *New Music Review.* vol. 12, p. 75. New York, 1913.

Coeuroy, André. "Concerning Arnold Schönberg." *Chesterian.* vol. 9, p. 141. London, 1928.

Erpf, Hermann. "Für Arnold Schönberg." *Neue Musik Zeitung.* vol. 42, p. 37. Stuttgart-Leipzig, 1920.

Engel, Carl. "Schönberg, as Poet, Considers Man's Destiny. *Musical America.* vol. 34, p. 3. New York, 1921.

Felber, Erwin. "Arnold Schönberg." *Musik.* vol. 23, p. 566. Berlin, 1931.

Fleischmann, H. R. "Arnold Schönberg." *Neue Zeitschrift für Musik.* vol. 87, p. 307. Leipzig, 1920.

Gray, Cecil. "Arnold Schönberg: A Critical Study." *Music and Letters.* vol. 3, p. 73. London, 1922.

———*A Survey of Contemporary Music.* London. Oxford University Press. 1924.

Green, L. Dutton. "Arnold Schönberg." *Chesterian.* vol. 6, p. 270. London, 1925.

Huneker, James Gibbons. *Ivory Apes and Peacocks.* New York. Charles Scribner's Sons. 1915.

Leichentritt, Hugo. "Schönberg and Atonality." *Modern Music.* vol. 5, p. 3. New York, 1928.

Machabey, A. "Schönberg." *Menestral.* vol. 92, p. 81. Paris, 1930.

Pannain, Guido. *Modern Composers.* London. J. M. Dent & Sons. 1932.

Schönberg Heft. Musikblätter des Anbruch. vol. 6. Vienna, 1924.

Seidl, Arthur. *Neuzeitliche Tondichter und zeitgenössiche Tonkünstler.* Regensburg. G. Bosse. 1926.

Specht, Richard. "Arnold Schönberg." *Der Merker.* vol. 2, p. 697. Vienna, 1911.

Stefan, Paul. "Schönberg's Operas." *Modern Music.* vol. 7, p. 24. New York, 1929.

Stein, Erwin. "Arnold Schönberg." *La Revue musicale.* vol. 12, p. 201. Paris, 1931.

Weissmann, Adolf. *Problems of Modern Music.* New York. E. P. Dutton & Co. 1925.

Wellesz, Egon. "Arnold Schönberg." Leipzig. E. Tal. 1921.

XIV. FRANCESCO MALIPIERO

Gatti, Guido. *Musicisti moderni d'Italia.* Bologna. F. Bongiovanni. 1925.

Jean-Aubry, Georges. "A Great Artist." *Musical Times.* vol. 60, p. 13. London, 1919.

Mitchell, Edward S. "Malipiero." *The Organist.* vol. 28, p. 18. London, 1920.

Prunières, Henri. "Gian Francesco Malipiero." *Musical Quarterly.* vol. 6, p. 326. New York, 1920.

Redlich, H. F. "Francesco Malipiero: Dramaturge lyrique." *La Revue Musicale.* vol. 12, p. 300. Paris, 1931.

Saminsky, Lazare. *Music of Our Day.* New York. Thos. Y. Crowell Company. 1932.

XV. ROY HARRIS

Ewen, David. *Composers of Today.* New York. H. W. Wilson Co. 1934.

Farwell, Arthur. "Roy Harris." *Musical Quarterly.* vol. 18, p. 18. New York, 1933.

Goldberg, Isaac. "Roy Harris." *Musical Record.* vol. 1, p. 253. New York, 1933.

Howard, John Tasker. *Our American Music*. New York. Thos. Y. Crowell Company. 1931.

XVI. RALPH VAUGHAN WILLIAMS

Colles, H. C. "The Music of Vaughan-Williams." *Chesterian*. vol. 21, p. 129. London, 1922.

Dickinson, Alan Edgar. *An Introduction to the Music of Ralph Vaughan-Williams*. London. Oxford University Press. 1928.

Erlebach, Rupert. "Vaughan-Williams and His Three Symphonies." *Monthly Musical Record*. vol. 52, p. 127. London, 1922.

Evans, Edwin. "Ralph Vaughan-Williams." *Musical Times*. vol. 61, p. 232. London, 1920.

Fox-Strangways, A. H. "Ralph Vaughan-Williams." *Music and Letters*. vol. 1, p. 78. London, 1920.

Howells, Herbert. "Vaughan-Williams' Pastoral Symphony." *Music and Letters*. vol. 3, p. 122. London, 1922.

Pannain, Guido. *Modern Composers*. London. J. M. Dent & Sons. 1932.

Rose, E. C. *Vaughan-Williams: An Appreciation*. *Sackbut*. vol. 6, p. 320. London, 1926.

XVII. GEORGE GERSHWIN

Ewen, David. *Composers of Today*. New York. H. W. Wilson Co. 1934.

——*George Gershwin*. *Gamut*. vol. 2, p. 30. London, 1929.

Goldberg, Isaac. *George Gershwin: A Study in American Music*. New York. Simon and Schuster. 1931.

——"George Gershwin and Jazz." *Theatre Guild Magazine*. vol. 7, p. 15. New York, 1930.

Osgood, Henry Osborne. *So This Is Jazz!* Boston. Little Brown & Co. 1926.

Woollcott, Alexander. "George the Ingenuous." *Cosmopolitan Magazine*. New York, November 1933.

INDEX

INDEX

2